Things Are Different in Africa

Things Are Different in Africa

◆

A Memoir of Dangers and Adventures in the Congo

Frederick Edward Pitts

iUniverse, Inc.
New York Lincoln Shanghai

Things Are Different in Africa
A Memoir of Dangers and Adventures in the Congo

Copyright © 2004 by Frederick Edward Pitts

All rights reserved. No part of this book may be used or reproduced by any means, graphic, electronic, or mechanical, including photocopying, recording, taping or by any information storage retrieval system without the written permission of the publisher except in the case of brief quotations embodied in critical articles and reviews.

iUniverse books may be ordered through booksellers or by contacting:

iUniverse
2021 Pine Lake Road, Suite 100
Lincoln, NE 68512
www.iuniverse.com
1-800-Authors (1-800-288-4677)

ISBN-13: 978-0-595-33204-5 (pbk)
ISBN-13: 978-0-595-77989-5 (ebk)
ISBN-10: 0-595-33204-8 (pbk)
ISBN-10: 0-595-77989-1 (ebk)

Printed in the United States of America

Contents

Introduction vii
CHAPTER 1   Pygmies in the Bush 1
CHAPTER 2   The Long, Long Road to Makoua 8
CHAPTER 3   Alone in Makoua 17
CHAPTER 4   Day Two in Makoua 30
CHAPTER 5   New Discoveries 37
CHAPTER 6   The Seventh Day 46
CHAPTER 7   Thieves and Wives 54
CHAPTER 8   New Confrontations 61
CHAPTER 9   Witches and Curses 73
CHAPTER 10   Uphill, Downhill 90
CHAPTER 11   Making Slow Progress 104
CHAPTER 12   Chaos in the City 116
CHAPTER 13   The Brick Attack 132
CHAPTER 14   Wheels and Ordeals 144
CHAPTER 15   The Trek to Etoumbi 157
CHAPTER 16   Crash in the Forest 175
CHAPTER 17   Evacuation 192

Introduction

Non-fiction is often like a picture of a quiet bay or lagoon, presenting a clear image of the subject but revealing nothing of the drama taking place beneath the surface. One best learns what Third World Africa is all about when one resides in that part of the world and actually becomes a part of the culture. The next best experience, is to read a book written by someone who has lived there, studied the culture, explored its mysteries, been exposed to its dangers and risks, and therefore understands the processes of day to day survival. And finally, one learns even more from a work that does not pontificate or lecture, that makes no attempt to be politically correct, and shows no hesitation to "tell it like it is". This is such a book.

1

Pygmies in the Bush

I had spent my working lifetime in white-collar sales, making money, driving fast cars, and burning myself slowly out. One day in 1992, fed up with the pressure and the lack of personal satisfaction from my achievements, I made a profound decision. I decided to give everything I owned to my three children and then I traded my comfortable lifestyle for a two-year hitch in equatorial Africa. There, I had been assured, my advancing age would bring special regard and respect from the people, and there, many of the rules and traditions to which I had been accustomed would not apply. I needed the change.

We Peace Corps volunteers had survived several months of extensive language training in Bujumbura, Burundi, some of us had visited Kigali, Rwanda and then our original troop of twenty-one had been scattered over the various countries of Central Africa. My own group of about a dozen was first flown to Kinshasa, Zaire (now the Democratic Republic of Congo), where we spent twenty-four hours before being taken by ferry across the big river to Brazzaville, Congo (Republic of Congo). Sixty days later, after yet another period of language and culture immersion, we all loaded into a British Land Rover for one last trip together.

Late in the afternoon we reached our destination of Sibiti, a town about three hundred miles west of Brazzaville. Exhausted from the twelve hour ride and covered by yellow dust, we were all ready to hang our mosquito nets, take a cold splash-bath, and crawl onto foam mattresses for the night. We had, for months, shared the coed "crash house" in Brazzaville or else stayed with African families in villages near the city. We had traveled over brutal roads, bunked wherever we were placed, eaten local foods and relentlessly slapped at mosquitoes, but it was not quite over yet. Sibiti was to be the focal point of our last training trip before finally being assigned to permanent posts somewhere in the Congo.

When morning came much too soon, we loaded into the truck along with the locally stationed volunteer, and started out to visit some remote villages where we were to learn what to expect in that "real world" environment. Thus, shortly before 11:00 A.M., we reached a village where mud-and-thatch huts housed some two hundred people. Because our visit had been prearranged, we met only briefly with the village chief and then began a hike into a deep valley. The farmer who owned that ground was the point man, while perhaps 30 more of us were strung out behind him. A dozen children were at my end of the line, all excitedly jabbering, eager to watch whatever it was that we were about to do. A girl about thirteen years old was busily knitting something as she walked just ahead of me and maintained her pace with an air of nonchalance. When asked what she was making, she looked over her shoulder and replied that it was a shawl. She was obviously pleased to have been noticed.

"What is your name?" I asked her in imperfect French.

"Anise," she responded with a big smile, and fell back to walk behind me, right on my heels.

I was still getting used to the reality that so many Congolese had names like James, Mark, Mary, or Anise. Because their culture had long been influenced by Western religions and Western cultures, the native population had come to be, superficially at least, about fifty percent Christian. Actually their faith was a blend of Christianity, geographic culture, and tribal superstitions, but it seemed to work perfectly well for them. I said my name to Anise, who repeated it back with difficulty.

"Fwed," she said, and the other children giggled happily.

We moved down the trail, Anise knitting, other children playfully following behind us, and adults ahead chattering in French. As they were discussing local history, I moved closer to eavesdrop and learned that Pygmies were still living throughout the forests of the country. We might even see some of them before the day was done.

Our safari moved deeper into the valley, descending over hard, slippery clay where falling would have been easy and the tumble to the bottom would have been fast and brutal. Momentarily we reached a clearing and suddenly I could see that we were on the very edge of a cliff. We were hovering about a hundred and fifty feet over a grand valley that was thick with banana, palm, and baobab, and short things and tall things and bushy things and sparse things, all forming a dazzling blend of greens. The sight was ominous and threatening, dark and powerfully beautiful and green. It was warm and breathtaking, enchanting and beckoning, and green. It was pure nature, life at its deepest meaning, and it was a hundred shades of green.

Regrettably the forest was nearly silent, for most of the animals were gone. Having hunted themselves out of reliable sources of game, villagers were compelled to go twenty-five miles or more to find prey no larger than antelope. Porcupine and rats were still about, and they were harvested, but even the serpents were largely gone because their food supply had disappeared as well. The Congolese, simply accepting life as it was, tended to boast about the taste of rat and something that resembled groundhog. But no matter what creature they served for dinner, they called it "bush meat".

We continued our descent to the swampy bottom where two very old fish ponds were nestled in dark, musty shadows. We learned that they had been there for many years, built by the French, but they had long since been abandoned because they had never been productive. Presumably, our lesson for the day was to examine efforts that had failed and to learn why. Having insufficient sunlight to promote algae growth, having a water source that primarily depended on run-off or upwelling ground water, the two ponds were little more than deep puddles in a large bog. We Americans puttered around for about an hour before conferring and agreeing that the site was entirely unsuited to fish farming, then we started back up the hill.

During the climb, several little girls were waiting with Anise who was still quietly knitting her shawl. She smiled at me as I approached but she did not meet my eyes directly. The other girls moved quickly aside, giggling, prodding, suddenly giving me the feeling that I had been chosen. Or at least that I was being given the opportunity to choose. An American man was considered a prize for a young African girl, because Americans were all thought to be rich. Even though I was already middle-aged, that only added to my "value". Older men were looked upon as "wise" and better able to care for their wives. When we reached the village again and we volunteers headed toward the truck, Anise was still beside me.

"When will you be back?" she asked.

"Probably never," I replied. "We will all be returning to Brazzaville soon, and I don't know where I will be sent from there." Anise continued for perhaps three more steps and then she fell back with nothing more to say.

Minutes later, when we had reclaimed seats in the truck and started to roll, I turned to wave goodbye to Anise who was standing between two huts out of sight of the other children, no longer knitting, no longer smiling. She watched us until we turned the corner but she did not wave back.

Later that afternoon after we had visited another village and studied more pond-efforts that had failed, we were all sweaty, hot, tired and would have given ten dollars for a glass of iced tea and a cool place to drink it. As we walked along the dirt road back toward the truck, we came to a field of orange trees where the fruit was a yellowish red. I asked the farmer if I might pick one. Nodding affirmatively, he stepped to a tree with low hanging branches and began picking and tossing oranges to each of us. I sliced mine open with my Swiss Army knife and bit into it, only to discover that it wasn't an orange at all. It was shaped and colored like an orange, but it was one the sourest lemons I had ever tasted. My thirst disappeared almost the moment the rich juice touched my tongue, but I ate it to the rind.

Thanks to yet another prearrangement wherein we Americans paid the cost and a Congolese woman did the cooking, we had a late lunch of saka saka (finely shredded cassava leaves), smoked fish, fried fish, pili pili (blazing hot pepper), manioc, and palm wine. All over Central Africa, manioc roots were eaten boiled or fried, and the leaves were chopped and cooked like turnips back home. The palm wine was an interesting concoction. It was opaque, pale green in color; it seemed to be naturally carbonated and it had a sweet fruity taste. It also had a strong alcoholic kick that tended to creep up on a person. Having sampled it before, I knew that it was only good when fresh, for within a few hours it would become sharply tart like vinegar. Pouring my third round of that very fresh wine, I stopped when two large flies flowed out of the jug and plopped into my glass. Staring at them for a few seconds, wondering who would notice my cultural insensitivity, I decided that I had had enough. I pushed the drink aside and left the table.

When the meal was done and we were back on the road again, we were driving toward our last destination for the day. We stopped to pick up another farmer who was about to take us to a very special place. Several miles into thick forest, we turned onto a neglected pair of ruts that were the remnants of a long abandoned dirt road. Thick brush swept across the windshield and slapped against the cab and raked both sides of the Rover, but we kept moving slowly until we reached a tree trunk that blocked the road. Surely someone had chopped down the tree to deliberately block the path, but none among us commented about it.

After leaving the vehicle and starting our walk along the trail, I saw that the sun was dropping rapidly and casting long shadows into which we were directly moving. But nobody called attention to that, as if to do so would have shown a lack of nerve or, worse yet, a lack of trust in the African farmer. As the thick woods closed tightly around us our "road" narrowed into a single rut of hard, gray clay that soon became a mere scar in the grass, more felt than seen. Minutes later when we reached a clearing that marked the end of the trail, we turned to the right and penetrated the wall of brush. And then, as we were easing rather sharply downhill again, I heard falling water.

We stopped at the top of a rock ledge, where the air was as fresh as mountain air after a snowfall. The lip of that ledge hung over a crystal river that poured from the forest and spread across an area about thirty yards wide, where the water was no more than a few inches deep. Rushing on from there, clear water pushed over flattened rock and then tumbled about sixty feet below us. Beautiful. Beckoning.

Carefully making our way down in the ever fading light, we were following the falls in dense shadows and thick brush through which I could see the man ahead of me and little else. Soon we were feeling our way along. As we moved over damp, slick clay next to the wall of the cliff, we inched along and clung to protruding roots. The man just ahead of me suddenly lost his footing and swung violently around until he was able to draw his legs underneath him again and reset them on the ledge. He paused there, took a deep breath and went on. The sounds of falling water had become a loud roar by the time we reached the spot where it slammed onto a wide bed of rocks, but to my surprise, we had only descended one tier of that magnificent place. My feet were at the very edge of a gorgeous pool from which rapid water streamed into a ninety degree turn, fell from another lip of rock and cascaded another twenty yards to the valley floor. Some in our group kept on toward the bottom, while others decided that was far enough. Stripping and wading into the icy water, my skin reacted to the shock like a tongue stuck to an ice tray.

After a few minutes of cooling off, I waded back to where my clothes hung on branches, took a seat on a huge root, and got dressed again. Momentarily I started back up alone. Climbing in the shadows, not knowing if a slithering beast might fall on my shoulders at any moment or if I might slip on a root and join the others at the bottom, I kept going to the top where the last hints of light still hovered eerily over the clearing.

A few minutes later, my return to the truck might have been a very uneasy walk. Failing light had already changed the appearance of everything and nothing looks quite the same going out as it looks going in. But I spotted the clay blemish in the grass and I followed it for perhaps a hundred yards. The truck, shrouded in the brush and the shadows like some lost metal relic, was invisible until I was only a few paces from the tree that blocked it. My plan had been to climb inside, stretch out on a seat and rest my tired muscles, but then I realized that all the doors were locked. Having little else to do, I climbed up to the roof, hung my legs over the windshield and waited.

When I first arrived on the African continent, I had expected that the jungle would be alive with the calls of a thousand creatures. But there, completely encircled by dense forest, there was silence. Momentarily, as my ears adjusted, I distinctly heard children's voices. Children! Minutes later, the African farmer who had led us to the falls came up the trail, evidently having seen the wisdom of an early departure from the woods.

"The others take too many chances," he said. "You and I are older and wiser." He smiled and I nodded my agreement.

"I thought I heard children," I said to him. "Is there a village close by?" He paused to listen for several seconds, then shook his head negatively.

"Non. Pygmy la ba."

"Pygmies?" I asked with evident surprise.

"Oui."

"Can you show me?"

"Oui."

We went into the dark brush beside the truck, stepping cautiously and pushing things aside. A few steps later, where even my guide had trouble finding his way, someone called out saying to go left, not right. He called back, bore left, and I followed. Suddenly, just inside the thick wall of vegetation no more than thirty steps from the road, we found ourselves standing in a little clearing where a dozen Pygmies, men and women and children, all half naked, were making a temporary home. They rushed around me crying out in delight and apparent surprise. They had to have known that the truck was out there, just as they surely must have known that I was sitting on it, but they had evidently not expected a personal visit.

Their camp had two thatched lean-to shelters. A low fire was burning between them, and a small animal was being cooked on a stick. A frail old woman, naked above the waist and wearing only a dirty wrap around her middle, was clearly the spokesperson for the group. She extended her hand and said something that I presumed to be a greeting and then she turned to her family and said something to them. Following that, all of them, adults and children alike, lined up and approached me for a handshake. My African companion spoke to them in some tribal language, no doubt explaining who I was and what we were doing in their front yard.

Hearing the word "American" and something that sounded a bit like "villagers," I presumed he was also telling them about the work we had set out to do with the rural Congolese.

"Hmmm," they grunted in cheerful unison, as if greatly pleased with the news.

It was surprising to me that the Pygmies were not tiny, fat people as the Tarzan movies had portrayed them. They were slight, perhaps only about five feet tall, but they were lean, muscular, and seemed to be quite normal in every physical way. It was difficult to understand why other Congolese so thoroughly disdained them, for they were considered to be inferior people. They were not allowed to attend Congolese schools nor even to be treated in hospitals. Thus the nomadic people of the forest stayed on the move and lived off the land as they had done for centuries. They were said to have no interest in towns, schools, houses, jobs nor money, but as they were mostly excluded from those things, it was hardly possibly to know which came first. Pygmies ate from the forest, they tended their own wounds, they knew the land better than any other Congolese, and they worshiped it.

Wherever I have traveled in my lifetime, an inferior population has always existed for the rest of the people to hate. It seemed sad to me that the Pygmies were in such a very bad position, for their jungle, their home, was disappearing around them and their sources of food were disappearing with it. Someday they would surely be forced to emerge from the bush, and to adapt even as third class citizens. Perhaps they would then function as little more than slave labor for the masses, but they would eventually cease to exist as an independent signature upon the landscape of third world Africa.

It seemed only a matter of time.

2

The Long, Long Road to Makoua

Six weeks after our trip to Sibiti, I got the news that I had been waiting for. Eric, the coordinator for the Congo fish project, told me that my final post would be a village called Makoua, located literally on the equator about three hundred miles northeast of Brazzaville. It was said to be a "town" of about five thousand villagers living in houses with shaded yards, where people enjoyed treated water and electricity and bought things in local stores for most any purpose that one might imagine. Eric, a tall and sturdy Tom Selleck look-alike who seemed to truly care about our project, also told me that the house chosen for me was almost finished and most of my furniture was already inside it, waiting for me.

"Oh," he said as an afterthought. "Tom will be driving you up, and he will be carrying the rest of the cash to pay your furniture maker in full".

It all sounded wonderful to me. After so many months of being under the control of others, I was excited to advance to the next level and to get away from our own bureaucracy. And regarding the money for the furniture, I was told not to release a nickel of it until the last of my things were delivered. That would be soon though, because the furniture maker had been paid a lot of money in advance. That piece of news aroused a flash of memory. Throughout training we had been told NEVER to pay in advance for anything in Africa, for that was a sure way to lose money and to get nothing done. Surely our leaders knew what they were doing, I told myself, and I put it out of my mind.

All of our Peace Corps officials resided in Brazzaville. They were all former volunteers who had actually competed to remain with the Corps as long as they could after completion of their own assignments. It was my guess that they hoped to win the ultimate reward of a Directorship somewhere, along with a fat salary of about $60,000 per year plus transportation, housing and living allowances. Bob was our Director, Tom was his Administrative Assistant, Eric answered to Tom, and Gary was the paymaster and accountant for the entire program. Although most of my day to day contact was with Eric, it was Tom who met me in the heavily guarded parking lot at 6:30 A.M. one Tuesday morning. I was already standing by, ready to load my boxes of food, pots and pans, dishes and everything else that I had bought for a long stay at my very isolated post.

"Good grief," Tom said with a whistle when he saw it. He was about five-ten, weighed probably a hundred-seventy-five pounds. and was as serious as a Montana cowboy. "I don't know if we can get all that stuff in here," he added.

"Well, a lot of it is what you folks told me to buy and the rest is to make my life easier. Anyway, I was told that this kind of stuff is a lot cheaper here than it would be in Makoua."

"Yeah, that's probably true. Most of what they sell there comes from either here or Gabon anyway, and they have to move everything by truck. All right. Let's get it aboard." I had already learned that no rails existed north of Brazzaville, and had therefore presumed that materials were trucked into that direction. I was about to learn just how significant that really was.

It did take some effort to get everything fitted inside or tied to the top of the Japanese Land Cruiser, but soon enough we were tightly packed and under way. Within an hour we were twenty miles from Brazzaville on an asphalt strip known as National Highway #2, speeding through long gentle curves, rolling hills and magnificent valleys. The weather was chilly and clear at that time, providing perfect conditions to enjoy the brilliant green of open plains that came in and out of sight between grand expanses of forest. Tom chatted cheerfully while I sat without much to say and watched the countryside roll by.

Occasionally there appeared a dotted white line down the middle of the pavement, but most of the time it was simply a dark strip on which two vehicles had just enough room to pass. When we had gone about twenty-five miles from the city, potholes began to appear. When another twenty miles had faded behind us, the holes were more frequent, much wider and decidedly deeper. A short time later, we had to leave the highway altogether, running in deep sandy ruts made by other four-wheel-drive vehicles.

"This is gonna get tricky from here on," Tom muttered as he steered through it. The six cylinder Land Cruiser had no problem with the terrain, but the highway had the distinction of being the worst that I had ever seen. When I commented about that, Tom shrugged indifferently.

"This is *good* road," he said, "compared to what lies ahead." He paused a moment and then added, "This country doesn't have enough money to maintain the roads, so the holes get deeper and deeper every year. Then the rainy season comes, and they fill up with water and hide what could be bottomless pits". The time was just at the end of September, right on the leading edge of the new rainy season.

When nearly three hours and the first hundred and twenty miles were behind us, we reached a village on the Lefini River called Mbouambe. Mbouambe seemed to be an ordinary village with a few thatched dwellings on the hilltops, but it played a special role for long distance travelers. It was Tom's routine stopping place for lunch.

"The river marks the outer edge of a huge animal preserve," he said, "which means there is plenty of game. You can usually buy all sorts of illegal meat here." He pointed to two open sheds just a few steps down from the road. "Highway buffet," he added. That day, the buffet happened to be, for no apparent reason, closed. Perhaps the hunters had missed their targets that day. We bought soft drinks and snacks at a tiny roadside kiosk and then moved on.

Miles later we reached a place where the pavement was entirely gone, having yielded to deep trenches, and once again we rolled into deep, barren sand. When we found asphalt again and were moving rapidly, we passed mile after mile of steep hills and deep valleys and open stretches of savanna bordered by forests as far as my eyes could see. When a loud pop sounded in the distance, Tom said with a grin, "Somebody just shot dinner." I envisioned yet another endangered creature lying in the grass, legs kicking spasmodically, blood seeping into the sand. I also realized that the thought was an absurd sentiment in a nation where the truism was, "If I don't do it, somebody else will."

As we rushed on, villages flickered past us like slow-motion frames of a travel movie and the colors changed from monotonous greens to the stark grays and browns of boulders and rugged cliffs. Soon we were riding above a splendid view of jungle canopy that went toward hazy hills far in the distance.

"This is big sky country," Tom commented without looking at me.

"Sure is," I said back. "Beautiful."

More villages came and went, boasting houses of mud and sometimes even plank, all covered with either thatch or tin, and all virtually lifeless as the inhabitants had surely gone into their fields or into the bush. Next we reached the river Nkini, an ominous body of dark, swift water with lush greenery on the banks. Carnivores came to my mind as I scanned the black mirror below. It was not a place where I would care to swim.

A hut still under completion, using bamboo strips and mud.

Barely one hundred and eighty miles into our trip, we drove through Gamboma, a pleasant little town with thatched houses scattered about the uneven landscape. Next stop, Oyo, which was the home of the former president of the Congo. We passed over the river Komo, where the water was quiet, black and sinister, then we crossed the wide, gray Alima River in Oyo. The broad, freshly paved roads and streets clearly revealed that someone of importance resided there. Beyond Oyo, the terrain grew flatter and far more densely forested. And, as we approached the equator, the air was growing hot. Very, very hot.

A round hut of bamboo. Such construction is less
common in the Congo.

Suddenly the pavement disappeared again under oblong lakes of muddy water. Little sections of asphalt still reappeared from time to time, but those broken segments were of no use to any vehicle. Sometimes we were forced to venture hundreds of yards off the road, traveling at about five miles per hour with sand flying beneath our wheels. We met a Nissan pickup with about twenty people packed in the bed, and with still others sitting on the roof and fenders while one stood on the rear bumper. Suddenly the vehicle sank into a deep hole and teetered to one side until two wheels lifted into the air and people started bailing out. Load lightened, it then settled back to the ground. The truck stopped beyond the worst of it to wait for the passengers to reclaim their places. Nine hours and three-hundred-twenty miles into the journey, we came to another stretch of smooth highway.

"We're almost in Owando,"Tom told me. "It's the capitol city of the Cuevette Region and the largest town this side of Brazzaville." Not waiting for me to react, he added, "We have to do a mail drop here."

We were about to visit another volunteer, a girl from Arizona named Anne, who lived in the heart of town. We drove a mile from the main highway on a smooth, curving road that was lined on both sides with huge eucalyptus trees. We passed a large playing field and several government buildings on the left and a post office on the right and then the pavement ended again at a place where empty sheds were bunched together on one corner suggesting a large and active daytime market. Several tables that stood on the opposite corner, were, according to Tom, where palm wine was sold by the glass every night. Every large village I had yet seen had such a morning market place (which we called the "grand marche"), and each also had a "night marche" that ran along its main thoroughfares after the sun went down. Typically, a night market was composed of a disconnected series of tables set up along the roadside, each lit by candles or lanterns, each selling whatever few items the displayers had to offer.

As we moved on through the intersection I noticed shiny aluminum poles bearing street lamps that stood about a hundred yards apart along the dirt avenue.

"Streets lights? Wow!" I commented.

"Those come on for a while most every night when the electricity is working," Tom said. "Pretty uptown, eh?"

"Doesn't the electricity work all the time?"

"No, not at all. It's generated with diesel power, the fuel has to be trucked here from the city, and it's expensive. So they only run it a few hours each night if it runs at all. Same in Makoua."

Wherever we had gone in Central Africa, we usually found at least one bar with its own private gasoline powered generator. Thus such bars, at least, were operational whether the rest of town was open for business or not. That day we rolled past several stores, shops, beer bars and even a bakery, beyond which I could hear a generator rattling in the background. And then we turned left, went two blocks down a shaded street, and finally pulled up in front of large whitewashed house.

Anne was a second year volunteer who had recently been transferred to Owando from another post in the opposite end of the country. When Tom hit the horn, she hurried out to meet us.

"Hello," she said happily.

"Got some mail from home for you," Tom said as he handed her a large stack of packages and envelopes.

"Great," she chirped back. And then she ducked to look at me in the other seat. "I heard you're going to be in Makoua. It will be nice to have an American neighbor only forty five miles away."

Her words caused me to wonder how it was that everybody always seemed to know more about my business than I did, again demonstrating that talk was free and open with everybody except the person directly affected by it. But I said nothing about it. She told me to visit when I could, she waved goodbye, and we rushed on. Reaching the national highway again where a service station occupied one corner, we stopped so that I could fill up a ten-liter container with kerosene. I had been warned that the supply of fuel was unreliable from that point on, and I did not want to risk being without any.

When underway again, still on Highway # 2, what lay in store for us came clearly to the forefront. The asphalt had terminated in Owando, leaving us to travel through the roughest conditions we had yet faced. As we persisted, sometimes the forest was so close that even a curve could take us into nearly pitch darkness. At other times, the road disappeared under loose mud and water for long stretches, making our way quite treacherous. Dealing with swamps in the low country and severely eroded higher ground or deep sand everywhere in between, our forward progress had become so absurdly slow that some of it would have been faster on foot. Yet Tom seemed to ignore his struggle with the wheel as if ours was only a casual Sunday drive. Another brutal four hours later we reached the outskirts of Makoua just at dusk, having averaged thirty miles per hour for one entire day of riding.

Cool in Brazzaville and sultry in Makoua, moving fast in Brazzaville and painfully slow in Makoua, fresh in Brazzaville and exhausted in Makoua, we were both eager to end our journey in the place that I was to call home for the next twenty months. First, however, we were to pick up a local Congolese named Herve who was to be my "homologue". That meant that he and I would work together during my stay so that he would be able to sustain the project after my work was done. Tom had already told me, "You will enjoy working with Herve. He was instrumental in getting things done on your house".

Obviously expecting us, as soon as we stopped near his front door Herve rushed outside as if greatly excited. The tall, pudgy coal-black man greeted Tom first, then he reached through the window and pumped my hand while speaking rapid French. Next he jumped into the back to direct us to my house. Situated only about two blocks farther down, it was a little brick abode on the last curve before crossing over the Likouala-Mossaka River and no more than a hundred yards from the equator.

I was shocked to first set my eyes on the place, for it looked more like ruins than a home. We stepped up on a little brick-floored porch where a locked door was to my left and a large empty space was straight ahead. That space, as if planned but never completed, had a gaping hole in the north wall that must have been intended to someday be a window. I only had a moment to glance at it while the door to my left grudgingly responded to Herve's weight. Following him inside, entering the dimness and taking a moment to adjust to it, I suffered another moment of shock. The room was large, maybe twenty by twenty, occupied only by a double bed with four narrow slats. The walls were crawling with insects and the floor was littered with bat guano under several rafters from which the ceiling had long been stripped away. If all of my furniture was supposed to have been delivered already, something was clearly amiss. Maybe the bed was all that I was to receive.

Not only would my 3" foam rubber mattress have to lie directly atop those slats, but it would only cover about half of the area. My mattress was made for a single bed, because that was what Eric told me had been built, and my mosquito net was also made for a single. While I stood there dumbly letting it all sink in, Tom and Herve hung my net with lines tied to large nails that had been left in the rafters. Quite pleased with themselves, the two men grinned and waited for me to say how happy it all made me. I was tempted to ask how I might keep insects from coming up around the spaces not covered by my mattress, but I already knew the answer. That was my problem.

Momentarily, after Herve fueled and lit one of my lanterns, dim light flickered under the tin roof and cast moving shadows all about the room. Spider webs hung everywhere with a variety of interesting carcasses clinging to them, and a roach bigger than my thumb scurried for safety underneath the bed. Dust rose in a ghostly orange haze all around my feet as a lizard rushed through a crack under a shutter.

A second room about four feet wide by about twenty feet long, accessible only from the bedroom, was rather like a large walk-in closet. That was actually my storage area and bathroom. It had one window in the middle, covered with rotten boards that had once been shutters, and it had a four by four square at one end inside which a person could stand and pour water over his body for bathing. The soapy waste would run directly to the outside through a hole in the wall that was large enough for rats to pass through, and signs suggested that they had been doing exactly that.

Startled by a fluttering noise overhead, I looked up in time to glimpse a bat heading out for the evening. Tunnels of light from the moon poured through a vent near the peak of the roof and seeped through holes along the tops of the walls and through cracks in the wooden shutters. I took a deep breath. My house was a sieve for light, for rain, and for the menagerie of insects and small animals that infested it. Maybe, it occurred to me, I was expected to thank Herve for being instrumental in getting it all done. While he was talking away, telling me how terrific the place was, my disappointment must have been evident. Tom started into a cheery defense of the place.

"You might have to have a door knocked through the bedroom wall for access to that other big room," he said. "Then the old entrance can be sealed up and the wooden door can be switched over." I was unmoved, but he kept on.

"A local mason can be hired to do all that, and to finish the window in the other room. He can also shutter it for you." I was still unimpressed. What he was really saying was that everything would be just rosy, if only I survived long enough to make it so. He also assured me that the rest of my furniture would arrive in the next few days. That was an interesting tidbit of news which meant he had known all along that it had not been delivered as I had been told. And then he dropped a fresh bomb. "Eric will come up from Brazzaville in a few days with the money to pay what's owed on it."

I almost asked why he was not carrying the money as I was told he would be, but I suddenly had the feeling that I had been suckered. Not even bothering to respond, I remembered Eric telling me that my house was "almost finished". "Finished," I thought, as in "done for!" The whole issue was a great joke, and the joke was on me.

When my things were unloaded from the truck and locked inside the bedroom, Herve joined us for a ride to the nearby river where we could all take a bath and cool off. Driving very slowly down a steep eroded hill at the foot of a bridge, tires crunching in the gravel, we finally reached the bottom and parked at the water's edge. Under a dazzling night sky, the white sand was almost luminescent as I followed them into the cold, swift water. By then I had given up on expectations and promises, and was counting only on statistics.

The odds were 66.6 %, that the crocodile would eat them first.

3

Alone in Makoua

Tom slept in the big open room that first night, lower body inside a sleeping bag with only a partial mosquito bar covering him from the chest up. That was in disregard for any snakes that might curl up with him or the mosquitoes that would attack any human tissue that touched the net. Maybe, I decided, he was just trying to make a statement that some of the safety lessons of our training were unnecessary after all.

Several second year volunteers had warned me not to expect much from our American leaders after being assigned to a permanent post. As we were supposed to manage for ourselves, being wise and self-sufficient adults, non-emergency assistance was seldom part of the procedure. I was also told that the routine was to abandon every "newbie" at his or her post as quickly as possible after delivery to it, so that the shock would linger a while. It was all rather a standard joke, a part of tradition practiced only because everybody else had been subjected to it. Just after dawn of that first morning, Tom led me across the road to show me the lone faucet from which I was to take water and then he disappeared in a column of dust, headed home. If the joke was true, then he must have had a great chuckle as he watched me shrink in his rear view mirror.

Actually, beyond the initial disappointments of the evening before, I felt relatively good about things. I was free to make my own schedule for the first time in many months, and free to set up camp inside four walls without a dozen other people sharing the space and eating my food. There would, of course, be disadvantages in my relatively pure camping experience. But the new adventure itself just might balance things out.

When Tom was out of sight, I set out one of my little kerosene burners to make some hot mocha and then ambled about, cup in hand, to inspect my new home. Only then did I notice that my house was a peculiar duplex structure, divided by a solid wall from front to back to separate tenants. That wall helped to support the tin roof, but many bricks were missing up high, making it possible for any creature the size of a baseball to pass from one compartment to the other.

Regarding my "bedroom," someone had recently brushed a coat of whitewash over three walls and part of a fourth, but no effort had been made to fill any of the holes, anywhere. All of the walls were pocked with insect borings, and several suspicious holes about the size of a snake sank through the brick floor. Several points of light shone through the roof where it was probably punctured by nails a long time ago and through which leaks would surely occur, but the leaks would likely be slow drips rather than steady streams. Webs hung from several of the rafters that ran the length of the house, front to back, and other webs decorated every corner with spiders clinging to them. One huge specimen backed into the shadows when I spotted him on the floor.

My lifelong impression had been that all bats hang upside down in cool places and sleep all day, but that certainly was not true in equatorial Makoua. The evening before, I heard high-pitched chatter when my bats prepared to go out for feeding. And I heard them again when they returned in the early hours of the morning. Looking for them in the light of day, aided by a flashlight, I could not see a single one. Yet I knew they were up there somewhere sleeping invisibly on the timbers that supported the corrugated tin. I was amazed that they were able to tolerate the heat as the sun bore down on that rusted metal, but they obviously did. Fresh deposits of guano were all over the top of my net.

Continuing the inspection, I noted that the bedroom had a pair of windows overlooking the dirt highway out front, each shuttered with wooden panels that could be swung open on badly worn hinges which squeaked and wiggled when moved. The shutters had been secured with cheap little dead bolts that would only have kept out an honest person, while securing the house against insects had evidently never been part of the plan. The boards over the back window had been nailed shut, apparently a long time ago, as if to protect the place from thieves.

The wooden door at the entrance was old, shaky and cracked, with spaces large enough for mosquitoes to pass through on the wing. The best news about my security system was that a burglar would have to make a lot of noise while breaking in. The other half of my house, the large room on the north side of that solid wall, had no door and no shutters in the spaces that had been built for them. Thus open to the outside world, acting as a haven for whatever creatures chose to set up housekeeping, it had become home for a variety of insects including a family of termites. A great teardrop of clay about two feet thick was securely fixed in a corner near the roof and hung down to within an arm's length above the floor. No life was visible around it, but, short of beating the thing down, there was no way to tell if it was inhabited or not.

My yard was also interesting. All but the front of the tiny lot was bordered by either elephant grass or manioc fields. The trunk of a palm tree lay across most of the back yard amid a heavy growth of weeds, while another tall but sickly palm stood in the southwest corner looking as if it too might fall in a strong wind. My toilet, located in the other corner, had been erected over a twenty-foot shaft that looked new, and a concrete slab had been positioned over it with a brick-sized hole for the passage of wastes. Aware of one volunteer who fell partially through such a stall because of shoddy concrete, I planned to use mine with the utmost caution. Making matters still worse, the walls had not been completed, no roof had yet been built, and no door had yet been hung.

The front of my house as seen from National Highway #2

A drainage ditch in the front separated the clay of the yard from the sandy edges of the National Highway, which went north another hundred and twenty miles through the thick of the rain forest to a place called Ouesso. "They don't use it much," Tom earlier told me, "because it's one of the worst roads in the entire country. Those that do use it are bringing stuff, or passengers, from across the border." (That meant from either Cameroon or Central African Republic.) A volunteer had told me a slightly different story about that road however, which I suspected was closer to the more complete truth. "They use it for moving ivory," she said. "The word I get is nobody cares much about it, except maybe the Makoua police and they get paid to keep it quiet."

Across the street where my water source was located, several buildings formed a square compound with a great courtyard in the middle. Tom had told me that it was the local station of the national police force, which was actually a part of the Congolese Army. When I walked over to fill my water canister that morning, two women were at work in the yard, one sweeping the soil with a brush-broom, and the other hanging clothes on a line. We exchanged greetings, but nothing else was said between us. Next I decided to take a walk to the Likouala-Mossaka River which was just across the equator and about a five minute walk from my door.

Standing thirty feet above the currents on a concrete bridge built by Germans a few years back, I could see perhaps a mile westward and half that distance eastward. The river was a pretty and soothing sight, but it was also as black as oil and filled with all sorts of creatures that I had yet to encounter. The road leading to the bridge was on level ground, but a sharp drop led to the water at both ends. On the far side, that drop opened into a low area, several acres large, that lay barely higher than the water. Also there were great stacks of metal pipes along with several road graders and bulldozers, all slowly sinking into the weeds and mounds of white clay. Another half dozen pieces of similar equipment were on my side of the river, parked close to a government building, but none of them looked as if they had been moved in quite some time.

That sort of waste seemed to be typical of Central Africa. Such machines were used until they broke down or the fuel ran out, then they were often abandoned to rust into ruin. I had once asked Eric about such waste and received an uncharacteristically straight answer, "Why should they fix anything when some Western nation will give them a new one sooner or later?"

Alone in Makoua

The "highway" as seen from my porch. This was actually taken after some repairs had been made to the wall. The equator lies about 100 yards beyond the woman with the load on her back, and the river is just beyond that.

The river, photographed from on the bridge.

Below me at the water's edge where we bathed the night before, clothes and dishes were being washed by women and girls. Several children were swimming in the midst of it all, young boys stark naked and girls in panties or dressed in traditional pagnes (a wrap-around garment made of lightweight fabric). And a few yards up from them, several men were bathing nude in the shallows where a dozen pirogues (dugouts) were secured side by side. Interestingly, tradition in much of third-world Africa dictated that women bathe downstream from the men, and nudity among adult females was entirely forbidden.

I already knew that it was not uncommon for girls to violate such rules if they were so motivated, bathing naked in open yards while someone poured water over their heads. They didn't even rush to conceal themselves when men walked by, and sometimes they would giggle when observed. One of our second year volunteers, the one in Sibiti, came home one day to find several teenaged girls bathing naked in his home made cistern. They left when he shooed them out, but shyness played no role in it and they came back as often as they felt they could get away with it.

The men's bathing spot was awkward to reach because of a hill of gravel over which one had to climb to get there, and due to the dugouts that were in the way at the river's edge. About a dozen men were using the spot that day, lathering themselves until their bodies were covered with suds like whipped topping. Few of them seemed to know how to swim, as they would duck beneath the surface to rinse but not venture more than waist deep.

Drinking water for Makoua was drawn from the river by diesel-powered pumps. Each day water was pumped into a pair of cisterns, from which it was redistributed across the community in underground plastic pipes. That was quite an achievement for a town so far from any important business center, but like most conveniences in the Congo, it was all built with foreign money, foreign equipment and foreign expertise. Evidently not everyone in Makoua could afford piped water, however, for women and children were hauling it from the river in plastic bidons (ten liter jerry cans) carried in wheelbarrows.

Just after finishing my walk and returning home, Herve rushed inside without knocking. He was, he explained, on a mission in the performance of his duty.

"I must introduce you to important people." he announced, meaning I was to go with him. I grabbed my hat and locked the door.

Our first stop was the police compound across the street. The several buildings there made up a "station," a jail, and a long structure with three apartments. A policeman lived there with his family, while other "unofficial" people inhabited the rest. A single faucet stood alone in the middle of the yard, hovering over a large puddle amid a rich growth of weeds. That faucet served the entire compound, and was to serve me as well. The main office, or station, situated all the way across the courtyard, was to be our first visit.

This shows two thirds of the building in which lived a police family.

The military man in front of whose desk I found myself standing seemed to be an enlisted person. Dressed in a jungle green uniform with long sleeves bearing stripes, he was seated behind an old wooden desk with carvings in its top. Behind him, taped to the unpainted wall, were several snapshots of unsmiling men and women who might have been wanted persons. The man's name was Norman.

Norman invited me to sit while he examined my papers and made a few notes. He had an uncertain look on his face as he turned the pages and then he remarked that something was not right. Herve, helping me with the language by rephrasing anything that seemed to have gone over my head, said that the officer in charge, a sort of chief of police, was out of town at the moment but I would have to see him personally when he returned. Acknowledging his words, promising to return, I followed Herve outside.

Next, as we left the compound, Herve explained that the town's water pressure was activated at about dawn each morning and it shut down before dark each day. "We don't have enough diesel to run the pumps all the time." He said,

"But the water is potable at the pipe." I chose to regard that declaration as a "maybe so, maybe not" sort of thing. We had been taught that the Congolese would always tell us what they thought we wanted to hear, and that nothing should be taken for granted. Underscoring that lesson, large water filters were standard issue for all volunteers, and we were expected to use them.

We moved on to the Bureau of Agriculture another block away on a red-clay street. That was where Herve and his associates worked, even though none of them had been paid in several months. One of the reasons that the national economy had collapsed during the time of the former President was the blatant corruption that had permeated the country from the top down. People at all levels of authority had been caught cheating in one way or another, such as assigning employment to infant children and fictitious people and then collecting the payroll for all of them. There, in the front office of the bureau, one man was seated behind a desk while two others were resting on a wooden bench in front of him. One of them was Calixte, Herve's immediate boss. The occupations of the other two were not mentioned. None of them stood to greet me, but they grinned broadly and shook my hand with vigor.

That building too was brick, and roofed with tin that had holes through which the clear blue sky was plainly visible. Herve opened the padlock that secured a door, pushed it open, and invited me to go inside my new office. There, in the dim light, a wooden desk nearly filled the room. As I opened the shutters behind it with a mighty effort, bright sunlight poured in through a fog of dust that had collected there for many months. Layers of old dirt lay on the desk, and splotches marked places where rain had dripped through the roof. But it was a desk, in an office, and it was mine to use as I pleased. So what if the building had no electricity, nor filing cabinets, nor typewriters. It did have a telephone, which Herve said occasionally worked. If I got lucky I might even be able to call my family back home someday. A deterrent was that such calls had to be arranged in advance through the local telephone office and the cost was $32.00 for about a half minute. I would keep that in mind.

Herve was a big man. He was upwards of six feet tall, big in the shoulders, and he walked with a long easy stride that forced me to stretch to keep up. Back on the main road again, as we went toward town, he said that Makoua was spread over a square mile, give or take, but he thought the population was not nearly as large as I had been told. "Maybe two thousand people now," he said. "Many have moved away."

Momentarily we came upon a place that actually astonished me. It was a large block building with plate glass windows in the front, on which faded letters mentioned something about a super market. Peering through the windows, I could see grocery carts still parked between long empty aisles.

"It has been closed a long time," Herve said.

"Why did it close?" He simply shrugged off the question and we kept moving. Evidently Makoua had once been a richer, livelier place with a far more interesting history than had been divulged to me, but nobody who should have known had explained a word about its past.

Two major thoroughfares divided the town, one going north toward Ouesso and the other almost due west toward Etoumbi, Kelle, and to the Gabon border. A dozen dirt streets flanked both sides of the main routes, all crossed by a dozen others to form remarkably correct blocks that suggested foreign influence. Some of those streets had been closed to vehicles for quite a long time, due either to erosion or collapsed bridges over ditches that carried rain water toward the river. Logs had been placed over some of those for pedestrian use, but because no trucks traveled there anymore, children ran free in the streets and even goats and chickens had no fear.

The "grand marche" was located in the heart of the community no more than a quarter-mile from my house. Because people deposited their wastes near the street, my first sense was that it smelled like a garbage dump. It was also a busy place that began shortly after dawn and ran until about noon each day. The market was a collection of flimsy tables where fresh vegetables and fruits, palm oil, candles, lye soap, cosmetics, toiletries and other such items were displayed in the open air. There was also a large covered shed where fish, chicken, bush meats, peanut butter, manioc, bread and other items were sold by whoever arrived first to set up shop. Perhaps a hundred people were there that morning, all of whom seemed rather indifferent to my presence as if I was already old news.

I browsed for a minute, then Herve and I went farther up the street to where several little boutiques featured fabrics, dry goods, hardware or canned or packaged foods, mostly imported from China, Japan or France. One of them was packed to the ceiling with household items including radios and cassette players, once again suggesting the prosperity of another time when people had the money to buy such things.

"You must buy a broom here," Herve announced. I bought a broom.

Makoua was a town of surprises and disappointments. Electricity did power a few of homes and the streetlights, although only for a few hours each evening. Running water was available to the privileged few, and even then only during the day after the cisterns had been supplied the night before. The town's only fuel depot, Hydro Congo, was a block from the grand marche just past a modern looking two-story building with glass windows. That was the local office of the national telephone company, in which only one room of the first floor was still used. Only a handful of telephones existed in the entire town, mostly for use by government officials, but even those were controlled by an antiquated wire-and-plug switchboard that generally sat idle.

The location of the "grand marche". This picture was taken at a time when the market was already closed for the day. Bush meat was butchered in the large covered building, while most of the open spaces were used to display vegetables, peanuts and small household items.

The building on the right was the largest food store in Makoua. Women often gathered there to display manioc for sale.

When walking back in the direction of my house, Herve at my side and broom in hand, we approached a place where several buildings bordered a grassy lot about the size of a football field.

"This is the medical center," Herve explained.

"You have doctors here?"

"Yes. Two of them," he said rather proudly.

We wandered through it for a closer look. The five room hospital was a dismal place, narrow and dark, with all the doors and windows open to fresher air. Across the lot from that, was the laboratory and another group of offices or sick rooms. Stopping there, I was introduced to the local Russian-trained medical doctor, a pleasant Congolese named Prosper. Doctor Prosper welcomed me to his town and assured me that if I needed medical assistance it would be available quickly and of high quality. His office had no electricity either, but it did at least have an old Underwood typewriter.

I was supposed to meet the "Chef du Makoua," a man who presided rather like an American small town mayor. Unfortunately he was not in, so we would have to reserve that visit for another time. When we returned to my own house again, Herve followed me inside without being asked and made it a point to open my boxes and rifle through my personal things. I had to bite my tongue. I had expected all along that serious adaptation would be forced upon me in my new environment, but it was sometimes difficult to distinguish between Congolese custom and rude behavior. Bidding Herve a pleasant goodbye I reinforced the hint by extending my hand. He took it reluctantly, as if to say he was not finished yet, but he got the point and made his exit.

I was eager to get started with house cleaning. I had unpacking and organizing to do, along with some bug killing, and I had to figure out how best to live out of cardboard boxes until my furniture arrived. My cans of food had to be arranged somewhere within easy reach, my water-filter had to be made operational, and a pair of single-burner kerosene stoves must be secured in a handy place for cooking. While hoping for a bit of privacy and a chance to settle in, I heard a noise out front.

"Kokoko," someone called at my door the Lengala equivalent of "knock knock". While French was the national language, the Congo had perhaps fifty different tongues that were specific to different areas of the country. Lengala was the one spoken in Makoua.

Because my guest was another stranger, I braced myself for another dose of Congolese culture and went grudgingly out to greet him. He was a fiftyish man who announced that he had five young daughters who would make fine wives and he wanted me to go with him across town to meet them. I could pick up to four of them, he explained, because that was the legal limit. "Legal limit," I thought. Back home that would refer to deer hunting or snapper fishing.

Thank goodness for limits in Central Africa.

4

Day Two in Makoua

During the evening hours of my first night alone, I went for a brief "promenade" to the night marche, which was a quite typical candlelit street market scattered along the road for a distance of about ten city blocks. Sold there were peanuts, manioc, day old French bread, or even fish that had been deep fried in palm oil and wrapped in pages from old magazines. Along the way I found a place to buy a cool bottle of cola, which helped to wash down the peanuts while I chatted with the owner a short time before wandering back toward home.

Mosquitoes chased me under the net shortly afterward. There I lay in dead air unable to throw off the covers because of insects and unable to relax beneath them because of the equatorial heat. Within an hour or two of drifting in and out of sweaty sleep, I awakened to find that my arms and neck were being fed upon by a dozen mosquitoes which had managed to find a way to reach me. It is said that they are attracted to the carbon dioxide that a person exhales. It is also said that some species are so highly adapted that they only feed on *sleeping* victims. Sometime later during the night I felt something crawling in my hair. My hand flew reflexively up to grab it, and I slung the thing toward the foot of my bed where it struck a board with a thud. First wiping the slimy residue from my fingers, I then searched for the carcass with my flashlight but was unable to locate it. Surely it had been a caterpillar, or perhaps the larval form of a large insect, but the mystery was never solved. Nevertheless, the experience reminded me that living in equatorial Africa would never be anything like home.

"Kokoko. Kokoko," someone outside my door yelled with enough vigor to wake me up at 6:05 the next morning, when dawn was barely sending little shafts of light into the room. Sleepy and grouchy, I managed to get the door open to find a middle aged man standing there. He was one of those introduced to me the day before at the agriculture center. His hand was extended in greeting.

"Herve told me to visit me every day and I am visiting," he announced. When we had shaken hands, he spun and walked out of the yard, no doubt pleased to have done his job so well. Just a little bewildered but wide awake then, I got dressed and opened up the house. Herve walked by a few minutes later while I was having my morning coffee on the porch, and he hurried up to greet me.

"What are you drinking?" he wanted to know.

"Coffee".

"Give me a cup," he ordered and then he watched me pour it. "Give me cream and sugar." He was staring into the black liquid as if something was terribly wrong.

"I don't have any cream or sugar. It is my custom to drink it black."

He tasted the coffee, made a wry expression. spat it onto the grass, put down the cup and walked away. That had just been another lesson in local culture, which taught me one way to get rid of demanding visitors. I was learning.

One of the chores from my official list of things to do was to explore my territory, to locate radios transmitters and airstrips, and to document a precise evacuation plan in the unlikely event that it would someday be necessary. Because Herve had already told me that the local Catholic Mission had a radio, and that an airport was located just beyond town, my main goal for the morning was to find the airstrip. I put on khaki pants, a long sleeved shirt and hiking boots, along with my wide brimmed black hat. Also carrying a canteen filled with filtered, bleach-treated water hanging from a shoulder strap, I headed out.

While walking through the eroded streets of town I encountered many people, some on foot, some on bicycles. Old women with empty baskets strapped to their backs marched toward their fields as little girls trailed behind them with little-girl baskets. Men stood idly in their yards, watching me cautiously, paying close attention to my camping knife. And boys, dozens of boys, were scurrying about as if they had somewhere to go without much time to get there.

I noted that some men would speak a hollow greeting, but most watched my eyes as if waiting for me to speak first. Others would look away and a few would spit into the dirt. I tried not to judge that, because spitting was such a common event in Central Africa. I had never been able to decide whether or not it was intended as ugly symbolism, so, just to be on the safe side, I never spat back.

This sort of paillote was found in most every village. Cooking was usually done inside, as was eating and relaxing.

When passing the last of the houses on the western route, a boy about fourteen years old, wearing khaki slacks, a clean white tee shirt and rubber flip-flops, suddenly appeared next to me and walked along with certain nonchalance an arm's length away. He did not look at me, but wordlessly matched my stride as if his presence had nothing to do with me at all. I decided to play the game.

We walked about two miles without exchanging a word, until we overtook two teenaged girls wearing ankle-length wraps (pagnes) and tee-shirts. The flowered pagnes had probably been a bright mix of red and yellow some time ago, but time and constant wear had turned them nearly brown. Their tee-shirts had surely been white when they were new, but they too had yielded to fading and to the many stains associated with hard labor. The three children talked noisily among themselves in Lengala, discussing something about the "mondele" (the white man), but my sense was that their words were not unkind. Just then the boy broke the ice, asking me where I was going. One of the girls, he claimed, was curious.

"I am searching for the airport," I told him in French.

"No problem," he said cheerfully. "We will show you the way."

They were all bubbling with talk then, firing question after question as we walked along four abreast. When I explained what I was doing in Makoua, they all nodded energetically and muttered sounds of approval. I learned that the boy's name was Prudence, a curious name for an African boy, but one which might have reflected some level of Western influence. The two girls were Patricia and Nadich, ages fourteen and twelve respectively, and they were on the way to their mother's garden. I found it interesting to observe once again that African children were usually tall and sturdy at young ages, for those girls were already taller than five feet and Prudence was about five-seven. None of the three had an ounce of noticeable fat, but all were muscular and sturdy and probably outweighed the average American counterpart by twenty-five pounds.

They said they knew all the farmers in the area, and they were going to spread the word to help me find interested people for my work. When we were about four miles out of town at the crest of a long hill, the distant forest had the usual but strange blue haze hanging over it as far as my eyes could see. So beautiful from that distance, it was yet a dangerous place for the inexperienced and not nearly so pretty from within. Someday, I promised myself, I would make it a point to see much more of it before so much more of it disappeared.

Soon reaching a fork in the road we followed the lesser used branch to the left. Momentarily we passed a mud house in a stand of trees, which my entourage advised me was the home of a farmer. Next, coming upon three smaller mud buildings, I learned that one was the home of the caretaker of the airport while the other two were the office and a shed. Just beyond those was an open shelter in which a diesel-powered generator sat rusting. (A thought flashed through my mind...Idle, idle everywhere and not a one will crank.) Beyond the rusted wire fence in front of it was a flat grassy field that appeared to be an old landing strip for small aircraft. The road ended there, giving way to a narrow trail that plunged into very tall elephant grass.

Believing that the object of my mission had been discovered, I was about to turn back when the children beckoned me to follow them on the trail. I followed. Suddenly, as we rounded another turn, I was stunned to come upon a long stretch of real asphalt that appeared to be in excellent condition. I simply could not understand what I was seeing. No road led to it, no hanger was in sight, no tower stood over it, no planes were tethered there, no machinery was to be found, no landing lights existed, but there it was, pavement to nowhere, used only by women and children with manioc baskets.

I had heard that a passenger aircraft had recently gone down with more than twenty people aboard, and that all flights to or from Makoua had stopped afterward. The story that the children told, was that "the mermaids took it". I never learned what "mermaids" had to do with anything, or for that matter, what an African "mermaid" was supposed to look like. The myth was simply one of many that spun out of belief in the dark spirits, and a person probably had to be an African to fully appreciate the strangeness of the symbolism.

I grew troubled over the perplexities that I had so far uncovered: an unused airstrip, a closed super market, a pair of rusted water cisterns, a few street lights, bicycles all over town, a fine concrete bridge spanning the river, vacant government buildings, and yet Makoua had no industry of its own and no significant commerce of any kind. Clearly the village had at some point been a far more vibrant place, yet no one had ever bothered to mention it to me as if full disclosure was entirely unacceptable. Indeed, our own bureaucrats tended to be evasive or downright deceptive about many such matters. It was possible, of course, that they neither knew the answers nor cared about them. It was also possible that keeping volunteers in the dark decreased the odds of early terminations. One things was sure. The mystery town of Makoua, as it then stood, seemed to have virtually nothing to offer the outside world.

Having to gather manioc roots then, the two girls said goodbye and stayed behind as Prudence and I headed back toward home under darkening clouds. When we reached the edge of town once again, we promptly came to a large house on a corner where a side street met the highway.

"That is my home," he said. "My older brother speaks very good English and he wants to meet you." He led me into the yard, dragged up a wooden chair, motioned me to sit and then he called out.

"Marin...Marin".

A tall, lanky young man, perhaps twenty or so, came out of the house with a grin and extended his hand.

"Hello," he said in clear English." I'm glad you have come. How are you?"

"Good, thank you," I replied. "And you?"

"Very well," he spoke through a perpetual smile that softened his sharply chiseled features.

"I am surprised to find someone who speaks English so well," I said.

"Yes, I speak it well," he responded. "I study it in school and I study at home." He produced a badly worn English dictionary from his back pocket and held it up for me to inspect. "I always speak it when I can."

"That's very impressive. I am happy to meet you." My remark seemed to greatly please the young man.

"The national radio told me you were coming," he informed me. "I have been waiting for you. I know where you live and what your work is all about. I will visit you tomorrow."

That was worth a chuckle, for I had no idea that my scheduled arrival had been such a news event. Even Herve had not mentioned it. But that was not the time for casual conversation even with an African who spoke English. Looking at the sky again and knowing that a big rain was coming, I stood to leave and bade him adieu.

"Come to visit me anytime you wish," I told him and then hurried on as the temperature dropped rapidly under threatening clouds.

Minutes after reaching my house, a pickup truck pulled up out front with a load of furniture on the back. Herve and Dr. Prosper had arrived with my table and chairs. Although I was ecstatic to have more of my things, I was appalled that the table was riding upside down on the metal bed with no padding underneath, where it had been sliding about and the chairs had been banging into one another during the trip. Prosper handed the chairs down to Herve while I went to clear a space for them. Even from the inside of my house I heard the terrible rasping as my table was being literally dragged off of the truck. It was as if the fine "rouge" hardwood was so much junk. My teeth clenched.

Within five minutes the table (with deep scratches etched through the varnish) and four chairs sat in my bedroom, cramped against that middle wall. Knowing that the two men were only trying to help, I made no comment about the damage even though I could not stop looking at it.

"Give me a rag," demanded Herve.

I handed him one of my clean socks expecting him to wipe off the dust, but he snatched it from me, grabbed my can of kerosene, doused the sock and slopped it all over the wood. I watched, utterly shocked, as both the scratches and the varnish simply disappeared. When done, Herve tossed the sock onto the floor, grinned happily to have helped me once again, pumped my hand, bid me a cheerful good afternoon, and hurried away to beat the rain.

I stood there another few minutes after they left, pondering what I had just witnessed. Mine was hand-crafted furniture made from fine locally grown mahogany, It took someone three months to build it, it cost many American dollars, and my homologue had managed to undo in thirty seconds what must have taken someone a week to accomplish. One step forward, I thought, and a half step back.

The wind was growing stronger, whipping through banana leaves beneath clouds painted black, and a wet chill was in the air. Glad for relief from the heat, I closed up the house, undressed and crawled under the mosquito net. At least I might take a cool nap while the rain fell, and maybe upon awakening, my furniture would not matter as much. As I lay back and listened to the first pecks on the tin roof, I reflected on the day with the best thoughts that I could muster. A good means of evacuation had been located, more of my furniture had been delivered, I was given assurance that the rest would arrive soon, and I had found someone who spoke a fair amount of English.

Not bad for one day. Not bad at all.

5

New Discoveries

My unexpected visitor the next morning turned out to be Marin, who had come to practice his English with me. While we drank mocha at my table, I asked him some of the questions that had troubled me about his culture and what he thought would be required to move the country forward. He was difficult to pin down, for his typical response tended to be either, "I don't know" or "The people are not interested". He claimed not to know anything about the former grandeur of his town or what might have happened to alter it. He would not discuss political issues at all, and he himself was entirely unmotivated to do anything he did not care to do. His goal was to attend college in Brazzaville and to become a teacher of English. He cared for little else.

Because I wanted to explore more of the community, he agreed to lead me to some interesting places that I might otherwise not see. As we walked through town and encountered a few people on bicycles along the way, I noted that all of the bikes were painted black, none had gears, and none had brakes. When a rider needed to slow down, it was necessary to drag the soles of his or her rubber flip-flops hard against the ground. We Americans called it "sandal brakes".

"I have seen many people on bicycles here," I told Marin. "Are they sold in Makoua?"

"Yes, in the hardware store," he said and pointed to a tin-roofed building at the intersection of the two main thoroughfares just ahead.

"But it appears to be closed."

"Sometimes it is open." Continuing, we passed a long narrow building with several doors. "That is a hotel," Marin said. It was a mud block building with several doors in a line. It did crudely resemble an American style motel, but not one in which I would care to spend a night.

"Do they change the sheets every day?" I asked him with tongue in cheek.

"Yes," he replied. "If they are dirty."

He led me to the outskirts of town past his home and then we took a narrow trail toward the river. Moving down the clay strip into the fringes of the forest where conditions were damp and cool, suddenly we were forced to pick our way over roots and to hang onto branches while sharply descending. The sounds of gurgling water soon came to my ears, but it was ground water, seeping from the side of the hill and then pouring over a man-made barrier. Marin said that the water was potable where it emerged from the ground, but the little pool into which it collected was used for soaking manioc to remove the cyanide. That process discolored the water and made it deadly to consume.

"Most people on this side of Makoua," he said, "take their water from the river because it is free. People die every year from drinking it. If a big animal is rotting upstream, disease floats with the currents."

"Don't they boil it, or treat it somehow?" I asked.

"No."

"But why not?"

"If they die, it is fate, and it is pointless to argue with fate."

"If a man steps in front of a truck and is run over, is that fate?"

"Yes. He would not step in front of the truck if it was not his destiny." As if giving second thought to what he had just said, he paused a moment and then added, "Many are killed by witches."

"Witches," I repeated dumbly.

"Yes. A girl was killed by a thunderbolt yesterday. She was sitting in her house and the thunderbolt came through the window and took her. A witch did it."

I was surprised to encounter that sort of superstition from Marin, but only because he had already told me that he was a Christian and a member of a local Evangelical church that met every Sunday in an open yard near his house. I also found it difficult to distinguish when he was being completely honest from when he was embellishing a point for effect.

"Why would a witch kill a young girl?" I asked, trying not to let my doubt show.

"Maybe she offended the witch, or maybe somebody else bought a curse to be put on her."

"Then I must be very careful not to offend anyone."

"Yes, you must. You were cutting your hair in your yard this morning. You must never do that again. If someone gets your hair, it can be used to make you sick or have you killed." Realizing he was quite serious, I thought about that for a long moment before continuing.

"How much does it cost to buy a curse?" I asked.

"Many different prices," he said with a shrug as if to say he was done talking about it. I decided not to pursue it.

We ventured another hundred feet through the brush to the very edge of the river where cold, glistening water swirled about trees whose giant roots were half in the water and half in the sand. Far from us in the middle of the currents, a man was sitting in a pirogue, dipping a plastic pail to collect water where it was generally thought to be cleaner. A woman in another dugout was standing upright, poling against the river from the other side.

"Fishermen drop nets in the river and work them from boats like those, except bigger. Maybe ten meters. Sometimes they catch deadly snakes and they bring them into the boats."

"Do the people then jump from the boats," I asked, seeing a comical picture in my mind.

"No. It is safer in the boat."

"Oh."

"One snake in the boat. Many in the river."

"Are there crocodiles there as well?" I asked, remembering that we were only about two miles from the bridge near my house.

"Yes, big ones."

"Then why are there none where the people bathe every day?"

"Because they are afraid of people. They have learned to stay away."

There was probably a lot of truth in that, I reasoned, but no crocodile was more afraid of me than I was of him and he could have the entire river all for himself if he showed up to claim it. As I looked at the sinister water, I had new respect for whatever denizens might lie beneath its surface. Surely there were many exotic creatures living there, both large and small, and surely there might be dangers that I had not yet heard of. I decided to remember never to fall into the trap of indifference concerning the unknown.

40   Things Are Different in Africa

A house under construction in Makoua. The system was to build a grid of bamboo woven together with vine. Next, mud would be applied from the inside, making a solid wall. Later, when that dried, a coat of mud would be added to the outside, making a very durable structure.

These villagers were making thatch by draping long strands of grass over a bamboo stick. The grass was secured (sewn into place) with thin slivers of bamboo.

"I will show you the Mission now, and also my school."

Every large rural town that I had so far visited in Central Africa had a Catholic presence in the form of either a church or a Mission. Makoua had both, representing two different orders of the same faith. The Mission was situated about three miles from town directly across from Marin's school.

Typical schools all over the Congo had benches but no chairs, no desks, no blackboards, no books nor other support materials, no lunchrooms, no drinking fountains, no electricity, no indoor toilets, no screens or window panes, and as often as not, not even shutters. Said differently, the average school was four walls with people inside. Students of all ages sometimes had to walk several miles to classes, and books, for most, were out of the question. But they could usually manage to buy little notebooks and a pencil or two. Thus the teaching technique for each course required the student to write down every word that the teacher said, for all learning and all testing was based on those words and they often had to be said back verbatim.

Small children were constantly seen about the streets and roads marching to and from their classes, seemingly carefree and unaware of the difficult time they were having. Lacking electricity in the vast majority of homes, students were compelled to study during the light of day, or by kerosene lanterns or candles at night. When testing time was near, it was common to see many of them sitting underneath street lights where they tried to study their notes.

Because teachers had not been paid in such a long time, their continuing participation in the process was based on the hope that pay would someday resume and all would be well. Besides, many of them had nothing better to do. Advancement from one grade to another and from one system to the next seemed routine enough, but if a student failed a single subject he or she had to repeat the entire year. Thus it was not uncommon to have boys and girls twenty-one years old still in high school. Many of them would someday drop out if they could not pass, and few seemed to care.

The Congo was generally considered to be 90% literate, according to something I read before leaving the United States. Which made me wonder exactly what the word "literate" meant to those who wrote about it. My observation so far, was that most Makouans spoke French and Lengala, and most of them could read to some extent, but math seemed to be a mystery even for storekeepers. Marin was an exception on all counts. He studied all of his courses, he learned because he wanted to learn, and he was quite proud to be the only Congolese in Makoua who truly spoke my language. He had my respect.

As we reached the crest of a hill and were walking beside a block wall hundreds of feet long, we came to a wire gate through which we could see several very pleasant two-story houses, seemingly of Spanish influence, positioned on beautifully flowered grounds. Actually they were not houses at all. They were the dormitories, the offices, the kitchen, a little chapel, and the barn-like storage rooms and chicken-sheds that comprised the Catholic Mission. A covered well was at the far end of a gravel driveway, beyond which a Caucasian woman dressed in white was directing the progress of two men working in a flower bed.

Across from us on the opposite side of the large field were a dozen other buildings of similar architecture, but which, Marin insisted, were not in any way connected to the Mission. Those collectively made up his school. The entire campus, obviously built during better times and most likely with foreign help, was constructed of brick and wood planking along with jalousie shutters and even glass in some of the windows. Unfortunately, it all seemed to be falling into ruin like everything else.

"Our teachers live here when school is in session," Marin said. "Many students come from great distances. They live here during the school year, but they are gone now because of the summer break."

Accommodating as many as two thousands students in its heyday, that school was among the largest on our side of Brazzaville, and had more to offer than most, including a kitchen that actually served lunch.

"We get boiled manioc and a green vegetable or maybe fish-salad." The fish salad, I already knew, was a green leafy dish served with chunks of fish that had been fried with bones intact.

"Every day?"

"Yes, but only the students who earn it are allowed to eat." He pointed out that it had to do with scholastic performance. Since those who failed the previous year were disqualified, eating on campus was quite a status symbol for those who enjoyed it. "I always eat here," he added proudly. "Many only get one meal a day. Some, if they are lucky, have money to buy food at the market, but most eat from the forest or from gardens behind the school." Walking on, we passed by the ruins of what looked like a bell-tower.

"Many years ago," he told me, "this was the front wall of a church. It was destroyed when the students turned violent."

"Why did they do that?"

"I don't know. Maybe a strike."

That bothered me some. I had heard many stories of the like regarding matters that people should have been able to explain, but it seemed as if extended exploration of some subjects was unacceptable or even forbidden.

"How can you not know?" I pressed.

"It is not my business to know," he responded. "But all of the students later died in terrible ways because God punished them. This wall is to remind us never to do it again." As we went by, I took one last look. The edges of all four walls were smooth. I was pretty sure it was an old bell tower.

Having finished our tour of the school, Marin took me back across the lot to meet some of the people at the Mission. We passed through the gate and went another fifty yards to the first building and then we paused at a breezeway that was sheltered by the floor above it. There Marin found a brass bell that rang a most delicate little tinkle, and moments later a beautiful Nun emerged, dressed in proper white habit. She smiled instantly at me and extended her hand with genuine warmth and welcome.

"I wondered when you would come," she said in flawless French.

"Everyone knows about me," I said back with amusement.

"Of course. You are a novelty here. And you are here to help the people, so you are of even greater interest."

She led us inside a brick chamber and motioned us to take seats in strangely cool air and then she left us momentarily. The walls were decorated with paintings of African women in religious posture, but there was also a television set, a VCR, and a shelf of popular movies filmed in America. When the Nun returned, she was carrying a tray with three glasses of chilled water, slices of lemon and several cookies baked on the premises. I quickly learned that she was German, and that she was fluent in several languages. English, however, was not one of them. Marin helped to translate her French when I was unable to follow as we all drank lemonade and nibbled on the cookies.

Momentarily, another Nun, an Italian, joined us and took a seat on the arm of one of the chairs. We all talked together for a while, during which I discussed my project and told them about my tenure so far in the Congo. Following that, I learned that both women were relatively new in the country themselves, and, to my great pleasure, they were both registered nurses. They seemed eager to exchange information with me, truly interested, and I was grateful for their company. When I stood to leave, they asked me to visit again soon, perhaps even at mealtime, no appointment necessary.

When Marin and I were back on the road again, I was struck by the irony of the situation. We had been in the company of two Nuns from two different nations, along with one American man who spoke only limited, basic, occupational French. But it was a Congolese boy who was the only conduit through whom we could all effectively communicate, beautifully demonstrating that which I believe to be a universal truth. No matter how disadvantaged the culture, it will always breed individuals who have the motivation and the tenacity to rise above the rest and to become anything they hunger to be. Marin would make a fine English teacher, because that was his singular goal and because he worked hard toward achieving it. As we walked toward home, a truck came speeding toward us with clay flying from its wheels. Inside it, clearly visible over the dashboard, were the white faces of three men.

"Priests from the church and the Mission," Marin told me before I could ask the question. As they skidded to a stop beside us, I saw that they were all wearing street clothes. A young blond-haired passenger greeted me with clear English. He was instantly quieted by the driver, an elder who held up his hand and then addressed me in French. He began asking me personal questions as if he didn't already know the answers, forcing me to respond with my ever so obvious limitations. Watching his smiles and nods, I realized the man was toying with me, being playfully sarcastic. The man in the back seat only looked at me and smiled.

"Oh, you're American," the driver said after I informed him of it.

"Yes. I am here to teach fish-farming to the villagers."

"Ah, fish farming. So you plant the fish and wait for them to grow?" He grinned at his two companions and waited for my answer.

"Of course," I replied. "We plant them in water and wait for them to grow."

He seemed to enjoy the answer. "And you will be here two months?" he asked.

"Two years."

"Hmm, it takes a long time for your fish to grow."

I decided that he was trying to draw me into a tongue-tangling discussion, not to learn about the project but to see me squirm. Since I couldn't effectively compete with him, I decided to end the talk.

"Yes, it does," I said back cheerfully. "Long time, big fish."

"Well," he said as he shifted the gears and made ready to leave. "We are all happy to have you. It is a pleasure to have an American here to help the villagers. You must visit us at the church sometime." Following those words, the engine raced, the wheels spun and the three were off again with their hands waving in the air.

It was a nice to learn that so many interesting people welcomed my presence. Furthermore I had discovered yet another person in the community who spoke English. And I had an invitation to enjoy somebody's else's cooking sometime.

Things were already looking up in my little piece of the Congo.

6

The Seventh Day

Certain birds that nested along the eaves of my house awakened me every morning as they precisely whistled the first few notes of *Mayberry, RFD*. As if that were not bad enough, they started before the chickens and their calls resonated underneath the tin roof in metallic echoes. Thus entertained, rising to beams of light that muscled through the roof while listening to Andy and Barney music, I tried hard to see the humor in that.

My morning activities usually began in a certain order. First, I would look carefully about the floor for snakes, then climb out, urinate through the drain in my bath-stall, shake my sheets free of whatever might have fallen through the net and then get dressed to go outside for a moment of dental hygiene. Next, while a pot of coffee was brewing on the kerosene stove, I would wipe the bat manure from my table, sweep the latest assortment of webs from the rafters, wash the rat feces off my favorite cup and then settle at the table to read my list of things to do.

While preparing my first cup of coffee one bright morning, Herve showed up with a man who claimed to be interested in fish-farming. We all shook hands, chatted for a minute and then we made an appointment to inspect his property early the next week. Herve seemed satisfied and the farmer seemed very pleased, so we all shook hands again and the two men departed together. The point of mentioning that moment is to address another interesting Congolese custom.

It was quite common to see grown men walking together holding hands, but that was only a gesture which underlined the cultural importance of touching. When one person encountered another, male or female, inside or outside, sitting or standing, shaking hands was an essential courtesy even if the parties had already met that day and even if they had already shaken hands before. The custom could actually interrupt serious, private conversations on the street, it could disrupt meetings, and it could be just plain silly when large groups got together.

Correctly done, two hands were clasped gently and they sometimes lingered. If in a group however, the hands met, quickly released, and moved through the crowd until every hand had been grasped or at least touched. When a hand was offered, failure to accept it was an insult that would not be quickly forgotten. If one's hands happened to be dirty or occupied, the right wrist would be extended instead, and it would be grasped in the same manner of shaking hands. Requirements satisfied, conversation might then follow or the parties might continue whatever it was that they had been doing. I found it interesting to watch when two groups met on the street. Each person of one group would shake the hand of every other person of the other group, it was all done rather simultaneously, and it was done both at the start and at the conclusion of the encounter. It seemed confusing, but somehow it always got done without the same hand being shaken twice or without a hand ignored. I was still getting used to the formality.

As Marin had been dropping by daily to practice his English, I used those occasions to learn as much as I could about local culture. During one of his visits we discussed the handshaking custom and my occasional failure to acknowledge it when I was in a hurry. He said it was rude of me to disregard the ways of his people, and I must not let it happen again. I paid attention to him but pointed out some of the many strange practices that seemed impolite by my standards, including having uninvited visits during the day and night, saying what people thought I wanted to hear whether it was true or not, gawking at me, shamelessly eavesdropping, begging, walking across my yard simply because it was the shortest distance between two points, often addressing me as the "white man" rather than using my name, and much, much more. Marin was unimpressed.

"You are in Makoua," he pointed out. He certainly had me there. Being both a foreigner and a guest, it fell upon me to make a better effort, but sometimes it was very, very hard. It crossed my mind that if I ever fully acclimated to the local culture, I would have to undergo deprogramming before the U.S. would let me go home.

Someone once told me that after a tour in the east, one goes home enlightened. Following a tour in the West, one goes home entertained. After a visit in Africa, one goes home drunk. That was the joke told to me by another volunteer the day we were sworn in, but first hand evidence had pointed increasingly to the truth of it.

One of our leaders once told me that drinking was a part of Congolese culture in which I must participate if I ever expected to be effective in my work. That remark seemed bizarre to me, because we had also been told that alcohol was one of the most deleterious influences in Central Africa. There in Makoua, it seemed that many if not most of the local men spent their days sitting in the shade, talking with friends and drinking, while their wives and daughters tended their crops, cooked for their families and hauled wood for their fires. When someone visited a villager, the host would often find whatever alcohol was on hand and the parties would drink. During the evenings, men gathered at the bars or street markets and they would drink. They had beer if they could afford it, or the harsh manioc-white-lightning when they had distilled it, but the most common beverage was palm wine.

Palm wine was not expensive, it was abundant, it was easy to make, and it was potent. The method of making it was to cut down a large palm tree, then whittle into the trunk near the crown to hollow it out. Next, they would force a pipe or length of bamboo through it so that it poked out over a collection basin at the bottom and then it would be left for a while. The carved opening in the trunk was usually covered with a cloth or palm leaves to keep out some of the bugs and then a supernatural spell was said over it to keep away thieves. Over the days and weeks that followed, the natural wine would collect in the cavity, flow through the pipe, and finally drain into the container.

A single large tree could produce several gallons before it ran dry. Thus it was collected every day to be sold before it soured, hauled to the market in plastic bidons, and sold by the glass to anyone with enough money to buy it. Makoua's universal price was forty cents per tumbler, so a person could walk to the market with hardly any money in his pockets and then go home a bit higher than before. If inexperienced in matters of drinking, he might later lean against something and vomit in the grass while the others laughed happily at him.

Scarce entertainment was available to the people of Makoua, which of course played a role in the popularity of drinking. While females didn't have much time for such pleasures, men and boys seemed to have plenty of it and all too often it was badly spent. Regular and persistent drinking was such a problem, it seemed to me, that it must be overcome if the people were ever to improve their lot. However, since I was supposed to drink with them, it was a cultural issue that was not my business to change. On the other hand, standing on grounds of principal, I refused to contribute to the problem. Hoping to set a notable example, I did not drink at all when work was to be done (or the night before it), I did not buy alcohol for anyone else unless the occasion was a social one of my own instigation, and I did not give away money. Some volunteers and staff members saw that as an "attitude," but to me it was sound logic and common sense. If I only attracted people who were serious about accomplishing something, we few would together build some fish ponds in Makoua, Congo.

One entire day, I worked both inside and outside my house without stopping even during the most intensely hot hours. Finally, when dusk lay over the area like a veil and the generator that powered the town had just begun to rumble in the distance, it was time for my evening promenade. As nighttime quickly fell, street fixtures cast a few patches of illumination over the dirt, but because the poles were so far apart there was no overlap from one to the next and the shadows between them were dark indeed. The two main streets were already alive with people, scores of them going in slow motion, drifting between burning candles that dimly flickered over table tops and on the faces of the women who displayed their wares.

Having witnessed a similar scene in several African countries, it had become clear that the night marche was actually a part of culture which summed up the night life in most villages and towns. There were actually two sections of it in Makoua, about ten blocks apart, but both selling exactly the same sorts of food, cigarettes and such. Some people spent hours going back and forth between the two major components of the market, visiting, flirting, and sometimes even buying, but usually with a social purpose in mind.

The palm wine was said to be the best in the large empty lot next to the Catholic church. It must have been exceptional that night, for an assemblage of perhaps twenty men were already at the fence where the talk and laughter was very loud indeed. Hearing my name called from the crowd, I scanned faces for the source. He was a military man whom I had met several days before, who happened to live near my house and who had always been friendly. Patting me on the back, he asked me to join his happy group.

"Have you found a woman yet?" he asked. "I have daughters I want you to meet."

"Thanks, but I need to wait a while," I responded.

"Okay, we will wait. For now, buy me a glass of wine."

I pretended not to have heard the plea. As I walked back home again in long shadows and orange circles of light, I thought about the cultural issues that I had so far observed and about my perceptions of the difficulties facing the people as they sought to change their status in the world. Short of altering many of their ways and adjusting the national attitude toward hard work, toward personal achievement and toward women in general, I could not see any way to painlessly achieve the goal. Dirt poor subsistence farmers were at the bottom of the ladder while very well-to-do people were at the top, with no stable basis in the middle upon which to build a truly democratic system. A goat ambled across my path a few feet away just then, calling out to the darkness with a sound that reminded me of an old man, sick from alcohol, emptying his stomach in the ditch. Baaaaaa. Baaaaaaa. As the walk toward home continued and it struck me that I had no friends to give me company, my thoughts shifted to the stillness and the damp heat, and to the long night that lay yet ahead of me. Unless I could put aside the increasing sense of loneliness that had hovered over me since arriving in Makoua, many future nights were destined to be very restless indeed.

Having spent my first full week "getting to know the people" as I had been ordered to do, I had already visited a nearby village and met with its leaders and even arranged my first preliminary site inspection for fish farming. I had also made some corrections to my regional map, worked to better secure my house, tried in vain to chase away my bats, and made some useful contacts. Mostly I was eager for Eric to bring the promised money with which my furniture account was to be closed. But as was said in Brazzaville, Eric was "on Africa time". That meant he would arrive eventually, on whatever schedule he happened to be honoring at the time.

Finally on the morning of the seventh day, while brushing my teeth in the yard, the familiar white truck came toward me dragging a trail of dust. Eric parked in the grass along the edge of the street, got out, took a long moment surveying my house and then walked up to me with a brief, almost reluctant greeting. My impression was he would much rather be somewhere else.

Taking him inside, I showed him the damage done to my table and chairs, since good American money had gone to pay for them, but he was not interested. Nor, for that matter, did he seem to care much that I was still having to live out of boxes. He also lacked any interest in the sloppy, unfinished work that had been done to the house before I moved in, but he did seem angry with me personally about something.

"They will deliver your furniture when it's ready," he said. He might as well have added, "And not a minute before."

He changed the subject then, evidently having more important issues on his mind. "I want you to get estimates from local carpenters to make repairs on your house. I'll be back in a few days, so you can give them to me then."

"I'll do that. But I've got a question for you."

"Like what?"

"What kind of work was done to this place before I got here?"

"Not much. Excepting the whitewash on the inside walls, it looks just about like it did the first time I saw it."

I was beginning to reach my boiling point. I had to bite my tongue to keep from unloading what I thought about "all the work that Herve had done," but I knew it would have been useless to get into it. I was not one to shy away from a disagreement, but I had already learned that nothing good would have come from having one. My impression was that our own leaders spent too much time covering their backsides, and probably about as much time getting even with those of us who confronted them.

"Well, how much was paid for the furniture in advance?" One of the cardinal rules that we had all been taught for the African environment, was never to pay for *anything* in advance. Since such money HAD been paid, my belief was that the common sense violation had helped to create local indifference to the furniture problem and I was stuck with the result.

"Don't worry about it!" Once again I detected a bristling undercurrent that said, "I don't want to hear it, so deal with it." Indeed his response almost took the form of hostility, as if inquiring about the matter would not be tolerated.

Monsieur Calixte, the local Chief of Agriculture, arrived just then as if by prearrangement, for he and Eric did not greet each other when he walked up. After addressing me for the usual handshake, Calixte led us into the back yard to discuss the palm tree that was ready to fall on my house. A short, slight man with a penchant for politics, he had always struck me as one never to completely trust.

"Two men of my acquaintance will cut it down and get it out of the yard," Calixte said. "They are highly competent and will do the job in short order." Eric nodded affirmatively, then Calixte added, looking squarely at me, "Your furniture is finally finished. All we have to do is pick it up."

Eric's thick brows rose at that piece of news, as if Calixte should never have said the words. But knowing perfectly well that I had no way to pick up the furniture myself, he must have felt compelled to assist. Five minutes later, we three were in his truck speeding insanely down rough streets as if daring a pedestrian to step in front of us. Calixte was in the back hanging on in silent desperation, eyes wide over a grimace that was frozen into his face, while I too was quiet, but more out of amazement than fear. Moments later we arrived at our destination where we slid to a stop next to a steep bank of clay. We all three got out and climbed up.

Momentarily we were standing in front of a mud house from which a man stepped with a look of surprise on his face. He came toward us with his hand extended, but it was obvious to me that he was either intimidated by our visit or else he just plain disapproved of it. He invited us into the shade of his work area and we followed.

The shop was nothing more than a tin roof fixed to poles that stood over bits and pieces of furniture in various stages of completion. Stacks of spare planks lined two sides of it, and a few basic hand tools lay on a table in the middle. I was mystified. The bed in my house with its finely turned posts must have been made under that shed, but I saw no lathe nor any other machinery that could have done the job. As I looked about for clues, I overheard the man say that my furniture was not ready yet, some of it had not even been started, and he did not understand why we were there. Calixte said nothing at all. Misinformation was routine in the Congo, but apologizing for it was not. He stepped aside as Eric spun on his heels and stormed back to the truck. Calixte and I followed and braced ourselves for another roller coaster ride back to my house. We certainly had one.

When we reached my house again and Calixte virtually jumped from the truck to hurry back toward to his office, Eric poked around in the back seat and came up with a package of mail for me. He also had some extra first aid supplies, as well as my long awaited technical kit from the U.S. That package had originally contained some basic surveying tools including a small telescoping device for use in sighting distances and elevations, several line-levels, a compass and a few other simple items for use in the field. Eric told me that some things were missing, but it was up to me to itemize them for the record. He then added that all of our kits had been opened "for administrative purposes". He did not bother to explain what that meant, but I assumed it to be African pilferage. He also had my replacement mosquito net, a double, which would cover my entire bed for the first time and give me adequate protection from insects in the night.

While I locked my treasures inside the house, Eric waited in the truck. We were about to go to a bar for a cool beverage and a chat, but my guess was that it would be nothing more than a tension break. Once there, seated in the shaded yard with bottles of Ngok and Primus (two brands of beer bottled in Brazzaville), he started our conversation. "Your furniture *must* be finished as agreed, because we have a written contract and a lot of money was paid in advance." He took a deep drink and began again. "If the man fails to deliver, he can be jailed for breach of contract."

"Well why didn't you talk to him while we were in his yard, face to face?" Unaware of any courts that might hear legal charges, or even any real law enforcement in Makoua, I could not see anything coming of the threat. "And for that matter why didn't you say anything to Calixte for misguiding us?"

"I don't have time to get into all that. I'm in a rush. I have to go to Etoumbi and Kelle to see Linda and Larry. But I'll be back in a few days."

"Well maybe you can take a minute to sort things out when you come back," I pleaded.

"Yeah, okay." The words were pleasant enough, but he still seemed to be tense underneath. Our little social lasted another minute or two and then he paid for the beer and left me to walk the mile home in the sweltering heat.

Angry about almost everything that had taken place between us but actually cooling off underneath the hot sun, I once again encountered the priest, Dominico, whom I had met near the mission. He was the driver of the truck that day when Marin and I were on our walkabout. Speaking through the window of his vehicle, he invited me to have lunch with him and the other priests at their residence near the church. Grateful for the offer, I climbed in for the short ride. As we pulled into the yard behind the place, two other priests were outside talking to several African boys. One of the men was Pelegrin, a tall, bearded, serious fellow who didn't seem to care much for my company. He too had been in the truck that day near the Mission. The other man was Eugenio, a tiny fellow who was exuberantly cheerful and who made me feel truly welcome.

I never saw who actually cooked our meal, but Dominico brought it to the table in large ceramic bowls so that we could serve ourselves. The lunch was spaghetti and meat sauce, the likes of which I had not tasted in a very long time, and our beverages were imported red wine and glasses of crystal clear water. The whole experience was absolutely wonderful.

"This is a fine way to finish my first week in Makoua," I said.

"Well," replied Dominico, "on the seventh day, He rested."

7

Thieves and Wives

"Donnez moi, donnez moi…give me, give me," seemed to be the national theme of the Congo. Each of my days had so far begun with visitors, most of whom had some dire excuse to brazenly beg. "Give me bread," demanded a husky young man who claimed to be a member of a starving family. "Give me ham," insisted another who was also hungry but only for imported items. "Give me clothes," begged a little boy of no more than six years. "Give me a red bandana," pressured a middle aged man with a machete in his hand. Give me boots. Give me postage stamps. Buy me beer. Give me money to buy whatever I want.

One morning as my second week began, my visitor was different. "Good morning," he said, repeating the words with which so many young men addressed me regardless of the time of day. It only took a moment to realize that his French was barely better than his English, but at least we were able to communicate at a most basic level. He had heard that I was one to take walks, and he wanted to show me the sights along the northern route. My guess was that he wanted to cultivate a friendship that might ultimately benefit him, for that had been the driving force of most who had preceded him. But the fact was that I had already planned to go along the north road anyway, in order to further test my regional map. I knew that the road went at least to Ouesso, deep in the rain forest, but my map indicated many other villages along the way. Bearing the names and locations of the communities known at the time it was printed, the map might yet need updating and that meant going where the trails might lead.

Wearing my camping knife on a webbed belt, I locked up and started out as my companion admired my Dickies work clothes and K-Mart work boots. He was barefoot, wearing tattered pants cut at the knees, and a tee-shirt that looked dirty but probably wasn't. In the U.S. he would have been seen as a tramp or a street person, but in his world, such clothes were typical for perhaps a third of the rural population. He talked endlessly as we went, speaking Lengala which for the most part was wasted on me, but that did at least give me a chance to try to pick out a few words.

Once we crossed the Likouala-Mossaka River and descended onto lower ground, the terrain changed suddenly and dramatically. The road was much wetter there as we marched into the fringes of the forest where the water table was higher and previous rains still stood in great yellow puddles. The constant shade and cooler temperatures offered welcome relief from the heat, but with it came the difficulty of negotiating long stretches of deep and slippery mud.

When we had gone about two miles, we reached a single mud and thatch house, all by itself in the middle of nowhere. My guide informed me that he did not know the name of that "village" but nobody was home anyway. Until that moment I had not realized that the word "village" could refer to a single house. If true, that was a critical piece of news that could change everything about the population estimates in my working area, not to mention the numbers of villages in which I was expected to generate work. Unenthusiastic about walking half the day to see more of the same, I asked my guide if a larger village might be anywhere nearby. He answered affirmatively and added that it was only two more miles away. Even sensing the unreliability of his words, I decided that it would not hurt to go a little farther. We moved on.

Thirty minutes later when all I could see ahead was more clay and mud, a very tall black man stepped swiftly from the brush right in front of us. Barefoot, shirtless and resting a machete on his shoulder, his sudden appearance raised the hair on the back of my neck. There was no trail where he had been concealed, and the greeting that took place between him and my companion was far too familiar for the circumstances. While his eyes drifted over me from my boots to the knife on my belt, I was already on defense. I spotted a long stick in the grass. It was hardwood, it was about four feet long, and it was heavy. Perfect.

With all of my senses on alert, my knife slid quietly from the sheath and begin slicing the end of the pole. My feeling was that the two men were watching the shavings fall before the sharp blade, but I did not look squarely at them. Something that I had learned wherever I had been in Africa, people tended to be more afraid of my camping knife than I was afraid of their machetes. That, I presumed, was because using the machete required drawing the arm back for leverage and therefore created an opening in which a knife might be used effectively. I had never fought with a knife in my life, but they did not know that. Certain that they were sizing me up, pondering whether the job might be an easy one or if it might come with a price, two more factors were working in my favor. They had already lost the element of surprise, and their hesitation had given me time to locate the second weapon.

"I'll be going back now," I said as casually as I could and then took several steps backward. The knife continued to whittle the point of my stick while, that time, our eyes met straight on. They remained where they were, simply watching my retreat as if a little confused. Nevertheless I kept them in sight until the distance between us eliminated most of the risk and then I simply walked on. As it turned out, they did not bother to follow. Maybe I had misjudged the moment.

A few Americans had been killed in Africa, mostly by disease or accidents, but others had been hurt in muggings and burglaries. One of our own volunteers survived an attack when a man held a broken beer bottle to her throat until she handed over her cash. I myself had learned a hard lesson in a Brazzaville market, when all of my cash was picked from my pocket. Thus, from that time on, I was generally on guard for the first hint of trouble and I tried always to move away from it.

A certain amount of violence had to be taken for granted anywhere in our part of the world, although it was usually African on African. Children were sometimes beaten by adults including their school teachers, wives were beaten by their husbands, women sometimes fought back or fought each other, and children tended to be very cruel to animals. Once I saw a man and woman fighting in a market, and from where I stood she seemed to be giving more than she got. Men did not seem to have fist fights with each other very often, so I was told, because such a confrontation could lead to somebody being killed, then or later. Thus if a man could walk away from a bad situation it was always wise to take the walk.

Continuing my trek toward home and crossing the river bridge again, I was approached by a young woman with a load of freshly washed laundry carried on her head. She stopped me in the middle of the bridge, adjusted her basket, and shared some news with me.

"That boy you were walking with is a robber," she said. "You must not trust him. He is a very bad person." I nodded in affirmation. "He steals," she went on, "and he knows others who will help him".

While grateful for the confirmation of what I already believed, I began to wonder how many other muggers were on the loose in and around the community and how I might best protect myself from them. Our leaders during training were almost forgiving when they spoke of such things. "The Congolese are very poor and we have so much," we were told. "You just have to use good judgment." Because I was a newcomer, I realized more than ever that I must tread softly while always keeping up my guard.

"Thank you for telling me," I said to the woman. "I will be more careful from now on."

"Yes, you must." She nodded and went in the direction from which I just had come. That was a mystery in itself, for I could not imagine where she might have been headed with her load of laundry.

The hour was still early when I reached home again, but the heat was so intense that I could not stay inside. Restless and needing to take advantage of every breath of fresher air, I decided to stroll toward town in search of a cool beverage. Just as I stepped out the door, two men met me in the yard. Because Herve and Calixte had spread the word for me, two carpenters were there to give me estimates for the work that was needed on my house.

I explained that I wanted competitive bids, and the lowest price would win the job. They looked at each other and again at me and then they smiled understandingly. They spent about ten minutes examining the outdoor toilet, the windows that needed shuttering, the door that needed to be moved and the place where I wanted a new passageway knocked through the bedroom wall. Following that they compared notes, jotted down some figures, and finally handed me one piece of paper. They would only work together and their labor would cost the equivalent of six hundred American dollars. Their expressions gleamed with optimism when I said that I would let them know as soon as their price was approved by someone above my rank. As they walked away together, chatting amicably, my guess was that neither of them had performed good paying work in a while.

A small house just beyond Herve's place usually had a half-dozen very young children playing in the yard who would always come to the edge of the street to greet me. That day the younger ones were quiet as a teenaged girl called to me saying "American, American." She motioned me into the yard where three adults and the usual children were all in the shade of a large thatched lean-to. One of the women, squatting in the dirt, hovered over a low fire and stirred something in a blackened pot. Accepting the invitation, I joined them under the thatch. The cook, a woman of perhaps thirty-five years, wanted to know if I would share their meal of fried fish and boiled manioc. More interested in a refreshing drink than food, I expressed my gratitude but declined.

During the next few minutes I learned that the teenaged girl was called Dani, while the others were her older sister, her mother, her grandmother, and her little brothers and sisters. Her father had died a few years before.

Perhaps fifteen years old, lighter skinned than most Congolese and almost as tall as me, Dani was quite attractive as she proudly showed her perfect teeth and wide smile. Her mother began asking me question after question. Did I like Makoua? Did I like my house? Would I be there very long? How was my work going? Had I met many prospective fish farmers? Was I married? When all of those inquiries were answered to her apparent satisfaction, Dani asked a question of her own.

"Are you going to a bar?"

"Yes," I answered.

"Then I will go with you."

I was amused at her frankness, but not entirely surprised by it. "Okay," I said back and waited while she drafted her older sister to join us. When in training, we were exposed to several sessions about social matters, but those sessions, for the most part, dealt with issues like objectionable gestures or body language, sexual harassment that females might encounter, common diseases and dangerous tribal medicines. Much of the rest was either romanticized or antiquated, making it largely useless to the unseasoned. Sexual behavior, for example, was usually addressed from the point of view of long term relationships, marriage, taking wives and husbands back home to America or trying to leave one behind. Some subjects were avoided altogether. One afternoon when Tom and Eric and several male volunteers were having beers at a Brazzaville restaurant, a question was raised about the age of consent.

"I don't even want to talk about it right now," Tom replied as Eric sat without a word and stared into his beer. The matter never came up in my presence again, for little was taboo in the Congo except to speak of it. Even our own second year volunteers steered wide of that particular issue, as if it might have been too revealing to mention. Many teenaged girls made themselves available in Brazzaville nightclubs, for a price, and some volunteers partook of their services without much regard for the risk of AIDS or the more prevalent social diseases. Once assigned to a permanent post, a man could only tread lightly until time and experience provided the wisdom that he needed to keep himself out of trouble.

The reality was that when Africans had the urge, they copulated, and age did not seem to have much to do with it. One volunteer in another part of the country had actually been approached by a father who wanted to sell his twelve year old daughter for $50.00. And several local men had already approached me about taking their young daughters for wives, companions or live-in maids.

Wedding dowries were customarily levied, which young African men were sometimes unable to pay, and which parents used as a tool to prevent unions of which they disapproved. But every American was assumed to be rich and would therefore pay a handsome fee indeed. Furthermore he would return to America someday, from where he and his wife would be bound by Congolese culture to send money back to the girl's family. She would also be expected to send for her others of her family sooner or later, one member at a time.

Another issue that we had to get used to, was the evident lack of any legal drinking age. Several boys as young as eight or nine once swarmed over some banana beer left behind by volunteers at an open air bar in Burundi, and I never encountered a youngster anywhere who would turn down a swig if he could get it. Dani and her family were probably no different from any others, except that they did not have a man in the household.

Not long after we three started out together, heading toward a place that Dani wanted to show me, we reached a restaurant on the other side of town called "My Cathy". (The significance of that name was a mystery to everyone I ever questioned about it, which added yet another layer of curiosity about my post). The large thatched building was situated behind a mud wall under the shade of a huge mango tree where the temperature dropped about ten degrees. Inside a room with long benches on either side of a pair of tables on a dirt floor, we took places near a window where the shutters had been lifted outward from the bottom and propped open with a stick. A large, balding man arrived promptly to take our orders, standing before us with neither paper nor pencil. He listened attentively as we discussed our choices of beer, which were Ngok, Amstel or Primus, then he advised that he only had Primus anyway. Primus it was, then, times three.

The girls begin talking to each other in Lengala. As they chattered and sometimes glanced in my direction, our beverages arrived, the tops were popped in plain view and then the waiter was gone again. The place was comfortable. The drinks were actually cold, and the change of pace suited my mood. I was perfectly happy to be in the company of the opposite gender and to rest quietly while the girls continued their secret discussion. Their voices were background noise, unobtrusive and private, like radio sounds on a day when radios didn't matter. A few minutes later, four African men came inside and headed toward the other table. They paused to greet us with "Bonjour. Ca va?" and the customary handshakes, then they sat down. They all knew about my work, having heard about it on the radio, but they wanted to know when I would actually start doing some of it.

"Soon." I responded with a chuckle. "Soon."

"Have you found interested people yet?"

"Yes, a few. But it takes time."

"Ah, time," one of them repeated. Momentarily, the subject advanced to a crucial point of interest without any subtlety at all. "Do you have a wife?" he asked.

"I'm divorced."

"Hmm." He got up then, stepped behind Dani and placed his hands on her shoulders as if about to demonstrate a nice garden tractor. "This one," he said, "would make a fine wife."

Dani did not look at me, but her eyes grew suddenly serious as if she approved. Also suddenly, since my suspicious nature had just kicked into gear, I had the unshakable feeling that I had been set up somehow. Surely no one could have known that we would wind up there, in that very place, on that very afternoon. On the other hand, maybe everything that the white man did was passed from one person to the next with the speed of electricity. Still I wondered.

The men and I all talked about nothing in particular until the first beer was gone, then the girls were ready to leave for another place and yet another drink. They called for the waiter and then motioned for me to pay the check. Perhaps being subtle, culturally correct, or honestly indifferent to my presence throughout the remainder of our afternoon together, neither of the girls spoke to me except when asked a direct question. I was, for the most part, the anonymous paymaster.

Early in the evening after Dani and her sister had been returned to their home and I had retreated to the privacy of my mosquito net, I pondered life in Makoua and how I was expected to fit in. I had repeatedly heard that pressure was always put on male volunteers to take African wives and to father children, and I had experienced some of that pressure several times already. Having been married twice before in America, however, I also understood the difficulties in holding a relationship together even if it began on solid ground. There in rural Congo where considerations were hardly complex, a marriage between a middle aged man and a fifteen year old girl would not be at all abnormal. Indeed, that arrangement made perfect sense in a culture wherein a wife must be strong to do all the work, and wherein having children was the principal means by which she would achieve status and recognition among her peers.

Much was yet to be learned about the ways of the people into whose midst I had been delivered. My own ways would eventually find a niche among them, but the process of learning must be undertaken with caution, observation and translation. The exploitation of cultural permissiveness in the name of personal gratification might have been easy, but there was one thing that I believed to be a fact of societies everywhere. The exploiter can sometimes become the exploited, and nowhere on planet Earth is there any such thing as a free lunch.

Sooner or later, the waiter arrives with the check.

8

New Confrontations

The morning kokoko came just at dawn, but after a few days of rising with the birds, I was already up and making oatmeal when it came. Herve stayed only a moment, having dropped in to let me know that my food locker, clothes cabinet and bookcase would be finished very soon. Because that sort of news had been delivered to me more than once already, I would not permit myself even a moment of anticipation. Instead, while drinking my second cup of coffee, I put the matter out of mind and once again read my official list of things to do. The "rules" were that I was not supposed to do any actual fish-farming or even heavy recruiting during the first three months of my adjustment to the new environment.

Ever more suspicious that my presence in Makoua might have little to do with the official propaganda taught us in training, a new glimmer of awareness began to poke through the fog. The whole experience might have been less about fish, and more a function of deeper politics that were simply over my head. Any aggressive person could have accomplished my list of duties in a week with only moderate effort, and I frankly had no idea how to stretch them into three months. Having thought long and hard about that, I decided to spend my time working at my own pace and if the Brazzaville bureaucrats objected they could send me home.

I spent the rest of that morning exploring the town. Makoua was divided into seven "quarters" each bearing a name like Mossaketa, Ohade, or Centreville, and each had a President whose job was to represent the people of his quadrant in matters of importance. The word "quarter" had nothing to do with fourths, as one might surmise, but simply implied "neighborhoods". Each of those was again divided into blocks, and each block had its own chieftain who was the problem solver for his jurisdiction. Walking through them, my purpose was to seek out the Presidents, meet with them if possible and then set the stage for more serious contact later.

A typical home made of mud-block. The blocks were made by mixing clay, sand and water and then pouring the mud into wooden molds. Next they were dumped into the yard to dry for a day or two. This particular structure was different only that the roof that was weighted down with such blocks.

Wherever I went, plenty of men were sitting about in shaded yards, watching me pass without hardly any apparent interest. And when less than two hours had passed, I had met the Presidents of all but two of the quarters and noted that their reactions were flawlessly predictable. Each invited me into a cool place, usually in the yard under a tree and then a chair was dragged up for me so that we could sit in the bare clay and chat about my work. My host always nodded his understanding as I talked, then he would invariably ask how much farmers would be paid to dig their ponds and if I would buy the tools to dig them. Because my response was always "no pay and no tools," the President would then say that we must talk again soon. He would stand, I would follow his lead, we would shake hands and I would move on. He was not being rude. He had simply said what he had to say.

Monsieur Itoua, Felix (the last name is said first) was a very unusual Congolese. Seeming not only pleased with my visit but excited by it, he invited me inside his home and motioned me to sit on an expensive sofa. He then sat across from me on a matching chair and leaned forward to engage me in conversation. His large brick home was spacious, clean, tastefully decorated and quite comfortable, clearly indicating the circumstances of a man who had done well for himself. And once again, the nagging question of "how" came to my thoughts.

Momentarily a teenaged boy brought out a bottle of brandy and two wine glasses that were immediately filled to the top. Monsieur Itoua said he had been hoping I would visit him. He knew all about the work I was there to do, and he was thrilled to have a "true professional" in the community. He also told me that he was in charge of a cooperative, a major fish-culture project, concerning which he desired my advice and assistance.

"Perhaps you have heard of it," he said. "The site is the lake on the other side of the river."

"Yes," I told him, "I know of it. I noticed a sign just past the bridge."

"Yes, yes, that is the one."

The truth was that I had indeed noticed his site and already concluded that it could never be successful as it stood. Actually it was against the rules for me to help him in any capacity, because the place could never conform to project standards. His "lake" was a product of spill-over from the river, which meant the water level was directly dependent on regularity of the rainy and dry seasons. Managing such a site would be impossible even if dikes could be built to protect it from flooding, or even if a regulated water source could be established for use during dry periods. Furthermore harvesting would be difficult unless the river-level dropped to cooperate, disease prevention would be out of the question, and keeping out predators and undesirable species would be beyond human control.

Mr. Itoua was not happy with the news. Actually I would have enjoyed helping to turn his lake into a viable project, but violation of the rules would have created problems for me with my own leaders. Mr. Itoua's elation of minutes before entirely disappeared and left him almost glum. As I excused myself, I was already wondering if it might have been better to work with him on the sly, outside official limitations, helping the man to make the best of what he had.

I could not help reflecting on the times during the last several months when various knowledgeable people from Burundi to Zaire had told me that fish-farming had never been and would never be successful as a Peace Corps project (even though it was said to be more successful than most others). That was attributed to a host of factors related to keeping the farmers on track. The dominant negative was the tremendous amount of labor required to build a workable site. Next was the matter of maintaining a pond after it was built, feeding the fish every single day, keeping birds and snakes away, keeping the stock of *Tilapia nilotica* completely pure, and harvesting only once every six months. *Tilapia nilotica* is a scaly, edible fish that looks rather like a Bream. The species was chosen for the African environment because it can survive high heat, low oxygen and other environmental stresses that would kill most fish. *T. nilotica* is also highly prolific, it eats microbes and vegetation and it grows rapidly. Thus it is a low maintenance animal, costing no money to feed, and it delivers a high yield of protein for the effort.

Finally was the matter of theft, which was a very serious problem indeed. Although a thief, if caught in the act, would be punished severely by other villagers, the only true deterrent was said to be the spell of a witch. I knew little about witches, but I did know something about human nature and I quite frankly had doubts of my own concerning the viability of our program.

I also could not help wondering if witches had decided to interfere with our rainy season. Rain was supposed to fall every day, but we had enjoyed only a few wet hours since my arrival. Unless that changed soon, people would suffer because the levels of wells would drop, crops would wilt, the river would not rise to normal highs, food supplies at the market would diminish and even small money would be harder to come by. That morning I was able to buy plenty of fruit and vegetables, all locally grown, but I wondered how long it would last if our weather did not soon change.

Once back at my dining table, sorting through the forms and papers that I was supposed to keep track of, I logged my accomplishments for the morning and documented all interest in fish-farming. Had I chosen to keep my papers at the Agriculture Bureau, anything left in my "private" office would almost certainly have been plundered and quite possibly removed. Even if that had not been a risk, their roof leaked like a colander and virtually guaranteed that my records would have been damaged sooner or later. Therefore destined to sit at my own table most of that day, sweating with no breeze and no possibility of escape, I wondered if my own grown children in Florida were enjoying air conditioning at that moment, maybe sipping a mixed drink poured over ice, perhaps resting on overstuffed furniture while watching a rented movie and wondering what kind of ice cream they would have after dinner. I tried not to think about it.

The policeman from across the street, Norman, came to my door with a message from his boss who had returned to town the night before. I was to go there immediately. Five minutes later, seated across from Norman in the station office, the chief appeared in his camouflage uniform with a forty-five caliber pistol fitted into a white plastic holster. Arrogant, brusque, and apparently accustomed to obedience, he passed between us as Norman snapped to attention. He did not acknowledge me at all. He entered his private office and slammed the flimsy door behind him, then I heard a chair sliding over the brick floor and a wooden desk drawer opening with a loud squeak. After several seconds of silence, the drawer slammed shut, the chair slid over bricks again and a hostile voice called out to his subordinate.

Norman immediately stepped to the door, opened it and motioned me inside the large but nearly empty space. Looking at me with disdain from his straight chair behind a cluttered desk, the officer grunted a greeting that was plainly hostile. He waved a hand as if shooing a fly, which was my cue to sit, then he looked over the document that Norman had filled out the day Herve had introduced me. An unhappy man, the chief vigorously shook his head. Norman had permitted me, a stranger, to take up residence in his town without the proper papers, and that was entirely unacceptable.

We volunteers had relinquished our passports to our Director in Brazzaville so that they could be stored in the office safe. That, Bob said, was to guard those critically important documents from loss or theft. Someone else told me that it was really to keep us from crossing borders, taking unauthorized vacations when we were supposed to be working at our posts. I never knew the truth for certain, but I had been given photocopies of my documents and those had been approved by Congolese authorities. Thus they were supposed to provide all that was needed for the verification of my status anywhere inside the country. Makoua's police chief was not buying it.

"Show me your passport, not useless sheets of paper," he ordered.

"I don't have it. It is in Brazzaville."

"This is no good." He shook his head again and scowled. "You must present me your passport immediately."

"That is not possible, because…"

"And you have twenty-four hours to complete a residency form and to furnish me two passport pictures." He shoved my photocopies back across the desk toward me.

"Passport pictures! I have been in your country for months, and we are nowhere near a border."

"You will provide them!"

"I don't have any passport pictures. They are all in Brazzaville."

"And you must pay me twenty dollars."

"Twenty dollars? For what?"

"Filing fee." He then looked back at some other papers on his desk and flicked his hand as if to say "You may leave now." As I stood to go, he added, "And you will pay me two dollars each month for water."

That one really burned me, for the water did not belong to him. The thought actually crossed my mind to tell him that I would simply leave Makoua, permanently, and let others of his own government deal with him. But no, there would have been no gain in crossing swords with the man if it was my intention to remain in town for two years. I left his office without hesitation, but by then I was both furious and concerned. We volunteers had been warned about exactly that sort of problem, and our instructions were clear. "Stand your ground and never pay any money to anybody!" Thus it was not entirely surprising to have encountered his attitude, but never could I have anticipated that the extortion attempt would be so brazen and so threatening.

Clearly the man was not going to let his opportunity slip away, for he was showing me who was boss, and he had the power to back it up. The entire matter should have been resolved before my arrival in Makoua, but like everything else that had come up, our own "leaders" did not care to get involved in the personal problems of mere volunteers. I was beginning to understand why some had terminated early, and why so many of the others seemed always to be right on the edge of it. Nobody in Brazzaville really wanted to hear it.

The air was choking hot when Marin paid me a surprise visit a short time later, but I was surely glad to see him. After listening to my plight, he informed me, "There is a place where passport pictures are made."

"There is? Here in Makoua?"

"Yes. Many people come from other countries and all of them must have pictures made for the police."

"But why? We're far inside the border here?"

"It is the way things are."

"And the twenty dollars?"

"You must pay it. Everybody who comes must pay."

"And the water? He does not own the water."

"No, but you must pay. The chief is a very bad man."

And so, I understood. The policeman had a petty but multifaceted extortion ring set up and it was evidently quite open for the rest of the village to see. "Why do the people of Makoua put up with this guy?" I muttered, feeling stupid for asking.

"We have no power over him."

I found myself liking my situation less and less, for I knew deep down that I would have trouble from that man before my tenure was over. If I paid him as he demanded I would be setting the stage for more of the same in the future. If I refused to pay, my own safety might eventually be at risk.

"I guess I should try to get the pictures made," I said, "and then see what happens next."

"You can only have pictures taken after dark," Marin went on. "They must have electricity. But you cannot do it today. The owner of the studio is out of town."

I found it amazing that people in every town I had so far visited, seemed always to know everybody's else business. They knew where other people were, what they were doing, why they were doing it and even when they would be back. While I went about making myself a cup of coffee and popping several aspirin to get over a tension-headache, Marin wanted to know if I believed there was a woman in the moon.

"Never having been there," I said back with slight irritation, "I cannot be certain. But I seriously doubt it."

"Well, you are wrong," he replied. "A woman went into the forest on Forbidden Thursday and she was taken into the sky and she is there even to this day."

"Forbidden Thursday?" That was one I had not heard before.

"Yes. It is forbidden to go into the forest on Thursdays."

"Do you know exactly why?"

"No. But I know it is not done by those who are wise."

"Well, who took the woman?" I asked, genuinely interested in his tidbit of cultural mythology.

"Witches. Witches are everywhere. Do you know that there is Voodoo in the United States?"

"No, I do not know that."

"Well there is. It is very common in California." Marin had my undivided attention then, as he continued his lesson about my country. He said that he learned all about it one night when he was in Brazzaville, watching television through somebody's window, peeping at a show called *Starsky and Hutch*". Chuckling in spite of myself and grateful to have some comic relief, I didn't even bother to explain the need for more reliable information. Surely none would have been adequate anyway. After all, it was *Starsky and Hutch*.

When alone again very late in the afternoon and my clothes reeked of sweat, I went to the river for my usual bath and cool swim. Several men were at the male only section, as was normal on those blistering days, some in the water and some on the beach. As I stood on top of the hill of gravel and slipped off my flip-flops, a tall, muscular man addressed me in rapid French. I understood enough to realize that he was not being cordial. He wanted to know where my knife was, and how it was that I dared to mingle with the men of Makoua without it. He punched my shoulder with a finger, provoking, testing me.

Many thoughts raced through my mind at that moment. He stood six inches taller, he outweighed me by sixty pounds and he was probably twenty five years younger. Furthermore I was a white man in a crowd of black faces, alone on their turf, ridiculously outnumbered and I had just offended the local chief of police. Too high the odds, too low the gains. I would walk away. The entire gathering had grown silent, but none of the others were looking directly at either of us. I simply told the aggressor that I did not understand his French and then I went down the hill and into the water. Even he fell quiet then, and the incident was over. Clearly a foreigner was at a huge disadvantage in such a dilemma, and for the hundredth time I asked myself why I bothered to put up with it all.

I stayed in the water a few minutes longer than usual that afternoon, bathing away the sour smell of my own sweat, cooling down the rush of my own blood, and clearing my head enough to face another hot night in my oven-house. But I had some serious decisions to make. The fact was that, early on, most every volunteer would face hard choices about whether to remain in the Corps. But, our leaders claimed, if a person survived the first six months he or she just might remain the entire two years. When we were all recently sworn in, a joke was circulated that if a person slept twelve hours a day, he would only have to spend one year awake in Africa. I began to appreciate the sarcasm. Clearly a good volunteer was patient, tolerant, understanding and dealt effectively with frustration from every corner. Equally clear, was that it would never be easy for me meet those qualifications.

Making my way back up the steep hill again, the rubber of my thongs squeaking as I went, the hot and humid air was already washing my body in sweat again. Several times before going to bed that night, trying to sit up for a while to read, I poured cool water over my head until insects forced me under the net. Twenty dollars, the police-thief had demanded. Before another hour passed that night, I would have given twenty dollars for an ice cube!

A monster storm awakened me just at dawn when rain was slamming through the attic vent. That vent was nearly twenty feet above the floor, it was only about twelve inches square, it was located just beneath the peak of the roof, and rain was washing through it like ocean waves through an open port. I was up in a flash, frantically jerking things around to a drier corner, but it was too late for the bed. The mosquito net, the sheets, the mattress, the wood itself was already soaked and I was standing in a puddle that was becoming a lake. Fortunately the violence only persisted about five minutes, leaving behind a soft rain that lasted another twenty.

Just as the weather cleared, Eric showed up with the volunteer from Etoumbi. Concluding his periodic tour into our part of the country, it had been four days since Eric first visited me and it might be months before he would come again. When his business had been completed in Etoumbi and then in Kelle, he picked up Linda for the return trip to Brazzaville. Throughout our African experience we were all required to submit to a host of precautionary injections. Some of those were administered every three months, which meant making the slow and arduous trip back to the capitol city each time they were due. Linda had gotten lucky to have hitched such a ride at that time on her calendar. "Wow!" she said when she saw the pond in my bedroom. Eric had no comment at all. I was reminded once again that the unwritten rule was "Deal with it, or quit!"

When I presented my leader with the bid for my home improvements, he silently studied it a minute or two with no reaction, then he did some figuring of his own. I explained that the carpenters had declined to bid on ceiling repairs using grass mats because that was not "proper work" for professionals. Anyway, grass mats were not routinely available within twenty-five miles of Makoua.

"Uh huh," he grunted, as if to say he didn't believe a word of it. When done examining the numbers, to my utter surprise he finally opened up a bit. He explained that we had a problem which was far more important than my ceiling. Millions of our dollars had been deposited into a Brazzaville bank, the government of the country was suddenly shaky, the bank was in serious trouble, withdrawals were troublesome except in relatively small amounts, and the future of our entire project was frankly uncertain. Those conditions, therefore, made it impossible to give me enough money to do everything that needed to be done. He would give me enough to repair everything except the ceiling, and I would have to make do with that as best I could. Picturing myself sweeping guano for a long time to come, I nevertheless held my tongue. At least he was being straight up for a welcome change.

"Well," I started resignedly, "where does that leave everything else, like the motorcycle I'm supposed to get and the safe shelter to keep it in?"

"We already have the motorcycles in storage. You'll get yours when the time comes."

"And the safe shelter?" Official rules dictated that the expensive machines must be kept under lock and key at all times when not in use, and our bureaucrats had the responsibility of paying for that security.

"There's no money for that kind of expense anymore. You'll have to keep it inside your house." While I took another bite out of my tongue and he counted out my money, I dared to inquire about his promised visit to settle things with the furniture maker.

"Oh, that. I didn't get around to it. But I'm sure you will be able to handle it." My tongue was already bleeding by the time I mentioned the local police chief. Eric shook his head as if to say that his day was simply not turning out well.

"The policeman is way out of line," he said with stern eyes. "Issues of that type have already been settled between our government and his. You tell him that!"

"I already did!"

"Well, you are definitely not to pay him any money," he insisted. "The most he can do to you," he added quite seriously, "is put you in jail". He poked a fistful of Central African Francs in my direction and then headed back to his truck.

A few minutes later, alone again in my front yard and thoroughly angry, I returned to the privacy of my bedroom and counted out the money. I had $435.00 to pay for my furniture and another $600.00 for the most essential repairs to my house. Fully realizing that my hands held the power to rid myself of some of the foremost problems, my temper eased a bit. But it did nothing to stop the churning of my wheels of logic.

The U.S. commitment to any post, anywhere in the country, was six years. The first two years were for development, the second two were for expansion, and the third were dedicated to maintenance. Following that, the local homologue (in my case, Herve) would take over and we would leave the community to its fate. Thus three different volunteers would eventually serve in Makoua, and all three would surely reside in my house. Assuming that everything was completed which needed attention, they would enjoy a relatively comfortable living space and adequate security without the problems of having to secure their own. Furthermore, the costs of necessary improvements, spread over six years, would make my residence a dirt cheap deal for the Corps and a prize for those who followed me! Why then, I wondered, had every issue been left up to me to solve? I decided to put a positive spin on it. Maybe Eric believed that I could handle it, while others might lack the capacity.

Shortly after securing the cash inside my metal foot locker, I walked to the Agriculture Bureau where I hoped to garner some assistance in dealing with the police chief. Herve was there, as was Calixte, sitting across from one another in the foyer, chatting the morning away. I explained my problems with the local authorities, but neither man was eager to get involved. They both suggested that it would be best to pay the bribe and let it go, for they lacked any power and they certainly did not want to get on the bad side of the military man. Anyway, what was twenty dollars to a rich American? I got the point and dropped the subject with a negative shake of my head.

Shifting the subject to business matters, Herve announced that he had set up a meeting with local villagers who might have an interest in fish farming. He wanted to know if I was ready for that sort of thing yet. I told him definitely yes. The fact was, that kind of diversion was exactly what I needed. If I could find productive ways to keep busy, I could deal with the rest of the headaches as they came. So it was agreed we would have the meeting in one week if I had not been arrested by then. I returned home to study French.

When Marin came over late in the day, we went toward town for passport photographs. The "studio" was a shabby little office in a shabby little building on a littered street behind the grand marche, where a four by six "waiting room" housed a desk and a short bench. There, sitting underneath a row of pictures that had been stuck to the mud wall with glue or tape, a customer was supposed to wait for a turn before the camera. The pictures were mostly the size of index cards, a few were wallet sizes and all were in black and white. The corners of most had curled over time, and the strained expressions of their subjects looked like the mug shots on the wall in Norman's office.

The photo room was a little larger than the other space, separated from it by a cloth that hung in the doorway like a shower curtain. The camera, an old crank-type box that looked like a relic from the fifties, was clamped to a homemade tripod made of scrap metal. While I sat patiently in front of it, the photographer tinkered with his equipment until the flash quite unexpectedly blinded both of us. Unexpected or not, that was it. We were done and he did not even ask me to smile. But he did tell me to pay six dollars on the way out. When he had his money, he gave me a little ticket with the amount written on it. The pictures, he assured, would be ready in another week. Another week? I saw myself delivering that news to an already hostile police chief, and listening to another volley of his demands.

I took Marin for a beer that evening. The place we visited was one where customers sat in straight chairs in a clay yard next to the street under speakers playing loud, fuzzy African music through blown speakers. Marin liked it very much. The street was exceptionally busy already. People were moving through dim lights or standing in the shadows, holding hands, talking, moving on, all of which somehow made me feel disjointed as if I were not there at all. I was like a ghost, seeing and hearing but neither touching nor taking part in the life that was in motion all around me.

An hour later, when I returned home in the thick of night, I had never felt more lonely and discouraged in my life. I opened my house to let the wind blow through while I took a cold splash bath. Fully refreshed, I tried to read at the table for a while, but the bugs were unrelenting. They were no longer a problem once I went to bed however, for the new net had been rehung, the mattress had dried out, and I had rigged a place for candles, matches, and books next to my pillow.

A while later, when I blew out the flickering fire, I settled back with my hands behind my head and listened to a pack of dogs fighting somewhere close by. Surely the mating season never ended in Makoua, as the fighting was constant over bitches in heat. It was good, I reasoned, for some of God's creatures to have a clear picture of what the fight was all about.

May the best dog win.

9

Witches and Curses

A few days passed without much happening, except for talking business with whoever would listen and attending the meeting that Herve had set up for us at the agriculture office. Four of the seven men present expressed interest in our work, and some asked for site inspections to be conducted soon. We took names and made appointments for times that suited each man, and, meeting over, everyone shook hands and left the building. Immediately afterward I delivered passport pictures to the police chief, along with the papers that he wanted and then we dealt with the matter of his extortion money.

"Give me the twenty dollars," he demanded once again.

"No. I will not pay you any money," I replied firmly as his large eyes grew larger and his puffy cheeks grew puffier.

"Then get your papers and get out!" he ordered and waved into the air. I got out.

The realization had finally sunk in that the only hold anybody had on me in Makoua, was my own personal commitment to remain there. If I were to abandon my post, the community would lose the immediate flow of currency that my presence brought to it, as well as the long term potential of the work that had been planned. And Herve, unlike all the other African homologues, would lose any hope of ever getting a free motorcycle. I did not believe the police chief really wanted to deal with the negative attention that might fall upon him, and he probably already realized that I would make it a point to blame him personally if it came to that. Thus I considered the matter closed no matter what.

Mid-afternoon, three days later, Calixte's men arrived to cut down the tree in my back yard according to the plan worked out the week before. The deal was that I had to pay Calixte twenty-four dollars. He would then pay the others for their services. Uncertain why we had to do it that way, I nevertheless paid and waited. Feeling a sense of relief when the men finally showed up, barefoot, barewaisted, axes in hand, I led them around back to the tree.

They walked boldly to it and studied it a long moment and then they conferred. Talking simultaneously, nodding vigorously, analyzing, noting the direction of the breeze and the slight tilt of the tree, they suddenly turned to me, pointed northward and indicated that the tree would fall in the weeds just behind my toilet. That would be very perfect, I assured them. Thus, they tested their blades, positioned their feet to balance themselves and they begin chopping, swinging in turns.

Twenty minutes later, as bits of wood were flying from the deep wedge they had cut, they were still swinging as mightily as when they were fresh and rested. Soon they paused, moved to the opposite side, and began cutting a new wedge that was lower than the first. Ten more minutes went by, and the tree began to groan. They worked excitedly then, swinging hard while watching for movement. More chips flew. They paused again, and appraised their progress. More swings were swung, more chips flew. The tree suddenly grunted and moved a little, then the men jumped out of the way. As it came down, it creaked, popped, and tumbled with a mighty crash into the neighboring manioc field. It had fallen exactly a hundred and eighty degrees in the wrong direction, landing on a great stack of cement blocks that had been stored among the plants in the garden of two old women. Dozens of the blocks were pulverized, and a forty-foot line of manioc was decimated.

I did not want to be home when those old women saw that tree trunk in their field. They had frequently worked there since my arrival, often laboring dawn to dusk, weeding, digging and nurturing until the manioc plants were knee high. But my tree had wrecked a good portion of it and parked a giant obstruction most of the way across it. I did not know where the women lived, nor what other garden plots they might have, nor when they might return to that one. But they would be back, sooner or later, and they would not be pleased. I wanted Calixte to see what had happened and to face the women himself. I would have gone to fetch him right then, but it was late in the day and he would have gone home already. Furthermore the woodsmen reassured me that their mistake would not cause a problem for anyone. Indeed, they seemed entirely indifferent about it as they strode out of my yard, mission accomplished. Not for one minute did they convince me, however. The whole thing felt like trouble ahead.

Working in my yard the rest of the day, digging a hole for burning trash in the back corner, I noticed that everyone on the road out front stopped to look at the tree in the field. Women observed it sternly, pointing to it and speaking all at once in rapid Lengala. Men stopped as well, but none of them talked much. They just laughed. As for me, my negative feelings grew helplessly worse.

A huge storm came late in the day, cooling things down and providing an opportunity to steal a good nap in relative comfort, but the weather conditions were unusual. Raining hard when I fell asleep and still pouring when I awoke during the night, I actually had to find additional cover for the first time since arriving at the equator. When dawn came I was refreshed, invigorated and ready to get some things done.

Giving me something to think about other than the decimated garden next door, my carpenters arrived an hour after sunup. One of them was pushing a wheelbarrow and the other was helping to balance the tools and the wooden objects that it carried. Among other things, they brought a door that was fitted inside a nicely made wooden frame. They too had a good laugh over the tree in the garden, but then they went to work. Project number one was the toilet.

Because cinder blocks were not sold in Makoua, they had to be made on site by pouring cement into wooden molds. Sand and gravel had to be transported from the river's edge, and water was carried in whatever containers might get the job done from whichever source was the most convenient. Interestingly, the blocks of my toilet had been made with too much sand and too little cement, which made them easy to break apart, punch through or knock down as needed. My two tradesmen used common hammers to beat notches into the tops of two walls, then they placed boards on edge from one side to the next, fitted crudely into the notches. A section of corrugated tin was nailed to the boards, and it was all strapped down with a length of insulated electrical wire poked through freshly punched holes in the walls and tied together on the outside. Finally, the time came to hang the door.

When the door frame was placed upright in front of the entrance, I could plainly see that it would not fit. The vertical part was too tight. A few pencil marks were made, the frame was set aside again, and the men began chipping away at the leading edge of the cement floor. The concrete pulverized easily, crumbling into sandy powder with little lumps of gravel and then the debris was simply tossed out of the way. When enough of the floor had been chipped away, the frame was uprighted again and beaten tightly into position. Finally it was secured with nails driven straight through the frame into the blocks. However because the frame was no longer plumb, the door which minutes ago hung to perfection would no longer swing freely. Even that was not a problem for my pair of experts. They planed the upper half of one edge until it swung back and forth with ease. Next, a little block of wood was installed on the inside to act as a twist-lock, and finally, a hasp for a padlock was secured to the outside (the toilet had to be kept locked to keep people from taking the paper). Less than two hours from the time they started, the project was done, and for the first time it was possible to use the toilet without an audience.

The day was still young, but the men were done for the day. My shutters, they said, would be next. But they hadn't been built yet and several more days would pass before they could be completed. Having already learned that men of the Congo preferred to labor when it was not raining or when it was not too hot, and because they were on Africa time, I knew they would get around to it when conditions suited them.

Cheered by the positive events of that morning, I went about preparing a late brunch of canned pork from China, fresh onions and hot pili pili peppers from Makoua, bottled soy sauce from Korea, and rice from heaven knows where. Soon, while settling down to eat and to read the last few pages of *Heroes and Villains*, I heard distant voices, loud voices, growing louder, closer. Moving to my porch, I watched about twenty women and girls moving in my direction on the dirt road, dancing, singing, and chanting loudly. They were all dressed in red tee shirts, typical pagnes and thongs, but all were additionally decorated with strange wraps made of leaves and dried branches that seem to have been pinned on rather randomly. All of them had pinkish makeup on their faces, again randomly streaked, and several of them were carrying rattles made from gourds. The older woman in front had a whistle in her hand, which she blew smartly as they halted in front of my house; then the noise stopped abruptly and their formation unraveled. A brief but vigorous discussion took place, after which the whistle chirped again, the women shuffled back into ranks, and off they went dance-skipping down the street. I was told later that the women probably made up a funeral procession, in which they were marching out of respect for the dead.

A short time later, Dani showed up at my door. She greeted me and walked into my bedroom, looked all about and then helped herself to a chair. I had been glancing through a copy of *Newsweek* magazine (routinely distributed by the Peace Corps), three issues of which lay on my table. Dani picked up one, thumbed through it, and asked if she might have it. Thinking she liked the pictures and might somehow benefit from studying them, I gave her the older issues. Broadly grinning then, she hopped up and grabbed my broom and began sweeping the floor as if to demonstrate her domestic skills. No more than two minutes later, she put the broom aside and demanded twenty dollars. When I flatly refused, she lowered the amount to four dollars and waited patiently. I then made it clear that I would not give her any money, and if she felt that she had earned it by sweeping my floor, she should have negotiated her price in advance. She stormed out of the house, magazines in hand, with nothing else to say.

Late in the afternoon a young man from the post office brought me a note from Brazzaville, a form of telegram, instructing me to go to Owando to open a checking account. The point of that was to facilitate electronic deposits each month, and therefore to eliminate the need for Tom or Eric to physically deliver monthly stipends. I didn't know they even had a bank in Owando, but, having nothing better to do with myself and having learned that Calixte was out of town, I decided to go the next morning.

That night at the street market, I found Dani sitting at a table, selling peanuts packaged in paper cones made from pages of *Newsweek*. Wandering back toward home for the night, I recalled something my grandfather had once told me: "Disappointment comes only from expectations. All disappointment is therefore a problem of your own making." Every day I was learning how to avoid disappointment in Africa.

Makoua's "bus station" was nothing more than a circular weed bed in the middle of the intersection where our two main thoroughfares met. A cement wall about twelve inches high surrounded a dirt filled pit about twelve feet in diameter, providing a place for people to sit and to wait for a bus or truck going wherever it was that they wanted to go. I was sitting with the crowd at six o'clock the next morning.

Never having traveled by public transport before in Africa, I asked one of the men if there would be a bus to Owando that morning. He responded, "Oui, bientot". Sure enough, after only another half-hour, a Japanese-made "Coaster Deluxe" pulled up and people scrambled for the door. When it was my turn, I asked the driver if he was going to Owando.

"No," he said curtly back. "This bus is to Brazzaville."

"But you must go through Owando to get to Brazzaville, mustn't you?."

"Yes."

"Might I ride that far?"

"No. This is the bus to Brazzaville."

I pulled back, intending to reclaim my seat on the platform, but the man I spoke to before told me there was a small truck that I could take to Owando. He pointed toward the grand marche where an old Toyota pickup was parked in front of a store. The battered vehicle did not look like commercial transportation to me, but I thanked the man kindly and started toward it.

A typical truck, typically loaded with both people and cargo, heading from Makoua to either Owando or Etoumbi.

Just as I got there with arms waving, the little vehicle was pulling into the street. The driver stopped for me, advised that he was indeed headed to Owando, and that I might ride there for only four dollars. Someone above me grabbed my duffel and yanked it up while I stepped onto the axle housing, gripped the crash cage, and pulled myself aboard. Momentarily on our way, we eight men with several pieces of luggage and six huge sacks of manioc roots, were coughing in unmuffled exhaust and leaning forward to catch an occasional breath of fresh air. The truck was a rattletrap, the likes of which would have long before been taken off the road back home. Having no shock absorbers, or at least none that worked, we took every bump noisily and hard. Stressed metal creaked and groaned as it struggled over the rough road, sounding as if it might disintegrate at any moment. But we sputtered on, heads bobbing with the bumps, bodies weaving with the swaying, all in motion, moving toward somewhere, and everybody seemed content to have it so.

Villages were located every few miles, and we stopped in many of them. We stopped to buy what looked like a smoked fruit bat and smelled like a very strong ham. Later we pulled over for boiled manioc, still later for palm wine, and twice more because the driver wanted to chat with people he recognized. All along the way, passengers yelled out to people on the ground, perhaps old friends or relatives not often visited, who waved back excitedly and sometimes ran along with us for as long as they could.

When we had covered the first twenty miles or so, a young man sitting on the cab turned to me and grinned rather sheepishly as he lit up a marijuana cigarette. Following a deep draw, he passed it around to the circle of passengers. I politely declined, to the great amusement of the others. But I already had enough problems without adding drugs to them. Anyway, even the RUMOR that a volunteer had used drugs was all the evidence that headquarters needed to send a person packing. And I knew full well that there were no secrets in Africa, for everybody talks and everybody embellishes. About four hours into the trip, when we rounded a sharp turn on the wet road, a concrete bridge appeared just ahead. Momentarily we could see buildings along the far banks of a wide, black river, that marked the end of our journey. Beat up and nearly suffocated from the ride, I was quite satisfied to walk the remaining mile into town.

Having been in Owando only once before, when Tom and I stopped there with mail for the local volunteer, I did not remember the street to Anne's house. But I did recall passing the grand marche on the left, the palm wine market on the right, and the long dirt street ahead with stores on either side. Walking on, I suddenly heard my name called and looked up to see a white face in the crowd coming straight toward me. She was Anne, headed to the bakery, hoping for a fresh loaf of bread.

Anne was an attractive woman in her mid-twenties, and a second year volunteer who had been transferred to Owando from her original post in the other end of the country. Because she had encountered trouble with a former friend who became a stalker, she had been shipped back to the U.S. for a few weeks and then she was moved to her new placement. She seemed both surprised and genuinely pleased to see me, but she was a little confused when I explained my reason for the trip. She had received no similar notification. "Par for the course," she breathed.

Because she decided to put off the hunt for fresh bread, we walked along the eroded avenue toward her house and turned our conversation to more personal matters.

"So, how do you like it so far?" she asked, as we stepped out of the way of an oncoming truck.

"Less than two years to go," I replied.

"Everybody says that," she laughed heartily. "I'm a short timer now. I've got less than a year."

"I don't know if I'll make it that long. Every day is such a challenge."

"I know exactly how you feel," she comforted me with another chuckle.

"How come you stayed this long?" I wondered aloud.

"Future benefits. Job opportunities, deferred student loans. Besides, the worst of my hitch is over now."

Her house was unusual compared to those of most volunteers, for it had several large bedrooms with jalousie windows, a huge living room, a kitchen with a long wooden counter, a separate dining room, a large storage room in which she kept her motorcycle, and a real indoor bathroom that actually worked. Furthermore, she had running water, a shower and a bathtub, and even electricity during the evening hours. The justification for all the grandeur, she explained, was that her residence functioned as a crash-house for any volunteers or staff-people who might travel her way and need a place to sleep over. That made sense, because buses or trucks ran every day to and from Brazzaville, making Owando the ideal stop for long-distance travelers.

Located on a corner where two busy streets crossed, the house was surrounded by the homes of local Congolese and by the street-noises of cars, trucks, motor scooters, and an endless march of people. A family lived in a small dwelling in one corner of Anne's front yard, while others occupied little mud apartments no more than three steps from her back door. Those latter units faced her kitchen and dining room, such that she and her neighbors heard each other constantly and saw each other through her windows whether they wanted to or not. I would not have traded places with her for anything.

Thanks to the national monetary problems that had recently surfaced in Brazzaville, the local bank was already closed for the day. And because my business could not be transacted until the next morning, when trucks and buses would already have run, I would have no choice but to spend two days in Owando. That suited me. It gave me a legitimate and much needed change of pace for an evening or two, and some relaxed conversation with a fellow American. Even so, I was yet wondering what my carpenters would do if I were not home to receive them when they returned with the shutters. Ah, well. Whatever was to happen would happen. I was on Africa time.

When darkness came and we had finished a dinner of pasta and local vegetables, Anne and I sat in wicker chairs on the front porch and talked for a long time about home and family and about all the things we were missing. A loud radio was playing fuzzy African music somewhere up the street and a girl yelled at someone behind the house, but because a storm was coming the streets were still and even the mosquitoes had taken shelter. Soon we were presented with a lightning-show that danced madly across the skies for an hour or more, flashing, dazzling, sizzling, as if putting on an elaborate show for those who might enjoy the fierce beauty of nature at its finest.

Early the next morning, Anne took me to a local restaurant for an omelet, which turned out to be tasty but very expensive, then we went to the bank. Following a man to his desk behind the counter, we took seats and waited as the paperwork was completed. Finally my account was opened, with eighty dollars on deposit, and the man said that my checks should arrive in a month or so. Checks! I wondered what I might do with them. Certainly nobody in Makoua would cash one. But if the account assured that my monthly stipend would be electronically deposited and always on time, it would not be tough duty to visit Owando now and then to claim it. Frankly, it all sounded too good to be true.

When my business was done, we strolled to the agriculture office where Anne introduced me to her Congolese counterpart, Luke, who worked with her as Herve worked with me. Luke thought he might be able to find me a ride back to Makoua that very morning if I wanted it. Thinking once again about my carpenters, I told him to do what he could.

Walking together a few blocks up the street, we three went into the office of Mucodec which was rather like a small loan company in the United States. A Congolese man in a business suit was seated at a desk in the middle of the room, concentrating hard on the records in front of him and working simultaneously with a calculator. At first, he seemed a little annoyed at the interruption, but he listened as Luke spoke, turned to look me over, then nodded affirmatively. I had a ride to Makoua.

Since we had a little time to spare, Anne and I went shopping for grass mats. Luckily, a few of them were displayed on the ground in the grand marche, and they did appear to be nicely done. Hand-woven from local grasses, they were thin, flat, lightweight, they could be rolled into snug bundles, carried anywhere, and used for just about anything that a cloth rug might have been used for. But they did not have to be cleaned except by shaking them in the wind, which was a great advantage in a place where everything captured dust and dirt. Each mat, on average, was about three feet wide by five feet long, which made them well suited for sitting upon, lying upon, or for displaying vegetables in the markets. And if installed properly, they might make passable ceiling material in my house. I bought the four mats, paid the equivalent of two dollars each, and scrolled them into a bundle to be carried under one arm.

My "ride" was supposed to pick me up in front of a hotel located on National Highway #2 near the river, so after a brunch of peanut butter, honey and bread, Anne went with me to wait. Claiming chairs at a patio table shaded by a colorful red and white umbrella, we ordered Pulp Orange (a local soft drink), and sat back in muggy air in search of comfort. To my surprise, the man showed up exactly on time. After a moment to toss my mats in the back of his truck and to say a quick goodbye to Anne, my new acquaintance, Jean Pierre and I, in a little four wheel drive Suzuki, were off.

I had found that I could learn more French in situations like that than at any other time, because I was able to concentrate on one voice. Jean recognized my language limitations, so he made a special effort to help me converse as we rode. As a traveling auditor for Mucodec, he made the trip from Brazzaville all the way to Makoua every few months. He had studied economics in Paris, he still had family there, and he had traveled in other parts of the world as well. He also seemed to be interested in my opinions regarding the problems that lay ahead for his country. Surprised that he seemed to agree with most of what I had to say, I found our drive to be very pleasant, relatively comfortable and highly beneficial. It was also quick and free of charge. He even delivered me all the way to my door without having to ask the way. Thanking him profusely and wishing him well, I felt that I had made an important new ally.

My two carpenters came again the next morning, arriving just after dawn, but only to let me know that there would be no work at my house that day. Because I had left town, they had not built the shutters yet. But, because I returned, they would build them that very day and install them the next. The younger man, probably in his early twenties, was named John. His middle aged senior was Andre. Andre, wearing a patch over his right eye like a bad guy in a "B" movie, rode a little green motor scooter here and there, and was polite to the point of being humble. When they left, John afoot, I had the feeling that good things were happening.

Too hot to stay inside the house, by nine o'clock I had already started digging weeds in the front yard when I heard an angry voice coming from the field behind my house. I looked around the corner to see a withered, leathery old woman standing next to the fallen tree, staring alternately at it and the sky above, wailing as if to the spirits. She raved for a long time without moving, then she made her way to the edge of the street and stationed herself there like a circus barker. As people approached, walking or riding bicycles, she launched fierce tirades aimed both about me and about her damaged field. The one word I kept hearing over and over, was "mondele". I needed no linguist to help me grasp the rest. I stepped to the edge of my yard and called out to her in French, but the effort was unsuccessful. The pitch of her voice rose as the speed of her Lengala increased, yelling to the wind, decrying the deeds of the foreigner. Long after I had retreated back inside the house, she continued, while the sounds of male laughter and the howls of female admonition emanated from the street.

Marin showed up late in the afternoon, thirty minutes after the woman's voice wore out, to find out why I had made the trip to Owando. Following my explanation and seeming satisfied with it, he then listened with amusement as I related the episode of the tree in the garden. Oddly enough, he claimed not to be acquainted with either of the women of the garden. Since he always seemed to know everything about everybody else in town, his denial seemed a bit strange to me. But I could only accept it as fact and move on.

"But," Marin insisted, "it was not your fault anyway, and you should not worry about it."

I simply could not grasp the masculine indifference to the plight of those women. Somebody owed them some satisfaction, and if I couldn't get anyone else to take care of it, I would have to take it upon myself to make things right somehow. I really wanted to unload on Calixte and his expert woodsmen. I wanted them to fix the product of their mistakes and to do so immediately, and I did not care much if my demands offended somebody. Marin listened to my little speech as he always did, even promising to help if the opportunity presented itself, but his lack of enthusiasm led me to doubt his sincerity.

Afternoon clouds started building up late in the day and a breeze swept across the tall grass, bending it flat as if pressed by invisible hands. Marin left soon after demonstrating the proper technique for mowing a lawn with a machete and then I dragged a chair out to the porch and leaned back against the wall to read a novel that I had been trying for a week to finish. My heart was not in it. I could not get comfortable, could not nap in the heat, did not want to swim in the river, and didn't want a beer. All of a sudden every ray of sunshine seemed to have been chased away by a dark little cloud.

I also found myself dealing with a problem that was driving me crazy. Everything tumbled! My plastic plates tumbled, enamel cups fell off their nails, wooden spoon splashed into my soup which then spilled into my lap, and the spoon tumbled to the floor. I bent over to pick it up with one hand and dragged the salt shaker off the table with the other. I spilled my coffee in the mornings, dumped my lunch in the afternoon, and inevitably dropped something into my dinner at night. A glass of kool-aid wound up inside one of my boots, a kerosene stove nearly went over and its fuel sloshed all over my sneakers. I dropped my soap when bathing so that sand was embedded into it, I knocked over lit candles, I could not find the matches, and on it went. The phenomenon had started the day before, and try as I might to control it, matters seemed only to grow worse.

I had no fear of any evil sorcery that might have been directed at me, nor did I accept that any local magic was a serious power. Yet I had great respect for mind over matter. If one feared something, the power was in the fear and not in any supernatural calling of evil. Conversely, having no fear, those who might have sought to harm me had no power at all. And, anyway, they probably didn't even make curses that caused everything to tumble.

My personal witch arrived shortly after dawn the next morning, but she came in the form of the younger, heavier woman, who was the other half of the garden team. I had seen her a number of times before, but she looked mean even when she was in a good mood. Like her associate the day before, she took a place near the street and there she spent the better part of two hours yelling to passersby about the "mondele". She did not look at me, nor did she draw nearer, but her unhappy chants drew attention and developed an audience. She was, if nothing else, beginning to get on my nerves.

This symbol of the dark spirits and warning to potential thieves, was found in the forest near a large garden. I was told that no rational person would dare to challenge its power.

Herve came to visit shortly after the woman finally left, but he only looked at the tree and giggled. That did it for me. I locked up my house and followed him to the Agriculture office. Calixte, having just returned from his trip, claimed to be in the dark about the incident. But, he said, he would have the men return that very day to remove the trunk. While all the men in Makoua were having a good laugh at my expense, I was not going to let him off the hook with a lot of hollow words but no action. I told him to either fix it or I would take up the matter with somebody of higher authority.

The tree cutters showed up within the hour, just after my carpenters arrived with two pairs of shutters in their wheelbarrow. Working busily, John and Andre paid no attention to the other two men. The lumberjacks, axes in hand, acted as if they had intended to take care of the tree all along, no problem. Two hours later, when the pair had cut the trunk into four-foot lengths, Calixte showed up to see how things were going. He watched as they rolled one of the logs out of my yard deeper into the manioc field and then as they tossed the axes aside and put their shirts back on. Calixte nodded at them in approval. "C'est bon" he told them.

"No," I corrected him. "It is not good. It is not good at all. They were supposed to get rid of the logs, not roll them around the field."

Just at that moment one of the women walked into the garden, saw the logs, and started yelling and chanting all over again. Calixte went to her, calmed her after a moment, and explained that the wind had caused the tree to fall in the wrong direction. That meant the problem was caused by an act of the all powerful spirits, and no mere human could be blamed for it. She fell silent for the moment, absorbing his words, but I had the feeling it was not over yet.

Meanwhile, John was done replacing the shutter in my back room, and he had gone to work installing the other one in the north room. Andre, by then, had removed my wooden door and frame, stood it aside, and was busy knocking a new passage from my bedroom into the north side of the house. Watching him work, I realized that my "brick" house was hardly more than mud, for the bricks had been poorly fired and would crumble with little more than a hammer strike. As soon as the opening was wide enough to facilitate the passage of a person, Andre went about sealing up the old entrance with bricks taken from an abandoned building at the police compound. He had heaped a pile of pure clay from the hill behind my outhouse and mixed that with equal amounts of sand from the street. The two ingredients were blended with water, and just like cement, it was used to hold the new bricks together. Soon John was done with the shutters, and was helping to maintain the pile of mortar. When not needed there, he went about sealing up the spaces around the new shutters in the north room, and to my utter amazement, he was done within an hour.

Again amazed, I watched the two men work together to completely seal the hole where the old entrance had been, and to fit the wooden door into the opening that had once led into the north room from the yard. Before three o'clock came, they were finished for the day and the usable space of my house had just been doubled. Furthermore, the entire place was relatively secure against burglars. When they were gone, I moved my dining table and chairs into the big new room and luxuriated in my change of fortune Not to mention my attitude. That night, I slept like a man who was satisfied with life.

Someone at the police compound had a particularly annoying electronic gadget which, on the hour, every hour around the clock, played a few very loud notes of some catchy little tune. During the night at 7:00 P.M., I noted "Clementine," followed at eight by "London Bridge is Falling Down". A few of the tunes were not familiar to me, but I happened to awaken at two o'clock in the morning to "Lullaby and Good Night". When morning came and I was having breakfast, I listened to a rousing rendition of "Happy Birthday," and two hours later I distinctly heard "Itsy Bitsy Spider". Surely the witches had planned in advance for my arrival in Makoua and sought to punish me in every conceivable manner.

The day was Sunday, which meant that Marin and his brother Prudence would probably spend the morning at their protestant church. And my new friend, Kevin, would probably go to noon Mass and not drop by until much later in the day. Kevin was a sixteen year old boy whom I met at the Catholic church the day I had dinner with the priests. He had visited fairly often, earning small money by helping me with various domestic projects, and he had become a helpful (although persistent) companion. And because the women of the garden were not likely to tend their crops that day, nor stand at the street to cry their woes, surely my little piece of the neighborhood would be fairly peaceful for at least a few delightful hours.

Kevin was one of the young men who became good friends of mine.
Here he was cutting the grass of my front yard with a machete.

I was very interested in Marin's beliefs and what he was taught at his church. He seemed to enjoy talking about religion, and he would even sometimes read to me from his Bible. I found it strange that a person could claim to be a Christian on the one hand, while at the same time being entirely nervous around the subject of black magic. He was very mature in many ways, yet sometimes childlike, primitive and hopelessly backward in his reasoning. He seemed truly convinced about the "woman in the moon" and once told me of evil spirits who shone bright lights over a certain place in the forest every night. He absolutely refused to show me where it was said to happen, however, and furthermore discouraged me from any notion of looking for it.

Marin also told me of his girlfriend, his fiancé actually, whom he could not afford to marry because he had no money to pay the dowry. Trying to beat the system, he said, was a dangerous practice. Sometimes a couple would make the mistake of living together without the formality of marriage, but that would always backfire. The woman would eventually become pregnant and then her family would demand the dowry anyway. If it went unpaid they would contract a sorcerer for the placement of a curse to kill the unborn child. "If God were not with me," Marin once told me thoughtfully as if hanging over a precipice between true love and simple survival, "I could not make it through the days".

I never really understood what burdens Marin had to carry, for he did no work that I could identify, his life seemed to revolve around his language studies, and he appeared to do only what he wished. He was secretive about his father, who was said to be in Brazzaville and was often gone for long periods of time. His mother was another mystery, if she was alive at all, for she was never mentioned by either Marin or Prudence.

Having passed most of the morning reading and resting, I sat on my little porch and leaned back to watch as clouds began to roll in. The skies were soon heavily overcast while a strong breeze warned of a new storm approaching. And far in the distance I could hear the first thunderclaps of the day. I wondered if witchcraft could affect the intensity of a storm.

Exactly at high noon, electronic music sounded from across the street.

"Are you sleeping, are you sleeping….?"

10

Uphill, Downhill

John and Andre came with the rising sun, but as their work was drawing to a close, John was pushing the wheelbarrow that held only a few tools and a partial bag of cement, while Andre was riding his motor scooter and carrying nothing at all. They set to work as soon as I received them.

Because the only major unfinished job was shaping and smoothing the new passage into my bedroom, they immediately started shoveling clay and sand into a pile on the floor. John then poured the necessary water and maintained the mix, while Andre worked his trowel to fill spaces and smooth surfaces. Favoring an unusual sort of look for my house, I asked that an eight inch elevation be left at the bottom of the opening. Andre thought about that a moment, shook his head as if he understood the plan but didn't quite get the point and then he went to work with a private grin on his face.

When less than two hours had passed, the completed opening looked like any other door-sized passage except for the step-over. Andre and John then went to the front porch where the old doorway had been sealed, they took the cement out of the wheelbarrow and they made a small pile of fresh mud out of it. Over the next half hour, Andre spread a very thin coat over the new masonry. He explained that failure to do so would guarantee collapse when wind-driven rain splashed against it and washed the mud away from the bricks. A coat of real cement, on the other hand, would protect it from the elements and guarantee that the job would last for many years. Because the rest of the house lacked any cement glaze, I presumed that it must have been built in the dry season.

Soon my entire house was secure, completely usable, and it was no longer a duplex. The only entrance then opened into the north room which had been transformed into a kitchen and dining area, and passage into the bedroom had a unique look of creativity to it. I was rather amazed to discover how little it took to please me after I learned not to expect so much. The carpenters were paid in cash, they gave me a receipt, and they went away happy to have done business with me. Soon, I mused with satisfaction, I would even have a portion of my ceiling covered with grass mats. What a grand life had I.

Feeling excited and ready to tie up more loose ends, I decided to take a walk to see about my furniture. Thirty minutes later, reaching the shed with parts of furniture crowded underneath, a tall, muscular black man was moving about without much purpose. The cabinet maker smiled and shook my hand, as if actually happy to see me again, but his composure faded rather suddenly when I asked about the rest of my things. He paused a moment with his eyes narrowed, then he answered without conviction, "Everything will be finished Sunday." Having received such promises so many times before, my purpose that day was not to learn the truth but to keep reminding him that I had not forgotten.

"Sunday it is, then," I told him. "I'll be ready and waiting."

Done there, I took the long way home in the direction of the Catholic church and then turned down the main thoroughfare toward the heart of town. I drifted through the grand marche, hoping to find something for breakfast, but most of the market was closed by then. My habit had been to go there every morning, usually to buy eggs if I could find them, and sometimes even pineapples and other fruits. Fresh potatoes were not available, nor were lettuce, tomatoes or corn, because those vegetables were not yet in season and because they were not as popular as manioc anyway. National distribution of perishable products did not exist in my end of the Congo, while apples or grapes, watermelons or cantaloupe were evidently not grown at all.

I found it interesting that chickens ran loose all over town, but eggs were not readily available to those of us who would have liked to buy them. The Mission was by far the biggest supplier, selling about sixty a day to stores and restaurants. But sixty eggs for several thousand people did not last long. Before buying an egg in the open markets, one had to put it to his ear and shake it. If the contents were heard to slosh about, the egg was assumed to be bad and it would not be purchased. Since even the good ones sometimes carried Salmonella, eating from the markets was always a challenge no matter how fresh the products seemed to be.

I had often thought of raising my own chickens, believing it would be possible to do so in a disease free environment to produce a better quality product that could then be sold for profit. I had also considered inviting Marin to work with me in a business to produce both eggs and chickens for sale. He caught up with me while I was buying a few pieces of hard candy that morning, and wanted to know what I had been doing with my day.

Walking toward home with him at my side and eggs on my mind, I made an offer. I would furnish the money to build cages, buy chicks, buy food for them, and handle distribution afterward. His role would be to build the cages, keep them in his own yard, protect them from thieves, and finally to harvest the eggs. When the day came that I would leave the country, the entire business would be his at no cost to him.

"That would be a lot of work," he said.

"Well, of course it would, but it would be profitable."

"I am not interested."

"But it would earn money for you, then you might be able to pay the dowry for your fiancé."

"It does not interest me."

"If I were in your position," I argued, "I would do just about anything to make money. At least for a while."

"It is not what I wish to do."

I gave up and walked along with nothing more to say about it. When we reached my yard, I was literally stunned to notice something that I had entirely missed when I started out that morning. Somebody had been busy! About one third of my yard next to the manioc field had been converted into part of the women's garden, complete with young shoots freshly planted. I was speechless. Marin, however, was greatly amused. As the elder of the two women was quietly working in the dirt at that moment, I took Marin with me to talk to her.

Hoping that our disputes could be put to rest then, lacking Calixte to make matters worse, I told Marin to explain how the tree happened to fall there in the first place, how the wind had nothing to do with it, and that it was not caused by an act of God, or even Satan. Next he told her that the men were supposed to cut the trunk up and move it, they were paid to do it, but they refused to finish the job. That said, we moved on to the subject of her taking over my yard. I had planned to use every inch of that small piece of ground for projects that could be beneficial to the community and I did not wish to give any of it up.

She said the tree was not a problem anymore since Calixte explained to her how the spirits caused it to fall there. However ownership of the yard was another matter. She claimed that it was her property, it had always been in her family, her son gave it to her, she had intended to farm it, and I was the one who had encroached. So we were stuck on a thorny issue. Ownership of property was accomplished simply by claiming it and not by filing papers in some government office. I could have won if the matter had been taken to the Chief of Makoua, but that might not have been the thing to do. I would live there only two years, while that old woman would stay the rest of her life. I needed about thirty seconds to decide. I told her that she was absolutely correct, I was in the wrong, and the yard was hers. Showing missing teeth, she smiled happily and shook my hand as if it was great to have resolved a dispute with such a wonderful neighbor. We would have no more trouble, I was certain. But some day, when no volunteers lived on that parcel anymore, the quarrel would probably begin anew and she would stand in the street yelling about the wrongs that local officials were trying to do to her. I only hoped that she would remember to tell them that the American gave it to her.

Inside my house once again and resting at my table, Marin had news to share. He had heard on the radio that a pickup truck had crashed on the road to Owando.

"Five people were killed and many others were hurt. The driver lost control going down a hill and turned over in the ditch." That came as no surprise to me, actually, for those trucks were always overloaded, most of them were in poor repair and most underwent no routine maintenance whatsoever.

"That is too bad," I said with my best sympathetic face.

"It is nothing new," Marin continued. "The truck will probably be back on the road again soon."

When we had spent about a half hour talking and we had gone back into the front yard, a snake about three feet long and black as midnight hurried across the grass and slithered into the house. Marin stayed safely out of range while I went cautiously inside and prodded about with a long stick, but it never appeared again. I was pretty sure it went through a small hole in the bedroom floor, for it had only been two days since I filled that hole with fresh clay and it was open again as if never disturbed. Having seen snakes in my yard several times before, I had always suspected that a family of them lived under my house. But that particular snake was the first hard evidence I had encountered. Marin said that I must pour diesel fuel around the outer walls to get rid of them, for snakes were common and that method of treatment was the standard.

"But what would happen if the snakes were all at home when I poured the diesel fuel about? Wouldn't that drive them into my house?"

"Maybe. But then you would know where they are." I decided to buy some diesel fuel one day and give the technique a thoroughly calculated try, but only at a time when I could stand in the yard to see what crawled out.

Not long after Marin left, I went with Herve to meet a man with whom we had an appointment to do a preliminary site inspection for a possible fish pond. The walk was about two miles from my house, but it was a welcome break because I had not been there before and because it was the first hands-on work that we had done together. When we reached the site, the farmer was standing in the shade of a mango tree, waiting patiently as if he had been there a while. Immediately he led us into a thick patch of forest where a strong brook bubbled from underneath an embankment and from there it swirled through a deep channel into a downward run.

The "science" used in deciding whether a given site was suitable for a pond or not was actually quite basic. Because the depth of the finished pond had to be one meter, to meet our specifications and therefore to qualify for our support, the first consideration was whether the water source was adequate to fill the dig. However because the back end of the pond would have to be dug out for draining and harvesting, that required the slope of the land to be at least one meter down from the water source. Other considerations had to do with adequate space, sunlight penetration (which was essential), and whether or not someone could be depended upon to feed the fish every single day after stocking. Beyond those issues, the rest was a matter of hard work.

That particular location was in a wide open area where the spring was plenty strong for the job. Also the slope of the land, sharply downhill, was excellent for draining and harvesting. Normally a formal survey would have been necessary, measuring the dimensions of the property and establishing the degree of the slope, but it was obvious that the man had a terrific piece of ground which would support at least one pond. Maybe two.

My next step, however, was to explain the rules. If Herve and I were to work with him, the man must agree to complete his task according to our official standards. He looked a bit confused. Clarifying, I explained that he would be required to clear an area of at least ten meters by twenty meters, completely ridding it of all the little roots and twigs that entwined beneath the surface of the ground, and turning all of it into clean sand and clay. His enthusiasm seemed to wane a little.

"When that is done," I told him, "I will lay out the pond with stakes and twine, so that you can see exactly how it must look. That way you'll know how to shape the pond and where to build the dikes."

"Ehhh," he grunted his understanding with the Lengala expression for "yes".

"And I will work with you to make sure the finished pond satisfies all requirements." Formal supervision was essential, because the fish needed sloped banks on which to build their nests, and the degree of the slope had been standardized for best results. "When everything is done, I will stock the pond at no cost to you. Then you must feed the fish daily and protect them from thieves and predators." The man was looking alternately at me and then Herve, as if not quite certain how to respond.

"How much do you pay me for the work?" he finally asked.

"Nothing. Your reward would be to have all the fish that you and your family could eat with many left over to sell at the market."

"Okay. I will let you know when I am ready," he said after a long pause. His former zeal gone, then looking grim and serious, he shook my hand and terminated our meeting. So, I said to myself, one up and one down!

As Herve and I returned toward home, walking briskly and wordlessly, my sense was that my homologue had never been told anything of our "rules" about working with villagers. Clearly he had expected a different outcome from that first meeting, and he seemed thoroughly disappointed with the experience. He had not realized that if we were to help someone perform work that was not in keeping with project standards, Brazzaville would not support it. They would neither pay for, nor transport stock for the finished pond, and all that labor would have been done for nothing. When I stopped at a boutique in search of batteries for my radio, Herve hurried on alone without having offered his hand for the customary courtesy. He and I definitely had our problems, and they were probably rooted in the fact that we simply did not like each other.

Home again and free of other work-related obligations, I was about to install four grass mats over my bed. Five of six rafters that once spanned the twenty feet from the front wall to the back were still in place, acting as my only protection from falling guano. Made of locally grown redwood that had been shaped about four inches square, they were quite strong and highly durable. Mine had been made even stronger by a matrix of braces, held in place by very long, very large nails. Climbing up on a crude homemade ladder, I pulled myself into the attic, eased out over the floor, rolled out one of the mats, tacked down one corner, stretched it tightly to another and secured it with little nails bent down over the edges.

A while later all four of them were in place and I had the makings of a rudimentary ceiling. Although the mats did not fit well, when they were overlapped and tacked down I began to see that they just might do the job after all. As they covered all of the space immediately above the bed, I felt that I had made truly significant gains in my little abode.

A typical Congolese woman, hauling wood home after a hard day of work in her field. This photo was taken in front of my house.

Early in the evening, I walked up to my favorite bar for a cold drink only to learn that the entire town of Makoua was sold out. No sodas, no beer, no nothing, and the truck was not scheduled to arrive from Brazzaville for another week. That was not what I wanted to hear, particularly when I had asked the owner to stock extra colas that I would buy from him exclusively. Somebody else must have been thirsty first.

Surely the moon must have been in the wrong position during the past few days, because my mood had been fluctuating all week long. One moment I was perfectly thrilled to have made progress with either my work or my residence, and the next I was aggravated or disappointed with just about everything else. Little things, like a kind word from anyone in my association meant a lot, while the frequently encountered spitting began to truly annoy me. Furthermore, canned meat products were collectively taking my appetite away, and I was not ready for mystery bush meat. Had I any mayonnaise to spice things up a bit, I would probably have poisoned myself because of the lack of refrigeration. The only pastries in town, little cookies that looked like vanilla wafers but weren't, were sold at four dollars for a two-pound sack and they had to be eaten quickly to keep them from ants. Some people, I supposed, would have accused me of being homesick.

When the rain came just before dark that day, I was leaning back on my porch feeling a little depressed, letting the wind blow spray into my face and drench my clothes simply because I felt like it. Street lamps cast amber spots on the road as great droplets of rain swirled through them and gave the scene a hollow and somehow spiritual sense of melancholy.

Just then a woman walked by with a basket strapped to her back. She was bent into the rain as she moved slowly, heavily, on bare feet under a load of firewood. The wicker straps cut into her shoulders as the rain streamed over her eyes and down her face and saturated her flimsy garments. Yet I knew that she was not crying, nor even complaining. She was simply living life as she was taught to live it, subsisting and serving as those before her had always done, but never expecting to improve her lot. One day she would work, followed by another and another and another. And then she would sleep. Such was the way of the land. As for me, maybe I had it pretty darned good after all.

The next morning, when the heat chased me out of bed at daybreak, I felt somewhat better about things and was ready once again to try to get something going. Then came my morning beggar. Marin had once warned me that some people would ask for water just to soften me up for something else, and he was right. While the young woman drank water on my porch, her eyes were peering past me into the house, exploring, assaying. "Donnez moi cinq mille," she demanded suddenly. When I refused to give her the five thousand Central African Francs, she threw the rest of her water into the grass, thrust the cup at me, and left without another word.

Marin came during lunch, looked through the barely open door, saw me cooking and walked in to take a chair at my table. He reminded me that I had asked him to try to find some beeswax.

"I found some, and I will bring it later today."

"Fine," I told him. "This afternoon then".

When honey was harvested in Makoua, which was seldom, nature paid a heavy price. First, in order to gain easy access, the tree was chopped down. Next, the bees were smoked heavily to suffocate as many as possible and then the trunk was then split open. The honey and comb were scooped into a tub, dead bees and all, and the catch was hauled away leaving the waste on the ground. The wax was ultimately squeezed by hand to extract the honey, which was then diluted with water to make it stretch, and, incredibly, the wax was thrown away. Paraffin candles were twenty cents each in the stores of Makoua, practically everyone used them, and yet they threw away beeswax!

Later that afternoon Marin returned with a plastic sack holding about four pounds of dirty, worm infested wax that smelled like rotted meat. Although there was little hope of extracting any significant amount of clean wax from it, I wanted to try anyway just to demonstrate the process. We made a fire in the front yard and put on a pot of water, the idea being to boil the water, melt the wax, kill whatever lived in it, then separate the components which would rise to the top.

After raising the water temperature to boiling and holding it there for a minute or two, we dumped the contents of the sack into the pot. Next, as the trash and impurities rose to the surface, we dipped them out and then poured in cold water to solidify the wax. That worked, of course, but because the comb was so dirty, we had to repeat the procedure several times before we could extract a few ounces of clean, good smelling, tan colored wax. The simplest way to rend pure wax, even in Makoua, would have been using a solar extractor that could easily have been made with a pane of glass and a wooden box. But our awkward system made the point for Marin and demonstrated what anyone might do if one went to the trouble.

The final step in the process was to melt the clean cake of wax one final time in an empty can. Using a crude wick that was made by twisting cotton from my first-aid kit, we started dipping and cooling, dipping and cooling. The wax built up on the string as it was dipped, until soon we had a candle in the making. When we were done, new technology had been introduced to Makoua and Marin seemed to be thoroughly impressed. I told him to spread the word.

"Don't throw away wax from now on. Teach others what to do with it. Do it yourself, and sell the candles!"

"Yes," he cried. "Yes!"

When the rain came that afternoon, as I was trying to relax with a book, I was promptly forced inside as a sudden wind slammed against my roof with mighty force. Minutes later I heard something moving on the porch. There, squatting in a corner while trying to free herself from the basket of wood on her back, a frail elderly woman was wet to the bone, dripping, and shivering. She looked up at me with timidity and uncertainty in her eyes, no doubt wondering if I would make her go away.

I fetched a dry towel for her, which she literally snatched from my hands, saying no words, expressing no gratitude. When she had dried herself the best she could, she wrapped the heavy towel around her shoulders and tugged at the corners. Yet she remained squatting there without looking at me and without speaking. When I took a chair to her, she grabbed it with nervous hands and then sat down on it.

When the storm abated a little, the woman handed me the wet towel, climbed back into her basket-straps and started across my yard, bending under the load in the still falling rain. Drawn to the sight of her, I stayed on the porch to watch as she struggled through the mud until she was out of sight. In some places, where physical strength ruled over intelligence, it truly was a man's world. I was beginning to feel less and less welcome amid Congolese culture and saw only conflict and dismay wherever I turned.

After my usual trip to the market the next morning, and after my usual breakfast of rice, canned meat, soy sauce, pili pili, and coffee, I spent most of the morning working with clay, filling up more holes in my walls, and drawing ever closer to having a dwelling without unwanted animals living inside of it. Using scraps of plywood bought from Andre, I had been working to seal the cracks in my door and in the shutters, so that mosquitoes would have to try harder to reach me. Because most of the places through which daylight used to shine had been plugged by then, one of my top ten remaining projects was to barricade those vents near the peak of the roof to block out the bats (whose number, by then, seemed to have multiplied).

I also had developed a problem with my water filter, for the flow had slowed to a drip even when the valve was fully open. The container was a tall, two-tiered, pear shaped thing, made of heavy blue plastic. The bottom portion held three liters of strained water, while the top held another three liters waiting to drip through the ceramic filter.

Taking it apart in the front yard, I reached inside, grasped the tubular filter, unscrewed the wing nut that held it in place and removed it. One look at it solved the mystery of the obstruction. Like the bottom of the Likouala-Mossaka River, the filter was covered with a layer of slimy brown muck. No wonder they wanted us to filter the stuff. And I was probably the only person in town who did.

Herve stopped by that morning to say that the rest of my furniture was finally ready. He had talked to the woodworker the night before when they were both having a beer, and was told that we could pick it up at anytime. Furthermore he had made some arrangements for a government truck to drive me there and to haul everything back. There was a hitch though. The truck was nearly out of fuel, the agency to which it was assigned had no money to buy any, and it could not be run as it was. If I would buy three gallons of gas, costing twelve dollars, the vehicle would be at my service. I agreed with a handshake and a promise to be ready and waiting when the truck came the next morning.

Back in my kitchen once again, wishing I had a few bananas to go with my oatmeal, I saw someone approaching my door. He was a middle aged man I first encountered one day in the market, and he was dressed exactly the same as when I first saw him...tattered pants, no shoes, a torn shirt, and carrying a worn-down machete in one hand. Stepping to my door with a pair of mange-infested dogs at his side, he was humble to the point of bowing. He laughed as if it was a great pleasure to see me again, some great person from another world, then he took my hand with both of his and bowed again. I had seen him a dozen times and his reaction had always been exactly the same. And yet, he had never asked me for a handout or even implied that he needed one. When we were done exchanging greetings, which must have been all he sought, he started away again. I called after him in French to say that I wanted bananas. He did not seem to understand so I tried the Lengala word.

"Lekemba!"

"Oh," his expression seemed to say, then he nodded and walked away with his dogs at his heels. A half hour later when I had finished my second cup of coffee and put on the water for oatmeal, the man showed up with a beautiful bunch of fresh ripe bananas and it was my turn to be humbled. I quickly dug in my pocket for money, paid him much more than the fruit would have cost me at the market and then he was on his way again, laughing happily, dogs trotting at his side. During my tenure in Makoua I had suffered many disappointments and angry hours, and several times I had pondered quitting. But moments like those with that old fellow gave me new strength and a renewed sense of commitment. Regardless of politics, hidden agendas, crooked policemen, thieves and beggars, it was possible to achieve a few positive and beneficial steps in small, personal ways whether fish farming had much to do with it or not. Mine was a grand feeling.

The man was hardly out of sight when another visitor came to the door. She was the woman who had crouched on my porch to escape the rain, and she had a beautiful ripe orange in her hand. As she presented it to me, she did not have to say what it meant. When we had shaken hands, each understanding the other, she went in the direction of the river and disappeared around beyond the curve.

And I once again felt a deep sense of caring for the poorest of the people who lived and worked in Makoua.

Feeling quite good about things by the time Marin showed up again, I asked him if he would like a beer. Of course he would. He would love one. Thus, for the next forty-five minutes we walked from bar to bar all over town, and everywhere the story was the same. Sorry, we are out of everything. Makoua was bone dry. Finally we gave up, and parted company.

What followed, was a different kind of night. At first, sweat drenched my sheets and soaked the foam mattress. And then the equatorial equivalent of a hurricane tore at my tin roof, slammed into the shutters, and chilled the air so that it was difficult to keep warm. The atmosphere was charged somehow, causing the hair on my arms to stand up, making my skin itch as if invisible insects were crawling all over it. Just at daybreak and shortly after the rain stopped, a river was running where the highway used to be and the police compound stood in the middle of a lake. Already, women were filing by, tiptoeing along the shoulders with baskets on their backs or balanced on their heads. Rubber thongs slipped in the mud as they went, threatening to throw them off balance and send them sprawling. One woman was pushing a bicycle through the muck, headed in the direction of the grand marche with a load of goods strapped to the seat, but she managed to stay on her feet as if the bicycle itself assisted her movements. A young girl, struggling with an empty wheelbarrow bigger than the child, was rushing to somewhere, probably to a field to help her mother gather manioc.

Herve came early that morning, riding in the front seat of a pickup truck, ready to take me to collect my furniture. Excited and eager, I climbed onto the bed where two other men were hanging onto crash bars, and prepared for a bumpy ride. We first went to Hydro Congo where a woman pumped three gallons of gasoline for us and then we headed toward the home of the furniture maker.

As soon as we pulled up beside the clay bank, I saw the man staring at us with an expression that once again seemed confused or perhaps even a little intimated. "Why are you here?" he asked Herve.

"For the furniture," Herve replied.

"It is not ready," the man spoke with agitation in his voice. "Some of it has not been started yet."

"But he bought fuel for the truck," Herve gestured toward me as he talked.

"It is not ready," came the final defiance as I strode out of the yard in anger and disgust. I was absolutely astounded that such misinformation could be spread time after time after time, as if people had nothing to do but chase their tails.

Probably Herve had been lied to as a casual reminder of the African truism, "They tell you what they think you want to hear." But that did it for me. I did not blame my homologue, for he had only tried to help, but even he seemed powerless to overcome a system that was geared to inefficiency and failure.

"Go ahead without me, Herve. I want to walk back," I said as pleasantly as I could muster when everybody was back at the truck.

"But it is two miles."

"I know, but I want to walk. Thanks anyway."

During my return hike, some serious thinking was done about what I was actually accomplishing in Makoua and whether or not the mindless difficulties would ever end. I did not wish to quit because the challenge appealed to me, but some changes were going to be have to be made and some people would likely be offended in the process. I wanted all of the locals involved to ponder the problems I had been forced to deal with so far and to worry that I might abandon the game altogether. My departure would be a disappointment and embarrassment to a few, including Calixte, and to anyone else upon whom negative attention might be drawn. Herve had the most to lose, for the promised motorcycle would have advanced his status in quantum terms and provided him with transportation the likes of which he had never before possessed. Since there were no new volunteers standing by to replace those of us already posted in the Congo, and since training new people took months to accomplish, any early termination always left a gap in the system that could go unfilled for a long time or even permanently.

Pressuring people did not seem to be done among the Congolese, just as accountability did not seem to exist. Which explained why excellence was neither demanded nor expected. The people were difficult to disappoint because they expected nothing. They shrugged off incompetence and failure in ways which only the most seasoned bureaucrat back home could appreciate, after which they shook hands and departed as friends. They knew that "it" might eventually happen, "it" would surely be good if it did, but in the meantime nothing could be done to force "it".

I almost felt a tinge of pity for Herve, as he was trapped in a culture over which he had little control. Yet, while he had not caused my problems in Makoua, he had contributed to them by failing to take a strong and productive stand. He had a role in the success of the fish-project, part of which was making things come together for both of us. Like it or not, Herve the Congolese, Herve the aqua-culturist, Herve the homologue, was going to have to become Herve the helpful, or he and I would have tough times ahead.

When back at home again with my mind clear, I packed up a plastic tub with dirty laundry and headed to the river. One of the women there took it upon herself to help me clean a pair of my jeans by soaping them up and pounding them on a rock while I observed her technique and applied it to the rest of my things. Just as I finished, I looked up to see Marin standing on top of the hill watching me like a bird of prey watches lunch. He was beginning to annoy me, always shadowing me, always aware of my business. If I ever chose to do anything secretive, Makoua would have been the last place on Earth to do it. When I reached the hilltop with my tub of wet clothes, he fell in right beside me.

As my thongs flopped in the sand and my feet collected a fresh new layer of dirt, Marin told me that two more trucks had crashed on the road to Etoumbi. No deaths had been reported, but that didn't mean there weren't any. He also said those crashes were deliberate acts of the dark spirits. I acknowledged his words but showed no interest in hearing any more. Indeed, because I failed to encourage conversation between us, he left just before dark and I closed myself in.

Muggier than usual and without even a hint of rain, the heat was suffocating as I lay back and peered into the darkness. Memories dancing in my thoughts, I could see people and places of my past, and I longed for some of them. And once again I wondered whether my presence in such a strange place justified the frustration. Surely there would be good days ahead, just as there would be many disappointments. However, unlike my homologue, I lacked the capacity to go through life without expectations.

I knew that I must soon find people of similar thought if were to make it much longer in Makoua, Congo.

11

Making Slow Progress

Nearly two months after the night of my arrival, a truck pulled to a stop in front of my house with a load of redwood furniture that had been banging about on the back like pinballs in an arcade machine. The vehicle was the same one for which I had purchased fuel earlier, it was driven by the same driver, it carried the same two men in the back, and Herve was in the front seat, supervising. The men unloaded my things immediately, but it was done angrily, wordlessly. They took everything inside the house and jerked it into place where I directed and then all but Herve left without so much as a grunt.

"Now you have one chest for clothes and one for food, you have a bed, a table to eat on, four chairs, and a bookcase," Herve said sternly. He was cocky then, arrogant, using jerky body language that demanded the physical question "Satisfied now? Is that the end of it?"

"Well it is finally done, Herve. Thank you for bringing my things."

Heading out the door, he stopped suddenly and turned back to me. "Tomorrow WE will go to pay the man the rest of his money. You must not go alone, for he is angry and there will be trouble unless WE go together." He spun on his heels without a handshake and hurried away.

Thirty minutes later, the cardboard boxes out of which I had been living, were empty. Their contents had been relocated into permanent new places, and I was done. For the first time since leaving Brazzaville, my possessions were relatively safe from falling manure and nesting rats, and I had easy access to it all. I even found things in those boxes that I had forgotten about, including four glass mugs and one large plastic bowl. I was absolutely thrilled, even though Herve and company were angry at me.

My beggars for the morning were two young teenaged girls. Seeming more timid than my usual visitors, as if they were uncomfortable with what they were doing, their manner disarmed me a bit. They told me it was commonly known that the American did not help people, but they were hungry and hoped I would feed them. I didn't quite know what to make of them. They were shabbily dressed and physically dirty which suggested they had been working in the fields. But girls like those usually had parents or husbands, or at least friends who would not let them go hungry. Even orphans in the rural Congo would be fed by someone.

I could not give them money, for their next expectation would be to move in. I did not want to cook for them either, so I did the next best thing. I offered them each a peanut butter and jelly sandwich, which was what I had already planned for my own meal. Admitting that they had never had such a treat, they watched the making of the first sandwich with expressions stuck somewhere between amusement and amazement. They discussed the situation in rapid Lengala and then turned back to me for another try. They had in mind something like ham (which was actually processed pork, imported from China and sold in cans like Spam). They would also like some fresh manioc and maybe a cold beer. I pointed out their lack of realism. If a peanut butter sandwich was good enough for me, it was surely good enough for two starving girls. They walked out in a huff.

I was quickly learning that there was no significant poverty among those strong, sturdy people. Perceptions all depended on definition. If a person had the ability to build a better house and yet chose to live in a lesser one, then that person had no housing problem. If people ate manioc and fish or bush-meat seven days a week because they liked it, then they had no problem with dietary variety. If they had good vision, perfect teeth and strong bodies, then their food was surely nutritious. If they drank bad water because they had no well, then they chose fetching it day after day over the one-time labor of digging for it. If they piled garbage in their streets and then ate the animals that fed in it, knowing the hazards that had been explained to them for decades, then they chose to violate reason. If they wanted nice things but turned down opportunities to earn money, they were accepting the things they already had. Summarized, if they wanted life to be better but chose not to do the things that would bring about positive change, then what they had was not poverty. What they had, was an attitude problem.

I could not altogether blame them for lacking the will to change their culture. No matter what an outsider might see as serious shortcomings, their ways had worked for them for hundreds of years and they had clung to them because it suited them to do so. The forest had nurtured them with land, and an abundance of foods and plenty of materials for housing. Their fields had provided all the variety that they cared to grow, and supernatural spirits had protected them and given them mystical powers with which to govern themselves and others. Proving that point, Africans had produced huge populations of beautiful people all over the continent who had survived natural and human-induced holocausts since the beginning of time. And they had thrived.

Millions of Caucasians in the United States spent grueling hours lifting weights, working out on machines, jogging for miles and adhering to special diets, all trying to achieve the strength, the fine musculature, the powerful bodies that those people had naturally, genetically, without having to work a lick. Male strength was not only a convenience in their culture. It was necessary, socially speaking, because a Congolese man was a purely masculine creature who was expected to accommodate his wives and father children. Conversely, if a woman grew fat, which usually happened at an early age, that was a sign of prosperity which elevated her status among her peers. When she lost her physical attractiveness due to child bearing and hard work, that was fair exchange for the recognition she simultaneously gained in her community. Because her personal status was directly related to fertility, physical appearance was useful in finding a husband but had little to do with keeping one.

Certainly most Congolese did not own material possessions that would bring joy to the average Westerner. The men wore jeans and shirts, usually cheap imitations of Western brands, but even the best dressed would usually wear rubber sandals. Women wore lengths of fabric, wrapped and tucked at the middle, and little girls wore real dresses when they visited their churches or socialized at the street markets. But all clothing was worn until it was threadbare, for a single outfit might have been all they had. The entire culture was driven, not by the desire for progress, but by the pressures of day to day survival. Subsistence.

As for me, I was ready for the next challenge and the next step up the ladder. I stuffed my pockets with cash, locked up and started out in the direction of the furniture builder. I would not wait for Herve to accompany me, nor even advise him of my plan to go alone. He needed to understand that I welcomed his help when it was the right thing for him to do, but I did not want him to think that he could use "protection" as a means to hold power over me. The woodworker was surely upset that I had never eased back on my demands, but I had been in the right and everybody involved had to have known it. Furthermore I still had his money, which he surely wanted in his own pockets even more than he wanted a confrontation. Thus, I would visit him one last time, pay him in full, and be done with the matter.

I decided to take the long route that morning, walking near the Catholic church because it was the drier road to travel. As I went past the grounds where the little priest, Eugenio, was strolling among the flowers, he saw me and called out a cheerful greeting. Meeting me at the edge of the street, he wanted to know what I was doing with myself so early in the morning. He listened with great interest as I explained what was going on then told me to wait right there. He hurried back across the yard, short legs moving quickly over the grass. Moments later he drove up in a truck.

"Hop in," he said with a grin.

Some days I had to believe that angels were in my camp after all, when they grew tired of playing little tricks on me. I climbed in, and Eugenio steered us rapidly in the direction of the furniture builder. We made the trip in less than two minutes.

Just as I thought, the man was happy to see me walking into his yard with 109,000 CFA in my hand. The pressure levied on him had caused him to work at a faster pace than he would otherwise have moved, but that same pressure had just increased his net worth by a bundle, and money talks in every language under the sun. We exchanged knowing looks and little half-smiles, but he made out my receipt, walked me back to the truck, and even shook my hand before we left. What had just happened between us broke new ground, which I suspected would serve both of us well if we ever happened to do business again. Herve, on the other hand, would probably be disappointed to hear of so much good will.

Eugenio the speedster delivered me back to my neighborhood in five minutes. There, at my request, we stopped in front of Herve's house to pass along the news to my counterpart. He would not need to accompany me after all. Thanks just the same. I thought I saw steam coming out of his ears.

Hours later, in the middle of the afternoon, Herve actually came to my door with another man who claimed to be interested in fish culture. He was one of those farmers who had attended our formal meeting a while back, and he insisted that he was ready to start a fish pond. He only wanted me to take a look at his site and make judgments as to its workability. Standing in my yard with him and my homologue, carrying on our business as if everything was simply grand, Herve appeared to have swept our mutual friction aside in name of getting some work done. I respected that. We made an appointment to meet the farmer at his home the next morning and from there to walk to his parcel. When the two men left me, slowly ambling toward Herve's office, it seemed as if another barrier had been broken. Surely good things lay in wait just around the corner, even though Herve might yet be unable to see them.

While some men and women in the community rode bicycles, and a few even owned scooters, it was a curiosity to me that Herve had neither. I had also heard that some of the very well-to-do even had television sets, for use during those evening hours when the current was on, but Herve lacked even a battery powered radio. His future as the local director of fish-culture, however, stood to catapult him far ahead of his current status if only he had the vision to pursue it and the stamina to stay with it. He had been college educated in Ukraine, learning to be rather like a county extension agent. Having been back in the Congo for several years, he had been employed by his government even though he had often gone without pay. He had no children that I had ever seen, and his wife was so private that she was almost invisible. He never offered to talk about his personal life and I certainly did not feel free to ask, but I supposed that he was doing the best that he knew how to do. Nevertheless, educational history considered, it seemed odd that he was so very much imbedded in the local culture and that he had not been able to rise above it. But his personal problems were his to overcome, for the opportunity was there for him to grasp.

The next morning, when it was time for our appointment, I started out early and stopped for Herve on the way. Ready and waiting, he saw me coming and immediately bounded into the street. Although we walked together for a common goal, he still had little to say as he moved with long, easy strides and I hustled along beside him. We were two men headed in the same direction on the same path for the same reasons, but each with his own thoughts. We reached Michel's house about fifteen minutes later and found our farmer eagerly waiting for us in his front yard. We hardly lost the rhythm of our steps, for Michel fell in beside us, led us past Marin's house to the highway and then took us in the direction of the airport.

Our walk was to be about five miles, round trip, but we walked along in no special hurry as Herve and Michel prattled endlessly. I understood enough of what was said to learn that Michel was from Makoua but he had been away for several months. He had recently quit a job in Ouesso where he had been employed as an assistant to some cartographers who were working on a project for the Congolese government. I would have liked to know why he quit, or why he was not pursuing more of the same kind of work; but Herve did not pry and I thought it best not to do so either. I was also curious as to why Michel wanted to make such a radical departure from his former occupation and to dig a fish pond, but that too could wait. When we reached a distant hilltop, we took a trail to the right that led us past an abandoned house that was nearly hidden in the brush. Members of Michel's family had lived and died here, he informed us, but the house had only spirits "living" inside at that time. Like a grave, it was undisturbed and would remain so until the forest reclaimed it.

Continuing through high grasses behind the house, we walked along the edge of a cliff about sixty feet above the valley floor, the sight of which came and went as the brush thinned and thickened. When we turned deeply into the forest and started our descent over a trail of hard clay, it was tricky going and we took care not to trip over any roots. Once at the bottom, Michel led us through thick vines and bushes to where we reached a spring gurgling from the side of the hill. The flow of the water had carved a natural bowl in the clay over the years, in which the deep, clear liquid seemed to stand still. But it was not still. It bubbled and poured over a lip of rocks before it wriggled through the forest and out of sight.

There at the floor of the valley, tall trees, vines and overgrowth solidly blocked the sunlight so that the place smelled musty and damp like the swamp that it was. Hearing no animals around us, I noticed that our own voices seemed somehow muted in the thick woods. My first impression was that such a site would never work for a fish pond because of the amount of labor that would be necessary to clear it and bring in the sunlight. Trees would have to be cut down and stumps removed. Vines and brush would have to be cleared completely away, and the deep layer of humus with all its little roots and rotting organic matter would have to be dug out and cast aside. Water would have to be channeled to the high side of the site for filling and then it would have to circle back around until it reconnected with the spring. Such a project would be a huge, laborious undertaking.

Advising Michel of my preliminary assessment, I watched his eyes as he pondered the words. Finally he said that he had no fear of labor and wanted to culture fish if the site was otherwise workable. Thus pleased to be in the company of a man with such an attitude, I went about exploring some more, probing the soil, forming balls of damp clay to test adhesiveness, and making educated guesses. Site selection was not a complicated process, but his place, as it stood, was too overgrown for sighting slopes, elevations or even distances. Because those had to be determined before final approval would be possible, such a chore would be extremely demanding and it might all be for naught. After spending about a half-hour there, I offered my final observations.

"If you clear enough of the brush for me to make unobstructed sightings and measurements, then Herve and I will come again when you are ready for us to take another look. We will be able to say definitely then, one way or the other".

"All right," responded Michel. "I will do that. The ground will be ready in a few days. I will go to your house to let you know."

Herve, never having been exposed to precisely what qualified or disqualified a site, was just as much in the dark as Michel. I told both of them that I would go home to write up a site-assessment in French. The paper would restate what we had done that day and clarify everything that must be done in the future. Both men seemed satisfied with that, and we started back up the hill for the walk back to Makoua.

Michel's residence was about three blocks off the main road just at the edge of town and only a few blocks from Marin's. The house was a small one, made of mud and thatch, and set back under a large mango tree in a typical yard of brown clay, but it was surrounded with beautiful flowers and shrubs. Because I rarely found yards so tastefully decorated, I commented about it to Michel and complimented him on his efforts. Pleased with the notice, he whacked some branches off a tree, one with yellow flowers and another with pink, and told me to simply stick them in the soil at my house and they would grow. We shook hands one more time before Herve and I started toward home as fast as our feet could carry us, bearing a pervasive sense of friction that stood between us like a wall of mud. The man's behavior was just plain weird to me. He seemed to be missing the point that I could get my job done without him, but he could not survive and grow in his position without me. Maybe, at that point in our relationship, neither of us cared much one way or the other.

That evening I found three grass mats for sale in the local market. They had been made in the village of Mohali, forty kilometers to the north, and transported to Makoua by bicycle. And fortunately, the price was the same that I had paid in Owando. I bought all three. Lacking any new obstacles that might pop up, I would soon add them to the matrix over my bed to slowly construct a completed ceiling. My house was still crude, but day by day it was beginning to resemble a home.

Using a strip of leather cut from an antelope skin the boys brought me, I went about nailing a strip of it over the long space at the bottom of my door. The door had been hung too high, which allowed crawling beasts free access into my house. Also, because the stiff hide dragged with a mighty noise as it scraped over the bricks, it would warn me if anyone tried to enter without an invitation.

Privacy and respect for another person's property were not parts of Congolese culture. To the contrary, every village was communal by its very nature and design, so that all space outside of the houses was shared by the entire community. Indeed, it was perfectly acceptable if a person's yard became a permanent shortcut for anyone and everyone. I objected to it at my house because I had gone to the trouble to plant a lot of flowers, some from local cuttings and some from seeds sent from the U.S. Even though I pleaded with people to watch where they stepped as they went into the woods behind my dwelling, the plea never seemed to sink in. Perhaps that was because the villagers didn't notice my plants, or maybe they did not see the point of growing them and therefore cared nothing for them.

Children, particularly the boys, were the worst trespassers of all. Evidently permitted to run wild from the time they were weaned, the small ones were curious and obnoxious while the older ones were often just plain rude. I had chased many of them off my porch when they probably thought I could not hear them from the back yard, and I once caught a little mob at my back window, when they were attempting to climb inside. I also once broke up a trap that some boys were making on the edge of the road. The hazard was a deep hole covered with a sheet of paper and powdered with a thin layer of sand, designed to catch a bicycle tire and to throw the rider. The boys bolted just out of my reach when confronted, but they stayed fearlessly near, taunting and laughing. Congolese children commonly addressed adults as if they themselves were adults, sometimes even butting into adult conversations, and they liked to taunt white people with the "mondele" word. And because so many of the villagers, children or adults, were quick to plunder and willing to steal, I learned to lock the house even to go across the street for water.

Some interesting stories about rude behavior, snooping, plundering and stealing, were passed along from other volunteers and staff members. The American then stationed in the equatorial village of Kelle, routinely chased rude children. He would catch them if he could and haul them before their parents. That did little to stop the rude behavior, but at least it got some of them in trouble for a short time and established the notion that some taunted people would fight back. Another episode, told to me by the man who was guilty of it, spoke of a particularly obnoxious boy who refused to go away even after being repeatedly asked to do so. The American pleaded with the boy again and again, even threatened him, and finally, in a moment of frustration, caught him, tied him to a tree and left him there.

Older boys, having nothing else to do, often sat around in shady places playing card games for hours at a time. They would slap their cards viciously onto the table while arguing loudly, giving a greatly exaggerated sense of value to the outcome of any given hand. And yet those same boys would turn down offers of work, even if they and their families needed the money. Conditions would always be too hot, or the hour too late, the job too difficult, or maybe it was simply the wrong day. Little girls, on the other hand, slaves for their elders, simply worked. Doing as their mothers did, carrying little baskets on their backs or balancing small loads on their heads, they worked. Carrying babies when their mothers could not carry them all, they worked. Even when school was in session, little girls worked before and after classes while their brothers played or drifted about the villages. That was simply the way things were.

I found it remarkable that gentleness, tenderness and sweetness were not openly displayed, if they ever took place at all. Punishment, however, was practiced for all to witness, and the punishment was often administered by an adult who was not related to the child. I once saw some boys chased out of a creek because a man drove up in his truck and wanted the place for himself. He told them he would "hit" them if they did not leave, so the boys went a short distance away and remained there until the man finally left.

When a boy made a serious mistake or deliberately did something that was unacceptable to his elders, a hard blow across the jaws might greet him. Simple intimidation and fear, on the other hand, seemed to be adequate to control the younger girls. Once when I was walking by a local house, several children ran to greet me. A woman rushed out to intervene. One little girl was warned to stay out of my reach because "The white man will put you in a pot, cook you and eat you". It actually made a lot of sense to protect young girls from too much independence, considering their value as workhorses and as potential sources of revenue at the time of marriage. But it hardly seemed fair.

Men laughed, joked and argued while women worked and chattered, and all of the children, even little girls, played when the time was right. If laughter was a suitable indicator, all of them seemed to be happy during those times. By and large the Congolese were passionate people who hated and fought, dreaded and feared, sympathized and mourned, and they probably had fewer and certainly less complicated problems than they would someday have when they joined the rest of the "civilized" world. One thing was certain. Theirs was the culture of the Congolese, it had always been so, and they liked it just the way it was.

Once back at home and planting the branches that Michel gave me, I caught a glimpse of something long and green crawling onto my porch. Following it to my door for a closer look while a nervous crowd was already gathering on the street, I spotted the serpent as it was making its way to the shelf where I kept my kerosene stoves and dishes. A man came close enough to toss me a long stick before he retreated to his safe distance, from where he offered advice on handling the beast even though he had no intention of helping me with it.

During the several exciting minutes that followed, as the snake and I engaged in a territorial dispute, I poked and prodded like a swordsman but gave it plenty of room to escape if it so chose. Having no idea whether it might have been poisonous, or for that matter whether it might have been a young representative of the deadly Green Mamba species, I finally seized a moment when it was fully exposed on top of the cabinet and knocked it senseless. When it fell to the floor, I beat it to death and then hauled it outside hanging from the stick. Even dead, the beast was not without power, for the people backed even farther into the street. Maybe they knew something I didn't know.

Another two days passed and I found myself struck with a fresh pang of loneliness. As if alone in a big city, I was surrounded by people but somehow outside the perimeter of the circle. Never a part of it when I was inside it, and usually outside except when something was wanted from me, my entire world was one of aloneness. Mine was also a world of fish cut into chunks, grilled until black, sold in dim candle light and wrapped in newspaper. Mine was a world of saka saka, chopped manioc leaves that were boiled and sold by the spoonful and presented in banana leaves. Mine was a world of baked peanuts sold by little girls with dirty hands who measured their wares in tiny glasses and then dumped them into cones of paper. Or of peanuts boiled in their shells and sold by the handful. Or of peanuts ground into peanut butter and sold by the scoop.

Before moving to my post, I bought a large can of peanut butter in Brazzaville for nearly $8.00. But I refilled that same can in Makoua for half as much at the grand marche. The reason for the difference was commercial preparation and importing. Locally grown and locally produced goods were always cheap, relatively speaking, but they were sold without labels, without nice packaging, and their quantities were never exact. Quality was generally good in the open markets, after a person got used to the dust and flies and unwashed fingers and wraps of inked paper. One actually grew numb to it, seeing but no longer caring, forgetting to be concerned.

While walking to the market one morning, hoping to refill my peanut butter can once again, I heard someone call out to me. Our local post office was situated directly across the street from the grand marche, which meant that I passed it every day once or twice. Most of the time the postal workers were sitting on the cement wall of the breezeway or leaning over it while watching the rest of the world go by, and doing no actual "work" at all. Any mail that was intended for me generally went into a box maintained at the Agriculture office, but it was not uncommon for it to be given to someone else for delivery to my door. That day, as I walked in front of the building, one of the postmen was holding a letter in his hand and waving it in my direction. It just arrived, he told me, only two days before.

Tearing the envelope open, I found that it contained a generic letter, copied to all volunteers from our Director in Brazzaville, and it had taken exactly thirty-one days to reach me. Inside was a typewritten note, reminding us to communicate with our leaders about matters of importance. Bob did not want to hear any "self centered whining and bitching," but he did want to maintain open communication. I folded it and put it deep in my pocket, for that one was going into my permanent collection. That was because it perfectly underscored the bureaucratic meaning of "keeping in touch," while the deeper message was "If it isn't an emergency, don't bother".

The market was especially busy that day. Shoulders bumped shoulders, feet stepped on toes while movement never stopped in the ever-floating dust. People elbowed past those who stopped to talk in the flow of traffic. Some pushed others with their hands. Wheelbarrows and carts hurried through the crowd, sometimes deliberately bumping people to motivate them out of the way. Women called out "mondele, mondele" from displays of hot peppers, fruits and loaves of day-old of bread. Fish and meats were being butchered underneath the shed, where bits of flesh and blood splattered into the air and flies thickly swarmed in search of a place to lay their eggs. I bought my peanut butter, two loaves of bread and a box of cubed sugar, then moved back into the open street where the air was not quite so strong. My mood was not a good one for close mixing with crowds, and besides, I had Michel on my mind.

Michel had sent word that he would be over later that day to get the promised site analysis. My hand written review, ready and waiting for him, explained how the site must be cleared before judgment could be made as to its workability, and it also reiterated the long and difficult labor ahead if a pond were built to Peace Corps specifications. The official rationale was to not waste time with a man who seemed unlikely to complete what was begun. Otherwise, when a person was finally overpowered by the job, he might blame the volunteer for the failure. That in turn might damage our credibility in the community, and the effectiveness of the project could suffer because of it.

Hours later Michel showed up at my door. We sat at my table while he examined my little treatise, but he had little to say as he read it. The analysis pointed out that I needed an unobstructed line of sight of about 100 feet from the water source. If the lay of the land was found to be satisfactory, so that the natural flow of the spring would be adequate to fill his pond and so that enough slope existed to drain it, then the rest of the issue was primarily that of hard work. If he still wanted to face all that, then he would have my support to the very end and he would be the first officially approved fish farmer in Makoua. Michel was pleased. He said he would have the site cleared for the formal inspection soon, and he would return to let me know. We shook hands and he left with a happy grin on his face. I had a very good feeling about Michel. Surely he was about to make local history, and Herve and I were about to justify our livelihood.

12

Chaos in the City

Approximately three months after my assignment to Makoua and just before Thanksgiving, all of the north-country volunteers gathered in Owando for a meeting with Tom, Eric and each of our homologues. Part of the point was to discuss accomplishments that any of us could brag about, and another part was the issuing of our long awaited motorcycles.

Second year volunteers already had bikes. Second year homologues were to finally be awarded machines, along with all first year Americans. First year homologues, however, such as Herve, were supposed to wait several more months before receiving the prizes of their lives. When the official part of our meeting ended after two days, we all helped to unload four shipping crates from the back of a ten-wheel truck that had traveled from Brazzaville. Three of the crates contained two motorcycles each, while one was a single unit that was lying on its side after bouncing loose during the trip. Eric was furious about that, but he said nothing to the driver.

The stenciled markings on the crates were:
Made in Japan
Model DT 125

Cameron was less than half my age, but we had become fast friends when we roomed together during language training in Burundi. We had not seen each other in months, but we both had a good laugh when we met again at Anne's house. Both of us had lost a lot of weight, I had grown a full beard and he was sporting a goatee that was intended to make him look older. The effort failed. He looked like a tall, skinny kid with a goatee. He complained about that, saying he was finding it difficult to get any respect.

He and I grabbed an assortment of tools and tore into one crate marked "Color CPR," inside of which were a pair of beautiful, shiny, fire-engine-red, brand new Yamaha dirt-machines begging to be assembled and ridden. We spent three hours mounting the wheels, connecting the cables, wiring the lights, charging the batteries, fueling the tanks, oiling the engines, and inflating the tires. When we fired up the motors, those sounds announced that the bikes were alive, they were real and we finally possessed them after all the waiting. Helmets were handed out, papers were signed, and we were off for a sanctioned test ride. Cameron and I headed to Hydro Congo to finish filling up our tanks, then we glided into the back country.

Flying down dirt trails with ruts barely wide enough for the tires, tearing through sand several feet deep or rolling through mud that was black and slimy, we sped on. We ran over grass and brush when we veered off the trails and then we raced over packed clay. We zipped down lanes shrouded with jungle canopy and then we cruised on dirt roads flanked by elephant grass that was taller than us and as thick as thatch. We wound through villages where people rushed out of mud huts to watch us tear by. We crossed deep trenches and rattled over bridges made of loose planks. We cruised to the top of a steep hill and stopped to view the forest canopy that ran endlessly through the haze and then we turned and headed back toward Owando in search of other roads and other sights to see. On the way, we encountered another volunteer whose ride had been delayed due to some mechanical problems. He joined us for an exploratory tour south of town, where we went in search of the local airport.

The lush scenery was beyond beautiful as we whispered through a mile of palm groves and then banana trees and thick, green brush. When we reached the crest of a hill where an asphalt airstrip stretched before us, the opportunity was too appealing to ignore. We lined up side by side, glanced at one another, started together, and cruised the length of the tarmac the way Marlon Brando would have done it. The beauty of the countryside around us, the feel of the motorcycles underneath us, the freedom to do as we pleased for a little while, all together made it an absolutely perfect day. Late that afternoon, we placed all of the motorcycles under lock and key in Anne's house and prepared to spend another night there. The next day, some of us were going to Brazzaville.

Because of the great distance and the time required to travel to the city, we were compelled to make the trip by truck. Tom drove up at 6:30 the next morning, with Eric close behind in the other vehicle. Some of us would ride all the way to Brazzaville for required vaccinations, while others would only go to a convenient dropping-off point from which other transportation could be caught to their posts. Once we were under way, Tom shared some news.

"Things aren't looking good in Brazzaville right now." He let that sink in before adding, "Five people were killed in rioting several nights ago, and the city has been tense ever since. Several main thoroughfares have been blocked and I don't know how everything stands right now."

Nationalism was hardly as strong as tribalism in the Congo, which meant the country was always divided. Although the recent free election of President Lissouba had been well received at the time, an underlying current of dissatisfaction had soon surfaced. When Lissouba announced that he would dissolve parliament, presumably to tighten his grip over the nation, that was just the stimulant that the factions needed to promote unrest. I had been getting some bits and pieces of such news in Makoua, albeit mostly from Marin or occasionally from Herve, so I already had an inkling about the current situation. However I never knew how much of it to believe and which to disregard, because my own little short wave radio had stopped working. Thus it was especially interesting to learn that even Tom was concerned about things.

"If we ever had to make a run for the border" I asked finally, "will it be okay to ride our motorcycles out?"

"Yes". Tom looked at me in his rear view mirror for a moment. "If we have to start running, motorcycle policy won't mean much anymore."

The "policy" he referred to, was, among other things, that motorcycles were not to be ridden out of our respective territories for any reason. Actually, they were not to be ridden *anywhere* except for work related business. Tom's firm answer, it seemed to me, clearly summarized the gravity of the situation in Brazzaville. I also suspected that the political problems effected the timing of placing the machines into our hands sooner than we had once been told to expect.

Arriving in the capital on the eve of Thanksgiving and driving quickly along busy streets, we saw absolutely nothing to indicate any trouble of recent days. Indeed, taxis and buses were running as always, markets were busy, pedestrians were everywhere, and Tom seemed to breathe a sigh of relief. When we reached the gates of our own headquarters and crash house, politics out of mind, we waited for the guards to let us in and then we parked and unloaded.

The most important items on my personal agenda for the rest of that day were to wash my clothes in the upstairs machines and to take a very hot shower. Several people went to local restaurants for dinner that day, and some went to the "super market" (called "Score") located in the heart of the city. A few others went just up the street to another American compound called the "Villa Washington". The Villa served as a retreat for people from the American embassy or from any of several foreign agencies (and their families), and it had armed guards to keep it safe and exclusive. There was also a swimming pool, a basketball court, a tiny "library," a small but fairly well equipped gym room, a kitchen that actually sold hamburgers and fries, a great open patio with tables and umbrellas, and a huge lounge with a big screen television set. Thus the Villa was the place of choice for most of us any time we were in town. That evening the kitchen was closed, the pool was empty and the whole place was silent.

The next morning felt exactly like any other day, except that our own offices were closed for the Thanksgiving "celebration". An American style holiday dinner was planned for those who wished to attend, following which, a party for volunteers and staff members was to be held at the residence of one of our staff members. None of our group seemed particularly excited about any of it, but I was the only one who did not plan to attend the private celebration. I simply was not in the mood.

By 10:00 A.M. most of our number had already gone to help prepare for the private party, which left me and the security guards alone at the compound. Knowing a food-run would have to be made sooner or later, and anticipating no better time than the present, I decide to take a stroll down the hill toward the nearest store. Something was up! Traffic on the boulevard was much heavier than normal, and crowds were gathered along the streets as if waiting for a parade.

Just as I approached the railroad tracks near the store, hearing a commotion behind me, I spun around to see a dozen cars and pickup trucks rushing in my direction. They all had banners taped to their doors, and all were all loaded with loud, wildly gesturing people who glared at me as they passed. Stepping quicker then, I hurried the rest of the way to the market, stayed just long enough to buy a few essentials and then started back up the hill. Another line of vehicles was coming fast, but that time from a side street. Because the first car turned sharply at the corner and nearly clipped me, I jumped to the opposite side of the ditch and waited while five others sped through the turn without slowing for the required stop. Even though I had no idea what they were up to, my instincts told me that something was amiss and I did not wish to be a part of it. As my boots crunched into the stones at the railroad tracks, my eyes and ears were very much in tune with the noises around me. The walk back up the hill was only about six blocks, and that, at least, appeared to be entirely calm.

The Peace Corps offices in Brazzaville. The upstairs was divided into bunk rooms, meeting and lounging rooms, and the nurse's office.

Having taken advantage of the air-conditioned crash house to nap in comfort and to watch a couple of taped movies without having to compete for them, I next went to the Villa Washington. Most of the people there were strangers to me, who did not seem particularly interested in mingling beyond their own little groups. I stayed long enough to enjoy a plate of good food and then returned to the large, quiet building that we volunteers called home in the city. When darkness came and Anne returned early from the party, she seemed unusually stressed. She said rumors of shootings and looting were flying. Earlier that morning while jogging on the street just behind the office, she had seen an army tank with several uniformed Congolese positioned on it. It was parked in front of President Lissouba's residence. Security had been tightened everywhere, she said, and entire sections of the city were behind blockades again. Whatever was fact and whatever it meant, Brazzaville, Congo had evidently become a very unstable place.

Things heated up even more during that night. The next morning our offices were open again for essential business, but the Director instructed us not to go beyond the Villa for any reason. "Actually," he commented, "I prefer that you don't go outside the compound at all. Shots have been fired in parts of the city, some near here. Also rocks and debris have been thrown at vehicles, and some looting and vandalism have taken place."

I had actually heard shots a few minutes before Bob shared his concerns, but those sounds had come from some distant place and meant nothing in particular to me. Honoring caution just the same, I would get my required injections when the nurse came in and then spend the day catching up on my reading. If the Congolese wished to shoot at each other, they would have to do it without me in the audience.

When it was mid-afternoon, rapid-fire weapons were chattering only a few blocks away. We knew that President Lissouba was under threat, but we did not know for sure who was doing the shooting, nor who was being shot at, nor even what the outlaw factions hoped to achieve. Nevertheless the situation was growing more and more serious as the hours passed, and the tension in our offices was already thick enough to carve. The Director was staying close to his telephone and radio, staying in touch with both the embassy and roving security personnel, but the only news we got was of scattered violence all over the city. No one seemed to know just what to do about it. While uneasiness was high in our midst, a few optimists were downplaying the whole episode. Such disturbances had happened before, they pointed out, and were no big deal. Certainly it was nothing like they had once seen in Zaire.

Hours later, when the city had been disconcertingly quiet for a while and all of the known danger zones were some distance away from us, four of us decided to break curfew and head toward the heart of town for a restaurant dinner. Our route, a shortcut that took us straight toward the heart of town, cut off much of the distance by leading us down a steep hill through neck-high weeds and piles of litter that were routinely deposited there by the Congolese. Having no lights, and so heavily obstructed, the hill seemed so dark and threatening that I personally wondered if we might have made a mistake. We all moved quietly on, but with quickened steps.

All of the downtown area was darker than usual that night, and uncommonly still. Even in front of the building that housed our restaurant, across from a large hotel and several bars, no cars were moving about the broad streets. Hawkers were not working the sidewalks with things to sell, and no people were there to buy them. We heard another round of shots rattling in the distance, perhaps miles away, but we said little about it and kept in motion.

Once inside the lobby of our destination, we took a very slow elevator to the eighth floor and stepped into a huge room where scores of cloth-covered tables stood vacant. A man in the back waved cheerfully to us, obviously happy to see a few customers, and directed us to sit where we pleased. Taking a table near an open window through which cool night air eased in, we had a good look over the sprawling night line of the city. Tall buildings, churches, embassies and thousands of homes were lit up far into the distance, but the lights seemed dimmer somehow like kerosene lanterns with the wicks turned low. Brazzaville was pretty, even beautiful at night, but that beauty, like an aging prostitute, was an illusion that could best be appreciated in the dark.

The owner came over to talk to us, as his situation had put him in the mood to converse with somebody, anybody. Lacking any prodding, he started into the problems that were plaguing the city and to business owners in particular. He said that the political issues of the moment were only excuses for bad people to be very bad, and they were hurting him and others like him because people were not coming out to spend money.

"This is so stupid," he said with resignation. "Such chaos can only benefit the politicians. Whoever winds up on top when it is over will gain much, while the rest of the population will lose, as always." The man was on a roll and he had our attention. "This is a disturbance created by those who like to make disturbances. But no long term solutions will come out of it. Maybe we will lose our President, maybe not. But either way, like bad weather, it will blow over when emotions cool down and then things will be still again for a while longer."

When we were done with our dinner and the place was about to close for the night, we four Americans went back down the elevator and said good night to each other on the street. Two were going somewhere else for a beer, and two of us would take the long way back in order to avoid that grass-covered hill. We would walk on paved streets, stay under the lights, and perhaps move faster than we did on the way down. When Darrell and I were back at the top of the hill, we parted company. He had planned to watch movies at the house where the Marine embassy-guards lived, only a few hundred yards away, and I was going back to the crash house.

My destination was only about ten blocks farther, but the street was so dimly lit that a great shadow was reaching out like an oblong beast sliding over the pavement. A short distance beyond the street that would take me past the Villa and on to our headquarters, I could see several men leaning against a car that had stopped in the middle of the intersection. They were laughing as I approached, speaking loudly and provocatively and gesturing in my direction. I kept moving without acknowledgment, even when someone called out amid an outburst of laughter, "Hey, white man!"

The guard at the compound let me through the steel gate without delay, although he seemed half-asleep and he was not holding his weapon. Only a few volunteers were inside the building at the time, but as the clock ticked others trickled in steadily, each with bits and pieces of news and rumor. An African doctor was said to have made the mistake of driving through one of the danger-zones earlier. He was stopped and beaten, and his car was trashed. Other incidents of the like were reported, all violent, as certain parts of the city had definitely fallen into a state of chaos. Additionally, the President's house was secured with a large contingent of soldiers armed with machine guns. They also had two tanks by then, several armored vehicles, and, strangely enough, two antiaircraft guns. Well, I mused privately, if the President needed antiaircraft guns, maybe it was time to take another look at just how safe we really were.

We had been in the city three days when the Director announced that he wanted all of us to return to our respective posts where he believed we would be safer. Thus the next morning, two of the women and I would try to catch a ride to Owando. We would rise long before daybreak and take a taxi to Talengai quarter, where we would try to hire transportation to the north. Uncertainties existed, of course. Some streets were still barricaded, debris from rioting was said to be scattered all over the city, and we could not be sure that the buses or trucks were even running. We were given our monthly stipends in cash and told to stand by. News was still developing fast, and, for the time being, we could only wait and see.

When morning came, our plans were changed, for more shooting had taken place during the night throughout the city. Also, conditions were still extremely tense in the Bacongo quarter, which was too close for comfort, and the President of the nation was still protected under very tight security. We were told to stay close and wait for a better day. Late that afternoon, someone moved the VCR in the conference room and a few settled there to watch *Home Alone*. Meanwhile four of us men were playing a game of hearts, which I was winning by a landslide.

All eyes turned when one of our security guards knocked at the door and came inside to announce that the Director was on the phone and wished to speak to any one of us. Without another word spoken among us, the movie was paused, cards went face down on the table, and all ears were alert as one of the women picked up the receiver. Avoiding the natural tendency to try to gauge what was being said based on her reactions to it, we all listened and waited. When she hung up the phone, she shared the news.

"Things are heating up again, and Bob wants all of us to get out of town. He wants us to be packed and ready before daylight. Somebody from here is going to drive us to our bus stops." Then she added rather incidentally, "At least we don't have to depend on taxis."

The movie was started again. The card game resumed. Fifteen minutes later the guard appeared at the door for the second time. The Director was on the phone with something more to say. The movie stopped. The cards went face down again. That time Matt took the call. He listened carefully and then acknowledged that he understood. He hung up.

"Well, nobody is leaving tomorrow after all." He headed back to our table. "People are coming down from the north and causing trouble on the highway," he said almost absently. Matt did not elaborate, but probably neither did Bob. That time we all talked freely and openly.

"If people are up to mischief in the rural areas, this could go on for days," Matt said softly. Matt was one of the people connected with the waterworks project, he actually lived in Brazzaville, and even he was probably stuck inside the compound until we received better news.

I then seriously suggested to the group, that those of us going to the north should be flown to Owando,. That would put us past the trouble spots and give each of us the means by which to continue to our respective posts. Since my motorcycle was in Anne's house, Larry could double with me the rest of the way to Makoua, and he could bunk with me until he could catch a truck to Kelle. Larry thought it was a great idea, but the others were not convinced. Democracy ruled, even there. The proposal died on the floor.

A sudden storm brought steady lightning that flashed across the world and thunder bombarded us and shook the windows. After a few minutes we were besieged by constant, pounding rain. The movie was turned on again, but with increased volume. Chairs were shifted back into place, cards were picked up and our game was resumed. I won another hand.

The day was Monday, November 30th. Thanks to a hard night of rain, the action in the streets had cooled down and conditions were generally quieter. News updates from the embassy were not very enlightening, however, as barricades on all the main streets were said to be still in place and the level of tension had not abated. Public rallies were scheduled to take place in two different parts of the city sometime that morning, thus putting the action on hold for a few hours while the factions decided what to do next. Analyzing that, our leadership concluded that it was probably safe to go to the nearby store if any of us needed food or supplies. But we were definitely to be back inside the compound within an hour.

We had all been eating most of our meals at the Villa Washington, because shopping and eating out had been so unsafe. One of the staff members brought several loaves of bread for us that morning, along with bacon and cereal, but we had no milk, no eggs, and virtually nothing else. Once again I started walking toward the store at the bottom of the hill.

The street going toward the railroad tracks seemed perfectly normal. Traffic was busy, taxis were rushing about, men and women were waiting at bus stops, and children were hurrying toward schools as if their world was entirely at peace. People noticed me walking along, but they did not react in any unusual way. Life was simply proceeding.

I found about six dozen eggs on display, brown shells still dirty from the nest, but they were large and they were cheap. They were probably produced right there in the squalor of that very neighborhood and then sold in bulk to storekeepers who did not bother to clean them up before displaying them. I grabbed a box of powdered milk, three cans of corned beef and a few eggs, all of which might come in handy if we did not get out of town soon and if our access to the stores was cut off. When I was halfway back up the hill again, I heard several quick gunshots from just ahead. Those were close! Pausing, listening for more but hearing none, my steps resumed with hastened rhythm. Only three more blocks to go.

Hundreds of people swarmed at the crest of the hill, as if the entire student body from nearby schools had emptied there. They seemed to be collectively looking in the direction of President Lissouba's house. Another burst of shots sounded just then, and the crowd scattered. Children by the hundreds poured like ants from a pestered hill, running into the street without bothering to look for traffic. Scores of adults and children were coming toward me, some walking fast and some running, but none taking their time. Still another burst of fire sounded somewhere ahead, and people surged toward me like a tidal wave. They ran to the opposite side of the street where a few trees might shield them, getting out of the way of whatever it was that they saw or dreaded to see.

Once back inside the compound, I reported what I had just witnessed to our General Manager. He went straight into the Director's office with it, as if he too knew something I did not know. Things were stirring! An order was then passed along that none of us were to leave the compound, for any reason, period!

Moments later the Director left in a station wagon, heading home to collect his own children. The mood in the compound had suddenly grown very somber indeed.

As soon as Bob returned and we were all assembled in the conference room, we were given an update. Evacuation of all Americans was being seriously considered! The notion of the moment was to fly everyone out of the country to either Zaire or Gabon, but nothing was definite yet. We were to pack our bags with enough things for one night just in case we had to move into the American embassy on short notice. Businesses all over the city had been shut down. Furthermore, government troops had been stationed at proposed rallying sites to block mass demonstrations. Some looting had just taken place at one of the big markets and a few fires had been started. I glanced at my watch. The hour was high noon.

A long night and another day passed without the situation turning more grave, but we were still in the compound, stuck with each other. Friction across the city had abated again, on and off, on and off, but uncertainty continued to prevail and no one seemed eager to take any unnecessary chances. If the current status held, everybody would get out of the city, headed back to their respective posts the very next morning. Making matters worse, I had fallen very ill.

During the night, I awoke several times squirming with nausea. Three times I crawled from under my mosquito net and went across the hall to try to vomit but nothing came up. Diarrhea visited however, along with intense fevers and cold sweats that lasted through the night. When morning finally came and the nurse was notified, she called the embassy doctor to pay me a visit. What followed was a diagnosis based on simple reasoning.

What did I eat that no one else ate? Eggs, from yard chickens, bought down the hill. Were the eggs thoroughly cooked? Yes, I cooked them myself. They were scrambled well-done and eaten with a loaf of French bread. Were my hands washed before cooking? Yes, of course. Did I wash them again after cracking open the shells and before handling the bread? Well, no, I might have been careless on that one. Yep, I had been careless all right, as well as incredibly stupid! I had Salmonella.

I was to drink nothing with caffeine, eat no food during the next twenty-four hours, sleep as much as possible and take the medication given me until the last pill had been swallowed. Because my disorder was caught in the early stages, it would probably be brought under control rather quickly. But I would definitely not be able to leave with the rest of the volunteers the next morning. If all went well for everybody else, I would soon be alone in the crash-house.

All day long, between trips to the bathroom and to the refrigerator for the carbonated beverage called "Pulp Orange," I slept as much as I could and sweated endlessly while my body ached all over. Late that night, two of the girls woke me up to say goodbye. They were planning to leave in a few hours while the city was quiet. I would not be able to travel for at least another night. They were sorry to leave me behind, but they were sure I would manage on my own.

Terrific. Just terrific! I didn't know where the bus station was, or how to identify the right bus or truck if I found one, or even how to buy a seat. Furthermore, I had been told it would be a long and miserable trip even for a healthy person. Any nauseated passenger who tended to get motion sickness anyway, traveling in a small bus packed with strangers for a twelve hour ride over rough roads, was likely to suffer. As my medication did its work and I drifted into another deep sleep, my last conscious thought was maybe, just maybe, I would get lucky and heal before daybreak.

The others left without me at dawn. One of the African staff members drove them to the buses, but with orders to return immediately if things looked too dangerous or if any barricades were still up. Anne woke me just before they started out, giving me one last chance to join the exodus, but I was on a sweat-saturated mattress and sporting a splitting headache. Maybe I would see her in Owando in a few days.

The sun had been up for three hours when I first began to move about in search of something cold to drink. My nausea had eased some, and my headache had subsided, so I guessed that I would live after all. And suddenly I was thinking I could have gone with the others, wondering if I should have, wishing I had. Just then Bob walked in to say that he was sorry I had to stay behind, but things could have been much worse. The streets were relatively quiet all across town, he said, and had been for the most of the night. My own trip out should be fairly safe once I was able to take the ride.

The doctor checked on me again during the day and decided that I could travel when morning came. Thus just before the next dawn, my Congolese driver tossed my duffel into the back seat of a project vehicle as I climbed inside and slammed the door shut. We had to hurry. We would have to be at the bus station by six o'clock or run the risk of missing my ride.

We were soon hurrying through sleepy streets past charred car bodies that had been pushed onto the shoulders out of the way of traffic. Barricades that had been constructed from piles of auto frames, fenders, and other such junk, had been dragged aside as well. Perhaps our episode of civil disobedience had truly come to an end. Taxis were whipping about already, recklessly as always, while pedestrians were venturing along sidewalks with no apparent trepidation. As we passed through Talengai, a mere twenty minutes into the ride, my driver pointed toward a road just ahead that turned to the left. Our destination was at hand.

The "station" was actually a huge dirt field, large enough for a football stadium. The paved street leading to it was bordered on one side by a line of trees and brush, and on the other by a line of trucks and buses that stretched bumper to bumper for a hundred yards or more. Down from those, down a slight decline, an improvised dirt road went through a frantic mix of vehicles and people. Several Coaster Deluxe buses were parked there, standing side by side as if making ready for a big race. A dozen pickup trucks with crash cages, and as many lorries with canvas-covered loads, were surrounded by people waiting for permission to climb aboard. Taxis were cruising between the rows of vehicles where hundreds of Africans were milling about, buying seats, tossing baggage here and there, saying goodbye to others. Dozens of other men, women and children were working the crowds to sell sodas, locally distilled whisky, bottled water, food items, belts, shirts and even jewelry, giving the field the atmosphere of a fairground.

Daniel drove me down the middle of the field toward the Coasters. A young man wearing stained jeans and a tee shirt yelled to us, "Owando, Owando," and pointed to one of the trucks. Others chimed in, trying to direct us toward their own vehicles. We keep moving. One man, as if he had recognized me somehow, called out "Makoua, Makoua".

Nearing the buses and slowing to a crawl, Daniel asked me which one I wanted as if I might be able to tell a good one from a bad one. Just then I heard the back door open. Jerking around, I saw my duffel sliding off the seat into the arms of a young man and then being hauled away at a run. The moment Daniel jerked to a stop, I jumped out and went after my bag. It was taken about ten yards before being plopped onto the dirt at the feet of three men who were engaged in a pushing and shoving match. Stepping into the middle of the fray, I grabbed my duffle with one hand and pushed on someone's chest with the other. When the bag was mine again, the melee stopped cold. One of the young men turned to me and said "Good morning". Only then, as they all laughed, did I understand. Nobody was trying to steal my things. They were only competing for another passenger.

When my thirty-six-dollar fare had been paid and my bag was safely on board one of the buses, Daniel wished me the best of luck and left me to my fate. Nobody was yet ready to collect for passage but I was still allowed to claim a spot, so I took the front window seat. Wide, comfortable, it was separated from the driver by a console. Apparently I had gotten lucky.

The Coaster, a Japanese made six-wheeler, was a cab-over-engine rig designed to haul thirty-two people if the aisle drop-seats were used. When we were finally under way, forty-seven people were aboard, two of whom were squeezed tightly between me and the console pressing me hard against the door. Those sharing my seat were a very large woman, and her suckling infant who needed a diaper change. My good fortune had run out again.

I was surprised at how good the suspension was on that little bus. We gently floated over the highway as we sped through curves at seventy-five miles per hour, giving the impression that the ride would actually have been pleasant had it not been for the overloading. By the time the first thirty miles had fallen behind us, we nearly struck an old man on a bicycle who plunged into the grass to get out of the way. We almost sideswiped a motorcycle that was already hugging the edge of the two lane road as it went. We nearly took out two pedestrians who were walking toward us, and finally we killed a family of chickens when we raced through a small village. Our driver sped beyond each of those events almost without notice, as if the sport hardly amused him anymore. An image crossed my mind of him pasting little chicken-stickers on his door and laughing crazily after every kill.

Our first stop was made three hours into the trip, probably thanks to that smelly baby who was too close to the driver's nose. Surely the driver would not have cared about the violation of anyone else's senses. The women took her child behind the bus, while the men wandered ahead a ways and stood along a wall of tall grass. We were about to enter that one hundred and twenty mile stretch of washouts known among volunteers as "The Ride from Hell" and we all needed to be in the best possible condition to endure it.

("Rest 'em here, boys, 'cause its gon' be a long ride 'fore the next waterin' hole.")

That little bus amazed me. Even ridiculously overloaded, it handled deep potholes, sand dunes and mud bogs every bit as well as some of the four-wheel-drive trucks that crossed over them every day. Once, we left the highway to enter a deeply rutted expanse of sand where getting stuck was a real possibility. The bus grew quieter as we struggled through the coarse, white sand, slowing as we went, until we ground to a halt axle-deep.

"Everybody out," was the call.

We all climbed out and walked ahead, while the driver rocked the bus back and forth. As the wheels of the vehicle found traction under the lightened load, it started to move again. When it had pulled itself free, spraying sand as it went, the Coaster passed us and continued all the way back to the highway. There, when we all caught up, everybody loaded into the same seats that we had vacated and we were off again.

Forty miles farther on, still speeding on a good road, we rounded a sharp curve where elephant grass blinded us to what lay ahead. Barely slowing for the turn, suddenly our wheels locked and we began to slide sideways. As I braced myself against the dashboard, we managed to jerk to a stop nearly at the feet of a man who was standing in the middle of the road, waving hysterically. Just beyond him was a pickup truck lying on its side with its crushed body blocking all of one lane and part of the other amid scattered cargo. The vehicle must have turned completely over at least once, for its fenders were pressed flat against crooked wheels, and the crash-cage was deformed like a toy stamped by an angry child. Glass that had been strewn about during those violent moments was spread over the road a hundred feet or more, and bits of plastic and metal lay about as little monuments to a hard lesson. Another man was limping about the broken vehicle, while five shocked and battered women were sitting side by side on the shoulder like birds on a limb. Amazingly, not a drop of blood was to be seen.

Our driver got out to talk to the bewildered man in front of us, but there seemed to be little we could do to help. Those who needed medical attention would have to hitch a ride to Brazzaville to find any, for we lacked even a first aid kit. Our driver kicked some of the debris out of the way, clearing a way for our passage, while chatting amicably with the other man. Momentarily he returned to the bus. When he had fitted himself back into his seat, he must have noticed that I was dumbstruck.

"Accidents happen often here," he said to me in a sort of verbal shrug. "These people are lucky. Everybody was thrown into the sand when it rolled. They will rest here until another truck comes along." He drove around the scene and accelerated again as if the matter was already out of his mind.

Central Africa is a land of realities, I said under my breath. That had been one of them. I recalled a story about a volunteer in another country who had been run over by a truck while she was helping someone with a stalled motorcycle. She had not gotten her own machine completely off the highway, probably assuming that people would go around her, and the bike was knocked flying into her. I was learning that one best survives Third World Africa, when one takes absolutely nothing for granted.

When we reached Owando just before dark, we had managed the trip without real trouble, without having met a single roadblock, and without having witnessed a hint of political difficulties along the way. I walked fifteen minutes from the bus to Anne's residence, with my duffel bag on my shoulder, straining under the weight; but I found that I had grown tougher under the rigors of Central Africa. Reaching the house, I was surprised to find Larry still there. He and Anne seemed equally surprised to see me again so soon. They had been able to pick up a little news through the day, verifying that some of the reports given us in Brazzaville might not have been correct. Evidently all of the violence had been confined to Brazzaville and a few places south, for life in the rural north had gone on virtually unaffected. And, they insisted, the unrest was over.

"How can it be over?" I asked cynically. "Nobody won!" Neither of them offered an answer to the question.

13

The Brick Attack

Because the equatorial village of Kelle was so remote, and because the road to it was so bad, the four-hundred-plus miles to or from Brazzaville was a major ordeal that could take four days or more to complete. One full day would be spent between Kelle and Etoumbi, another from Etoumbi to Makoua (a distance of only 63 miles), a third from Makoua to Owando, and finally the fourth would be consumed while traveling the rest of the way to Brazzaville. Ever since Anne had been posted in Owando, Larry and Linda had both enjoyed a break. Having an interim place to stay as long as they needed, they were able to be more selective in their rides. Thus, after having spent two extra nights at Anne's place while waiting for just the right ride, when Larry found passage all the way to Etoumbi, he took it.

While he was catching his truck, I was at the local bank closing my checking account. Things had become too unstable to trust it. Bank officials protested, albeit weakly, assuring me that my money was perfectly safe and that I should leave the account as it was. I was unconvinced.

"Well if it's all the same to you...."

Lacking automation, the clerk had to research and cross reference his handwritten logs before my money could be given back, which took a while, but late in the morning the job was finished. I was eager, by then, to climb onto my motorcycle and head back to Makoua, but a storm was already building in that direction, compelling me to stay in town another night.

When the next morning came and the skies were clear, I was ready to ride. Fueled and oiled, cranked and tested, my shiny new machine was propped on its stand and I was strapping my forty pound bag onto the rear of the long seat. When I straddled the bike and fired it up, Anne gave me a motherly farewell and reminded me of the official rule that the headlight must be switched on at all times when the engine was running. I turned on the light with a grin, fitted my helmet into place, lowered the visor and was off. Rat-a-tat-tat!

Even though the motorcycle was small, it was perfectly suited to the roads of Central Africa. Reasonably powerful, relatively fuel efficient, adequately fast and made for the dirt, it had the capability of handling deep sand, thick mud, eroded hills, steep inclines or most any other conditions, and it could run in lower gears for extended periods without damaging the engine. Furthermore it was designed to withstand hard falls, coatings of slime, and the shock of cold water on hot metal. Its only drawback was that the tires were not "knobbies". Mine had been made for the street rather than the dirt, which guaranteed a significant loss of traction and diminished the power of the machine to perform at its best. That also made it much more difficult to ride.

When terrain changed from sand to gravel, hard clay to soft mud, or from sand to standing water, traction also changed rather suddenly. One had to be ready. Thus as I sped across Owando's river bridge and approached the end of the pavement, the throttle was eased back and the road ahead was observed with renewed respect. I was alone then, and on my own if an accident happened. Anyway, there was no need to rush. I had all day to get home.

That first few miles were even worse than they had seemed from the trucks that I had ridden. Tiny pebbles on the clay between washouts and puddles acted like a lubricant, forcing me to veer constantly back and forth across that natural obstacle course. And sand, often powdery and deep like a West Florida beach, required much greater speed and entirely different riding techniques.

Just over three hours later, when a little concrete bridge appeared at the foot of a long hill, I knew I had made it to Makoua. A few minutes later, cruising slowly past the grand marche while looking for familiar faces, I waved to cheering children who ran after me as though to see if they could keep up. Herve, having heard me when I rolled past his house, rushed out to follow me home. The morning after our big meeting in Owando, as we Americans left for Brazzaville, Herve and the other homologues caught rides to their respective villages. He had probably been waiting for me with the same kind of excitement with which a child anticipates the arrival of Santa Clause. As I rode across the drainage ditch in front of my house and pulled up near the porch, he was approaching at a fast walk.

While I untied my bag and then removed it from the seat, he walked around the motorcycle several times. He was wearing a huge grin, touching the machine with longing, surely picturing himself on one just like it. He said he was pleased to have me return "home". He also said that I had been missed, and several potential fish-farmers had inquired about our services and asked for help.

While we were talking, Norman the policeman ambled over to admire the motorcycle, closely followed by a crowd of women and children. His wife and unmarried daughter were with him, along with another woman whom I had not seen before, and a little girl about seven or eight years old. The children had to be warned to stay away from the hot engine, while the women were only slightly more subtle about their own excitement. Norman's teenaged daughter told me with out-of-character good cheer that she had never seen such a beautiful machine and she had never ridden one at all.

Just to prevent misunderstandings that might arise, I explained as pleasantly as possible that the motorcycle was only to be used for work, and passengers, even Herve, were expressly forbidden unless they had an "approved" helmet. Following that declaration, Herve's smile faded and the former coolness of my neighbors quickly returned. As they all strode out of my yard, my sense was that none of them believed a word of it. The notion struck me then, that I might have just witnessed the first of a host of new issues that could arise between Herve and me. When I went to bed that night, realizing that nobody had ever explained the motorcycle program to him, I was bothered by thoughts of the new problems that might arise between us. Well, I thought, he would just have to get over it.

Having wheels for the first time, my official explorations could finally broaden to the borders of my territory. Even though my geographic area was limited to a radius of about 20 miles, not much was known to Americans about life within that circle. According to my old map, the northern village of Aboua was shown to be within the range, and Herve had already told me that Aboua was a large and thriving village that might even have some old fish ponds. I planned to ride there the next morning to investigate.

This nook was part of my front porch. The dark rectangle behind me was the original doorway that had been sealed up. The new entrance was to the side at my left and just out of the picture.

After a good night of sleep with the motorcycle locked inside the house, I was up before dawn, dressed and ready to ride. I didn't even bother with breakfast. Months before, when walking north with the young man who was said to be a robber, I went only a few miles before turning back. Only ten minutes on the Yamaha took me past the "village" we had visited, the village that was composed of only one family and then past the farthest point that seemed familiar.

Penetrating ever closer to the rain forests where rain fell more regularly and the road was like the bottom of a wet canyon, it was even more dangerous than the highway from Owando. The washouts were more frequent, wider, deeper and far more treacherous where standing water was more common than dry ground. I took it easy, more conscious than ever that an accident so far from help could spell disaster.

Several small villages appeared on the way, each with a few residents who would come to the road to watch my approach. But they all seemed more interested in the illuminated headlight than in the white stranger on a shiny red motorcycle. "Lumiere," they called out angrily as they pointed to the light. During my first test-ride in Owando I had experienced the same response,; and other volunteers claimed to have encountered the same. None of them seemed to understand what that was all about, but several of the second year people admitted that they routinely ran without the light. Life was, they said, more peaceful that way. I simply waved back to the gesticulating villagers and continued my ride with the light shining brightly.

The terrain soon became hilly as well as thickly forested, but the high ground presented a breathtaking panorama of peaks and valleys and of grasslands and jungles that give me a fresh sense of appreciation for the country that was my temporary home. Easing along the narrow and often shrouded road, I was still moving faster than any truck could have taken me, for my forward motion never stopped.

Looking for a side road, a right turn going to Aboua, I was beginning to think no such road existed. Worse yet, I was nearly at the edge of my range. When 18 miles from home, I stopped in a little village and disturbed a man who was napping in the shade of a mango tree. Listening as I explained where I was trying to go, he then said Aboua was several miles to the southeast. If true, that should place it inside my territorial limits. The man pointed to the hill behind me. I was to go back to its top and look carefully in the grass. Thus, I backtracked, moving slowly with eyes wide open, and sure enough discovered an old trail that was nearly invisible in the tall green that surrounded it.

The new path soon widened into a pair of dry, sandy ruts that must have once been a road. When I had gone less than a quarter mile, I reached a crest that overlooked the canopy of a long expanse of forest. Green hills in the distance seemed to melt into the blue of the sky, uninterrupted by any sign of human intervention. I then descended a slope into thick brush where the air turned suddenly damp and cool. That usually meant that water was near, perhaps even crossing my path ahead, and if so, I would probably find a log bridge spanning it. Slowing in anticipation, I eased along until the road became a pair of trenches that were deeply cut between banks of clay. Huge rocks occasionally poked through dark shadows and dangerous roots were nearly hidden under layers of leaves. Low hanging branches swatted my helmet and grabbed at the handle bars, until the anticipated bridge appeared just ahead. The bridge was made of two logs that were secured about two feet apart. I was able to walk on one of them while wheeling the bike across on the other.

Although this was not the "road" to Aboua, it was a quite typical trail in the bush. Wherever such a path appeared, it generally led to a village sooner or later.

Soon reaching a place where the road gradually smoothed out and widened again, I crested another hill and that time completely stopped to switch off the motor. I was looking directly over the most gorgeous valley I had ever seen, where the forest seemed hundreds of feet below me. Some said that gorillas were still found in that rich expanse of green, and that hunters would often go there to illegally kill game. Some of that meat was said to have been sold in Makoua, while other animals were killed for the hides, horns, tusks and anything else that commanded a price on the black market. I remained several minutes at that spot, spiritually moved, trying to commit the sight of it to memory.

Thirty minutes and eight miles later, I reached Aboua. There, in a clearing of several acres, stood about fifty huts and a small school, all lined up on either side of common ground about a hundred yards across. Palm trees threaded a line down the center of it, and banana and papaya were scattered throughout its length and casting great shades over the dark ground. The paillotes were made of thatch mounted on poles over bare dirt, but the houses were the same as the squares and rectangles of mud found in Makoua. Some even sported new roofs of tin. Bicycles were propped against the walls of several houses, behind which, colorful garments hung on lines, drying in the cool air.

A dozen boys running on either side of the motorcycle were dressed in western style pants and tee shirts while all the girls that I could see were wearing traditional skirts of imported fabric. The grounds were swept clean, as was typical, but the entire place suggested a hint of prosperity that made me wonder how that could be. Many villages, large and small, still thrived in that isolated part of the country and many of the villagers managed without much contact with the more progressive world. One might see western style clothes and metal pots anywhere, where money was available to buy them, but "jobs" did not exist so far from cities. Perhaps the local teacher made a little money, when the government could afford to pay him, and it was possible that a few tradesmen were able to generate some cash by selling lumber or dugout boats, but that did nothing to explain the look of middle-class contentment in Aboua.

As the children yelled "lumiere," I rode all the way to the far end of the village, deliberately letting everyone know that a stranger had come and then I rolled slowly back looking for someone chief-like in appearance. As expected, a very old man came from a mud dwelling toward me. He was shirtless and barefoot, wearing a sleepy look as if someone had just aroused him. I stopped at his side and removed my helmet.

"Mbote, Tata," I greeted him in respectful but limited Lengala.

"Ehhh, mbote," he said in return and extended his hand.

Propping the bike on its stand, I dismounted and addressed him in French, but he did not seem to understand. He replied in lengthy Lengala, leaving me just as lost. The two of us were by then surrounded with both children and adults, male and female, and others were approaching. Trying to communicate with a combination of words, sign language and pictures drawn in the sand, everyone seemed to understand "Makoua" and "America" but they all appeared to be much amused at my picture of a fish drawn in the dirt. The effort simply was not going to work.

I would have to return some other time with Herve, if I could figure out how to get him there. As I climbed back on the motorcycle, I noticed grass mats on the ground in front of one of the houses. I pointed at one and blurted out "Litoko". A murmur rose from the crowd and teeth showed as heads nodded approvingly.

"Ehhh, litoko," several of them chimed back. Yes, they were agreeing, it was a grass mat.

I pulled a one thousand CFA note from my pocket, said the word again and waved the bill. Another effort failed. If they knew what I was trying to say, they did not seem interested in making a sale. I shook hands again with all who wanted to shake it, and strapped on my helmet. When the engine started up again, some of the boys reached out to touch it and then they watched me ride back out of the village.

Having been at my post barely three months, more of the obstacles that lay ahead had suddenly been made quite clear. One issue was the need for cultural compromise, which meant finding a middle ground where the Congolese and I could meet without stepping too far out of our respective comfort zones. Another was to clearly grasp the needs of a given village before trying to affect it. Still another was to identify people who wanted progress badly enough to try something new to achieve it. And more importantly, if I was to be effective, I must either learn to speak their languages or somehow I must work more with Herve. There simply was no way around it. I needed his help.

"Lumiere," people called out to me as I rode through the several villages on the way home. "Lumiere," they yelled and pointed angrily at the light.

"Yes," I called back in French. "I have found the light."

A day later and exploring again, I was riding almost due west toward Etoumbi on a road that was relatively good compared to most others of my African experience. The first few miles were wide and comparatively straight, mostly dry and only occasionally covered with deep sand. But my interest faded soon, because I had found only a single village along the way and it appeared to be abandoned.

During the return ride through Makoua, dozens of people watched my approach while pointing vigorously to the headlight and yelling at me to turn it off. I had logged one hundred and eighty miles on the motorcycle already, and found that every African thus far encountered reacted expressively, almost furiously, about that light. That made no sense to me. People on motor scooters ran over the streets of town every night, weaving through crowds of nearly invisible pedestrians, and those machines had no lights at all. No one seemed bothered by that, and yet a light used during the daytime drove them to distraction. I had already asked Marin about the phenomenon, but his response was only, "Lights are for the night".

During the next several days as I continued to explore my territory, I found villages that were not on my map and found the remains of a few that were charted but no longer existed. However, no matter where my wheels took me, villagers were always encountered who knew of me and my work. A few of them actually claimed to have interest in fish farming, but my sense was that their hearts were not in it. Maybe my best and most practical working area would be in and about Makoua, where Herve could work with me without wheels of his own.

Another mud-block house in an outer village.

When the rain came late one blazing afternoon, I took full advantage of it to get some truly restful sleep. Suddenly I found myself sitting up in bed with cold chills racing along my spine because something had just jerked me from a sound sleep. Whatever it was, it slammed into my roof with the subtlety of a lightning strike. Something bounced a time or two, then slid down the tin and hit the ground with a thud. I was wide awake then, trying to understand what was happening and how to react to it.

A few streaks of yellow were still shining through the remaining cracks in my shutters, which meant the streets lights were still on and the time was not yet eleven o'clock. Surely it had been a brick, I thought. And if it was a brick, somebody had to have thrown it. But who, and why? He must have been some practical joker, or maybe a drunk. Or maybe the meaning was somewhat more serious. I did not want to alert the assailant as to how I might react, no matter what his intentions. I sat rigidly up and waited.

Something I had learned months ago was that my bed would creak loudly every time I moved, even simply to turn over in the night,. Getting up in the morning was a public announcement. I sat still and tried to think. My camping knife was hanging on a belt near the window. Where was my machete? On the kitchen table in the other room. Where was my flashlight? Somewhere under the net with me, close to the candle and the book I had been reading. I reached out carefully and located it. Where was my three-fifty-seven magnum? Locked safely away in a relative's home in Florida. Unarmed and under attack, all I could do was remain still. Wait.

If I moved very, very slowly, shifting one foot at a time to the sturdy side boards, maybe I could work my way from under the net without making much noise. I decided to give it a try. Working the material free from the mattress and letting it hang over the side, I then pulled myself gently to the edge of the frame. So far so good. Arm reaching down, fingers touching the floor, I eased my hip up onto the frame and rested my weight there for a moment, then slowly swung both legs out. I was up, and no one on the outside could have heard me.

The second brick hit sharply and bounced down the metal roof, creating noise that reverberated through the bedroom like an echo chamber. Taking advantage of the racket, by the time the missile hit the ground I was on the floor and rolling over to my knees. I got to my feet in the darkness and eased to the window, careful not to bump or kick anything on the way. Found my knife. Slipped it from the sheath. Peered through one of the narrow slits in the wood, looking toward the light.

I could see the shoulder of the road, but nothing more. Whoever was out there had no fear of being seen, for he was under the street light and probably knew he was in plain sight. But what in the world was he trying to prove? He surely knew that I would not open the shutters and present my skull to a sailing brick. Thinking the view might be better through cracks in the front door, I felt my way there, pausing on the way to find my machete. A nail hole in the door was the only place I had not covered up. Blinking to focus through it, I found the angle to be worse than that from the bedroom. I needed a plan of action.

I might have crawled out the back window and sneaked around the house in the shadows, if the dead bolt could be slid without noise and if the shutters could be opened quietly. But I had no way to know how many people were out there, nor what their intentions were, nor whether they were men or boys, big or small, drunk or sober, armed or not, or even if they might be in the back yard waiting for me to do exactly what I was pondering. I needed to know what I was up against before making any sort of move.

The third projectile struck the bedroom shutter with full force, as if the assailant expected me to be hiding behind it. I was under siege! That blow came directly from the front of the house where the light was the brightest, and furthermore directly across from the police compound. The policeman and his family had to have heard all of the noise! Looking through the crack in the shutter again, I saw a man's feet and forelegs moving deliberately on the road as if positioning for another toss. Suddenly, the world fell dark as street lights went out.

I definitely could not go outside then, for they could be waiting for that and they would see me before I could see them. I waited a few more minutes, saw nothing and then noisily pulled back the dead bolt on the front door. Another minute passed, and all remained quiet. I threw the door open then, and flashed a beam of light over the street. Nothing! Nothing.

Believing the incident was over but clutching the machete just the same, I went outside and looked all around. The police compound was dark and as quiet as a tomb. Only a fool could have mistaken the message there. Only a very brave civilian would have dared attack someone next door to a police station, unless that person had no fear of the police. And it would have taken a dunce to launch his attack from a lit street, in clear view, unless that person wanted to be seen. No doubt about it. My assailant was a police officer and he had dared me to see who he was. He must have lost interest in his little game when the lights went out. Perhaps darkness removed the challenge.

Many sleepless hours later, the rising sun brought a brilliant and hot Sunday morning. I walked up the block to find Herve in his back yard, working in his garden. Seated in a shade, talking and watching Herve sweat, were Dr. Prosper and another man whom I had not met before. I explained what happened during the night, and told Herve that assistance was needed to get something done about it.

"If I tell my leaders in Brazzaville what happened," I said, "they might pull me out of here. And if they do, that could mean the end of the program in Makoua." Herve and his friends were listening intently, Herve frowning, the others nodding their heads seriously. "It would be better if we could handle this locally, but you know your system and I don't."

"This is not serious," Dr. Prosper remarked, as if bombarding people's homes went on all the time.

Realizing he had to do something, Herve dropped his hoe and went inside the house for a clean shirt. When he returned, he and I left for a visit with the chief of Makoua. The chief lived in a sprawling government house on the river bank, not thirty yards beyond the concrete post that marked the equator. As Herve and I approached, the chief and another man were standing on the front patio watching us come.

Herve went up the steps ahead of me, he quickly went through the hand shaking ceremony and then asked the chief for a private audience. Perhaps recognizing the seriousness in both of our faces, the request was instantly granted. The chief was a slight man, perhaps five feet eight inches tall, light complexioned and about forty years old, but he appeared to be all business. He led us into a large room and took a seat behind a very businesslike mahogany desk. Herve and I took places in wicker chairs that flanked a glass-top table with water rings on it. While the chief listened intently, Herve told my story. His head was nodding, his hands were slicing the air, his facial expression were strained.

For the second time since my arrival, I almost felt sorry for Herve. Clearly written in his eyes was that he knew beyond doubt just how delicate the situation really was, and just how much he personally had to lose. The chief was quick to recognize it as well. He looked back and forth at us while Herve talked and then he assured me that he would notify the police and see to it that any "strangers" were rounded up and questioned. I smiled at that, knowing exactly what he meant. Absolutely nothing would be done. Nevertheless I had taken the proper steps, made the proper authorities aware of the situation, and put them on notice. That might force them to notify the real suspects, and the police would be forced to take my side even if it was against their will to do so. I would notify Brazzaville, of course, just for the record, but I honestly believed that the matter was finished. And if Norman or his crooked boss had expected me to leave town, they were about to be sorely disappointed.

My resolve, all of a sudden, was stronger than ever.

14

Wheels and Ordeals

A new day came, and running water was unavailable in Makoua. Hydro-Congo was out of diesel fuel and none had been stockpiled for emergency use, so the pumps had simply quit when the tank ran dry. Villagers who lacked access to deep wells were forced to carry water from springs in the forest or from the river, and sometimes for great distances. That morning the road in front of my house was bustling with women and children carrying plastic containers, while still others were pushing wheelbarrows loaded with them. Even Norman's wife and children were forced into action, but the woman looked as if she dared me to notice.

Marin claimed that the well in his yard had been deepened every year since it was dug, but the falling water table was not his only problem. Some of his neighbors routinely took his water without permission. The rate for access to any water supply, public or private, was five hundred CFA per month, or roughly two dollars. Marin had warned people they must either pay him or stop taking his water, but when the well was unguarded they took it anyway.

"If they don't have the money to pay," I attempted to reason with him, "why not demand labor in exchange for well-privileges?"

"Because they would not do it," he replied.

"Then why not cover and lock the well?"

"Wood is expensive, and so are locks," he said.

"But the people are stealing your water. That's illegal. Why not speak with the police or the chief of Makoua?"

"Because someone would hire a witch to get even."

"Well then, why not just give people the water and stop fretting over it?"

"Because the well belongs to me, and I don't want them to use it." Having cleared up that issue, maybe he would soon be free to tackle some other significant local mysteries for me.

Entering the second week of December, and having visited every known village within the boundaries of my territory, a considerable amount of interest in fish farming had been generated all over the region. Several site inspections had already been conducted and a few had been approved, but little had taken place since. I didn't worry. Everybody was on Africa time.

One day at the market I saw Dani there, selling peanuts, and noticed that she appeared to be about six months pregnant. Which perhaps explained why so much attention had once been directed my way regarding her potential as a wonderful wife. Having given up on me, and apparently with some bitterness, she had actually become hostile when in my company. Either speaking boldly and discourteously or simply ignoring me, she made it quite clear that she wanted nothing more to do with the "mondele".

The situation was not much different with Herve. His attitude toward me was tolerant one day and insufferable the next. He never offered to discuss issues that bothered him, but the biggest problem between us, I was certain, was the motorcycle. I was sorry about that, but it was not within my power to fix things short of blatantly violating rules that I had agreed to honor. Thus, I continued to work alone while Herve stewed, and I continued to learn about local culture.

The Congolese tradition was one of sharing. If a villager was unable to provide for himself, other family members and friends would keep him or her from going hungry or going without shelter. However that system of sharing seemed also to mean *obligatory* giving, even if it worked to the detriment of the giver. If, for example, one person had a little money, then others had no reluctance to demand shares of it. Furthermore, if the donor was out of money or refused to part with what he had, that was a cultural slight which would be seen as selfish and unforgivable. That could also lead to great sorrow caused by the spell of a witch.

Being a stranger did not exempt me from that system. Quite the contrary, because I was a "rich American," I was fair game to anyone who might desire something for nothing. I supposed, since the Congolese culture had created and maintained the policy of sharing-on-demand, that in part explained why people were not very aggressive in any quests for personal wealth. They would have to give it away, so what would have been the point?

Even Herve had tested my generosity a few times, making hard and fast demands for kerosene, or bread, or cash, but I continued to refuse him with no attempt to disguise my resentment for it. He must have gotten over it though, for he suddenly was all smiles and good cheer again. One of the men who had attended our group meeting at the Bureau a while back wanted a site inspection as soon as we could get to him.

Michel, in the meantime, visited me after lunch one day to let me know that he was not yet ready for me to inspect his site. The reason? He had not finished digging his pond yet! I was stunned. All of my efforts to write down exactly what he had to do before a formal evaluation could take place, had been an exercise in futility. Just then it struck me that he probably couldn't read a word, and that he had only pretended to know what my papers said.

"Michel, you must stop your work," I told him. "I only wanted you to clear enough of the brush to allow me to make a formal inspection."

"But I have worked very hard," he replied angrily.

"I know, and I am sorry about that, but I'm sure you don't want to do even more work for nothing. Let me return to your place tomorrow and then I'll see what must be done. Maybe the work is not all lost."

"Tomorrow then". He went away in a silent blaze of temper.

"Midmorning," I called to him.

Early the next morning, I went to a fork in the road near the Catholic Mission, early as usual, where I was to meet Herve and Monsieur Okeni Mathieu. Neither man was anywhere in sight, so I quieted the motorcycle to wait. Mathieu soon arrived on a bicycle, alone, with no word of Herve. He said that his property was only a short distance away, and that I should follow him to it. Thus we went uphill on a dirt road that took us away from the direction of the Mission and then down a trail heading toward a patch of forest. We parked near a spring at the bottom and crossed over to a field of grass that waved in the breeze. There, on the side of that long, gently sloping grade, Mathieu hoped to build a pond or two. Unfortunately, because the entire hill was overgrown with the tall grass, he must clear a good portion of it before any judgments could be made.

Because his water-source was a fast spring that ran about three feet below the ground's surface, I doubted that he would be able to barrage the water high enough to serve the purpose. Mathieu insisted that he could do it, however, and that he did not mind clearing the field for the inspection. Asking me to return the next Friday, he thanked me for my visit and wished me a good day.

I rode from there to Michel's site, parked the motorcycle behind the abandoned house, and walked the rest of the way to the valley floor where Michel was waiting for me. I was amazed at what I saw. The man had dug a gigantic rectangle in the earth that was probably two meters deep, with walls that went straight down to the bottom. The hole would have better served as a swimming pool than a fish pond, and I told him so. He was furious with me.

"You should have come sooner and worked with me," he insisted.

"I would have, if I had known what you were doing. Michel, you were only supposed to clear some of the land for a formal evaluation. I told you that. I expected you to come back in a few days to let me know you were ready."

"I wanted to finish it before you came," he said, voice quivering with a mix of anger and frustration.

"I respect you for the effort you have made here, Michel. You did the work of ten men. But it won't work for growing fish. Now you are angry with me when this error was no fault of mine, so maybe you should work only with Herve from now own."

"No, no," he said adamantly back. "I will work with you! Just show me what to do and I will do it."

One thing was obvious. His property would definitely support a pond or two. I spent the next two hours showing him how he must channel a stream of water higher on the bank so that several ponds could be filled on demand without interrupting the flow of the main spring. I showed him where to start the next dig and what dimensions to follow, and how to slope the dikes. And I promised to work with him more frequently until the job was completed. He was not a happy man, but at least he was not furious anymore. When I made my way back up the hill, he was busily digging a feeder channel on the bank. We had suffered a setback, but he was still with me and I was eager to work with him. Things would be okay. I hoped.

Back at home again, I spent the afternoon wondering whether Andre the carpenter would return as he had recently agreed. I wanted him to enclose my front porch from the top of the half-wall to the ceiling, so that the motorcycle could be kept there during the nights. Specifically I wanted a grid of wooden bars, and a similar door that could be locked with a chain to keep intruders out. He did finally show up with the materials in his wheelbarrow, and before the afternoon was done, I was able to roll the machine out of my kitchen into a relatively secure enclosure. The bars were not intended to guard against burglars when I was not at home, for the motorcycle would be kept inside during those times, but it would do nicely to keep out the opportunistic thief who would have been forced to make a lot of noise if he tried to steal it while I was there.

Looking from my kitchen through my new security system made of wooden bars.

Ten days before Christmas and long before daybreak, I awakened to thunder so deafening that it propelled me from my bed and drew me outside for a look. Standing on the porch, I was able to watch the most spectacular display of lightning I had ever seen. It was horizontal, cloud to cloud, as if the great wires connecting the heavens had been jerked apart while the current sizzled between them. When the winds began and the fierce rain came, I locked up tightly again and returned to bed where I lay back and listened to the sounds of nature and thought of things philosophical for a long time before drifting into a deep sleep.

Two more sites were inspected the next morning, one seven miles out of town and the other only two, but Herve chose to boycott both visits. The closer place was the property of Monsieur Boreffe, who had a pair of hogs grunting in pens at the top of the hill overlooking a vast garden on the slopes of a three acre site. Five very old fish ponds, long abandoned, lay in a line at the bottom.

Boreffe was a husky, good natured Congolese who grinned constantly and laughed with his head back when anything amused him. The man was also driven! He was employed as a government agent having something to do with medical care, even though he worked without pay, but it was the garden-site and those hog pens that actually provided for his family. Boreffe said he wanted to rejuvenate the old ponds if it could be done, and he claimed he was willing do whatever it took to make it happen. I believed every word.

An outside look at my new enclosure, made for the motorcycle.

The old ponds were located on a broad, flat bottom where a fast spring rushed toward the river on the far side, while a second slower stream ran higher along the other. The slower water had almost surely been the original source that fed all five ponds, but because of time and neglect, they had largely filled with sand and the entire place had become a marsh. The greatest difficulty faced there was that the site would have to be drained by channeling all of the standing water into the main flow.

Obviously, without any measurements necessary, Boreffe had a terrific place for several new ponds. I waded about in the mud for a while, putting poles in the ground to mark where the work should start and where it should end. Boreffe took it all in and then laughed with his head back and said it looked as big as a soccer field. His was indeed a giant job for a man working only with hand tools, but he assured me he would do the work, spirits willing, and, of course, with a bit of technical guidance. When I walked back up the hill toward the motorcycle, I turned back to see him working alone in his marsh pushing the blade of his shovel into the wet soil. I realized then that I had been hasty in my impressions of the men of Makoua. Those early judgments might have accurately applied to most of the masculine population, but I had already met some outstanding exceptions. I was excited to work with them all.

The next site was located west of town. Monsieur Laurent and I walked through heavy brush and ankle deep water for more than three hours before we finally found a place that likely had enough slope and adequate water flow. Just as several times before, I could not take measurements due to the overgrowth, but Mr. Laurent promised he would clear it and I could return in a few days to see the results. And once again I was impressed. We shook hands, and I left him to his work.

Pleased with the way the day had gone but thoroughly disappointed that my homologue had not participated, I had to devise some sort of scheme to include him even if it was against his will. As he was "the man" chosen by higher authorities, and as he would continue to be the man whether I liked him or not, something had to give. Nearing home but thinking of nothing else, I made my decision. I would park the motorcycle at home and walk to my various jobs from then on, if that would enlist Herve's cooperation. Maybe he would feel better about the job if he and I were absolute equals, on foot, treading over the roads mile after mile after mile. When I rolled the machine onto my porch, I locked the handlebars and put the key on my bookcase. I would approach Herve with the new notion when I next encountered him.

The day I returned from Brazzaville, I noticed two new faces among the policeman's family. One was a child about eight years old. The other was a woman whom I guessed to be her mother. That woman disappeared after a few days, but the child stayed behind as if spending a summer vacation with relatives. Having observed her during the weeks that followed, I began to wonder exactly what was going on. Every morning she would sit on a little bench in the yard, and there she would wash dishes in a pan. Sometimes she would even do laundry there. Sometimes, when the spigot was dry, she hauled water from the river, and sometimes she walked to the market. But she always seemed busy with chores. While she worked the morning hours away, the larger children were gone to school and the younger ones played all around her without including her or even seeming to notice her. Practically everyone gave her orders, and she seemed to heed them as if disobeying them might not be a wise thing to do.

Situations like hers disturbed me, but it was not possible to get involved without running the risk of digging myself deeply into cultural issues that were not my concern. Once passing her on the street while on my way home from the store, I handed her a little piece of hard candy from a package that I had just bought. Eyes lighting up and grinning happily, she took the candy and skipped toward her destination. I happened to be working in the front yard when she returned and noticed that when she went into the compound, she showed the candy to the policeman's wife. I could not hear what was said between them, but the candy was taken by the larger hand and then the child glanced sheepishly in my direction before she sat down again to do her chores.

Marin told me it was not uncommon for children to be passed around from family to family when their parents could no longer care for them. Sometimes, he said, they were even sold to whoever would buy them. Selling children was clearly against the laws of even the Congo, and no person would ever admit to having done it. Certainly not a policeman. But when a child was turned into servitude in exchange for food and a place to sleep, I only knew of one word to describe it. We Americans don't talk about that sort of thing much anymore.

Two days later, having planned another visit to the site of Monsieur Laurrent. I told Herve that I would leave the motorcycle at home if he would walk there with me to participate in the process.

"No!" he angrily refused.

"But why not? If I am willing to walk with you, what is the problem?"

"You have a motorcycle that is for work. We can ride it together, but I will not walk like the white man's servant!"

"Herve, it is not my motorcycle, and you cannot ride it until we can get you a proper helmet. That is the rule, and I will abide by it."

"Other volunteers don't have such rules," he argued.

That was actually true in some cases. Some of our number did use the machines for social purposes, hauling passengers around as they pleased, and even riding long distances from their respective posts to visit other volunteers. Their homologues broke the rules too, rather constantly, and everybody knew it. Keeping such matters secret was an impossibility in the rural countryside where the motorcycles stood out like Corvettes in big city slum. That sort of disregard for the rules, made it a lot tougher for those of us who respected our agreements, but that was the way it was.

"Well, if you won't walk with me tomorrow, I might as well go alone and ride." Herve went away then, his face swollen with anger.

Irritated with Herve, I decided to go back to Laurent's place right then and look around a bit more on my own. I rode the several miles out of town and pulled to a stop near the beginning of a forest trail. Concealing the motorcycle in the brush, I locked the wheel and got off. As I started down the dense hill, I stopped to watch a wide swath of ants that were marching directly across my path.

The Congo has several species of ants, some massive and dark, others red and almost microscopic, some slow and precise as they move in perpetual lines, and others frantically erratic. Driver ants were, to me, the most interesting of all. Like Army ants, they seemed menacing, deliberate, calculating and thoroughly organized as they went about their work. Unlike Army ants, however, they do not sting. They bite, chew, and rip flesh from the bone.

Sometimes I had watched them in my own back yard when they were scattered over a wide area as if somehow confused. Then via some unknown method of communication they became organized, falling into tight military-style formations. Following that they would cut a path with seven or eight ants abreast like soldiers marching to battle. Fearsome members of their ranks, those with gigantic heads like Nazi helmets, typically flanked both sides of the line, holding positions an inch or two apart while facing outward from the direction of the march. If an intruder dared to test their defenses, they would instantly attack. If a human moved too close to such a line and somehow disturbed it, he or she would be swarmed in a matter of seconds. Some of the insects would march up the inside of one's clothes to the highest possible point, and there the attack would begin. That morning, I watched them for several minutes and then finally crossed over without bothering them.

The densely covered path that I had to follow was a tunnel in a green and brown world where strange insects thrived and reptiles scurried noisily but invisibly about. I watched above me and on both sides, always looking for snakes, for some that lived in the brush could have been fatal to encounter. Deliberately making plenty of noise with every step, I saw no more animals all the way down.

Laurent had been busy! An impressive number of the smaller trees and a large quantity of brush had already been chopped, piled and burned. Conveniently, that gave me an unencumbered view of his grand parcel in the jungle, and clearly showed just how much labor yet remained before it could be transformed into a suitable place for aqua-culture. Dozens of trees, a few of them two feet in diameter, towered over a rich abundance of vines, scrub and long-standing puddles that had been maintained by saturated ground and the lack of an escape route.

The primary water-source was a network of trickles that came from the side of the hill and gathered into a pool, from which a run began. The flow widened as it went, forming a serpentine channel that eased down the grade to where it ran out of sight into the forest. The entire place was marshy, but it would surely dry up once the channel was deepened and the puddles were trenched toward it.

If a pond were dug one meter deep from the level of the spring, it would fill up over time and support a full growth of fish. The question for me was whether the slope was such that the pond could be completely drained when the time came to harvest the catch. I began placing poles cut with my machete, spacing them several meters apart and running heavy string between them. A line-level was fixed to the line, and I measured and cut notches on the poles to indicate the ever increasing slope.

Placement of the last stake was going to be tricky. The ground was especially boggy there, making it difficult to move through the mud without sinking ankle deep. Looking for dry places to land my feet, I chose certain spots in advance so that I could jump from large roots to thick clumps of grass while carrying my string in one hand and a pole in the other. Close to the channel of moving water then, pausing catlike on a large root, I was readying for one last step.

Suddenly I felt a burning sensation on my calf, then another. Then there was another higher up, and something was crawling inside my pants. Looking at my feet, I saw hundreds of Driver ants. My boots were covered with them and thousands more were moving toward me. I had to move! Looking for a place to run, I saw that the entire bog was literally blanketed with ants, disorganized, scattered thickly over a thousand square feet of damp ground. And they were biting me, chewing my flesh, eating me alive! No longer thinking, simply reacting, I turned toward the little canal and jumped. My feet plunged into sediment as soft as runny oatmeal and I was sinking. Knee deep and going deeper, the ants inside my underwear were gnawing on me while I was stuck solidly in the muck, hanging by my elbows from the sides of the trench.

Splashing water over the ground to discourage more of them from coming after me, but sinking deeper as I did so, my options were limited. I would have to ignore the approaching ants and somehow get out of that canal. Leaning backward and slowly lifting one knee up, my foot moved a little closer to the side where it struck something solid. I was lucky to have found leverage. Very slowly, the other knee came up, and inch by inch I was pulling myself free.

I spent several agonizing minutes working my way completely out of the bog and then, muddy to the chest, I was right back in the middle of the ants again. I had no choice. That time I didn't look for dry spots. I simply ran as hard as I could go. Bogging, sloshing, stumbling, lunging and nearly falling several times, I finally made it back to high ground near the valley wall and found a place which, luckily, was ant-free.

The muddy pants fell past my knees, followed by my underwear and then I started picking off the ants. After a minute, making certain that no others were approaching, I plopped down in the dirt to get the rest of my clothes off. Then standing in the thick forest alone, stark naked and still pulling insects from my flesh, I had learned two important new lessons about Central Africa. First, I did not know enough about the forest to trudge around in it alone, and second, Driver ants were nasty tempered little beasts.

When I reached home again, a man was waiting in the yard for me. He wanted a site inspection as soon as I could get around to it. Discussing his property, he informed me that he had very strong, fast moving water running through the bottom of his little valley and that he wanted to build a pond above it somehow. I took him inside to draw some simple pictures, indicating that the water must be above, not below, his pond site. Could we achieve that somehow? No, not unless he could build an amazingly effectively dam. Hmm. Well, thanks anyway. He shook my hand with a grin and left, walking without haste toward the market.

Having listened to second year volunteers who had considerable experience trying to motivate the Congolese, I knew that most of them had never finished a single pond during their tenure and some had not even started one. Nobody seemed to have an explanation for that, leaving a person to draw whatever conclusions he or she might care to draw. And our own officials did not seem much concerned, one way or the other. Based on those facts, however, I could hardly believe the interest that had been generated in Makoua, or that it had happened so quickly. Feeling a burst of optimism, I went to see Herve for one more plea.

Because our second meeting at Mathieu's site was scheduled for the next morning, I told him once again that I would leave the motorcycle at home if he would join me. Perhaps deciding that his failure to participate might be catching up with him, his resistance weakened and he promised that he would go. We would meet at his house at seven o'clock.

Herve was probably in his middle thirties and seemed healthy and strong even though he had a few pounds of extra flesh around the middle. When we started toward the mission from his front yard, and the chilly mood between us resurfaced almost immediately, he was setting the pace with long quick strides, hopping briskly over obstacles as if his objective was to leave me behind. Hustling along beside him with shorter steps nearly at a run, realizing what he was up to, I praised him on the his brisk walk.

"This is excellent," I said happily. "Wonderful exercise." Herve only grunted in return.

We were certainly making good time. Nearing the point where we would turn off the main road, Mathieu came up behind us on his bicycle. "You are walking very fast," he said as he rode by. He went on ahead and then waited on the shoulder overlooking his land. When Herve and I caught up, we three descended together. The amount of work Mathieu had done was astounding. The grass that once reached above my head was gone, clipped close to the ground and piled out of the way like bales of hay. And it was done with only a machete. Large rocks that had been hidden in the grass, dozens of them, lay at the borders of the clearing. The entire field was clean and ready for the determinations to begin. The man was a marvel.

We started at the level of the spring. Helping me by holding poles, stretching the string and leveling it for new marks and more poles, Herve did whatever I asked him to do without complaint. I was secretly pleased to notice that he was studying my technique and simple tools, figuring out for himself exactly what was going on. He asked no questions, but at least he was interested. We spent three hours at the site before giving it a failing report. The water would have had to rise a meter or more before our system could work, which was clearly impossible. I wished the news could have been better, but the place was hopeless.

Mathieu revealed no hint that he was offended, or even terribly disappointed. He said he would plant corn or something there instead and maybe find another pond-site later. I regretted that his place was not suitable, for I would have enjoyed working with that exceptional man. He obviously had no fear of labor, and he had a wonderful attitude that I believed would lead him to success one way or another, whether luck was on his side or not. We shook hands before he led us back up the trail.

When Mathieu started his ride back toward home, the walk-race between Herve and me began anew at a pace just short of jogging. We crossed a ten foot long footbridge in three rapid steps. Going beside a line of shrubbery, he pushed a branch out of the way and let it swing back with a swish and a pop. Seeing it coming, I was already ducking when it flew toward my head. Herve did not look back.

Twenty minutes after leaving Mathieu and having probably established record time for the distance, Herve and I were standing in his front yard. We were both breathing a little hard and were probably both about whipped, but I would have suffered a heart attack before letting him know it.

"Thanks, Herve. I really enjoyed the walk. Let's do it again tomorrow on the way to Msr. Laurent's site."

"You can count me out," he fired back angrily. "I am not going six miles on foot when we could be riding the motorcycle. It's stupid!"

"I'm sorry to hear that, but I don't make the rules and I won't break them just because others do. If you change your mind, I'll wait until seven o'clock at my house."

I was frankly surprised at the resumption of his negative attitude. Clearly he did not understand my hard line about the motorcycle, and nothing else that I might have said would have resolved that. However I could not give in to his demands without making more problems for myself, and perhaps with a host of other people, and that was simply not going to happen.

Thus, for reasons entirely beyond my control, I had won the battle, but possibly lost the war.

15

The Trek to Etoumbi

Having received word from Brazzaville that we volunteers were to visit the posts of others in order to view whatever work was being done, I decided to go on a "walk about" to the equatorial village of Etoumbi is a village-town located in the high country sixty-three miles west of Makoua. Because I lacked any sure way to notify Linda that I would visit her, I could only assume that she would be home when I arrived and that she would be able to put me up for a night or two. Never having been to her post, it would be a great new adventure and a chance to clear my head of all the negatives that currently filled it.

When the day came for my departure, dawn found me hustling about with eagerness and anticipation. A breakfast of peanut butter and jelly on French bread satisfied my appetite, and the moment was at hand. My attire was composed of boots, a long sleeve cotton shirt, a red bandana tied around my neck, and a brightly pink baseball cap that someone back home gave me as a joke. My camping knife was secured on the leather belt around my waist. A machete, sheathed in goatskin, was strapped to the pack in case I had to camp in the wilderness, and my Swiss Army knife was clipped to a loop and stuffed inside a front pocket where forty dollars in small bills were tightly folded. A dozen pieces of small money were inside the other front pocket, intended for trading in villages along the way. The pack held my tent, sleeping bag, rubber bed roll, a change of underwear and tee shirt, my first aid kit, a compass, and a few tins of potted meat. My canteen was full of Gatorade, sent from home, and I had extra packets of the powder for later mixing,. I also had a few iodine tablets to treat whatever water might have to be taken from untested sources. My house was snugly bolted, the motorcycle was locked inside the kitchen, and I was out the front door without looking back.

Before reaching the grand marche, I was already creating a spectacle. Children who had seen me a hundred times before rushed to the street to stare at the mysterious things mounted on my back and then they grinned and waved excitedly.

Men resting in hammocks lifted their eyes but not their bodies, watching suspiciously as they usually did. Little girls got out of my way, giving me a wide berth while adult women moved to the sides of the street. They all turned as I passed and observed me with critical eyes, but they did not speak. Making my way through the narrow passages of the morning market, being careful not to snag my gear on drooping tin or jutting nails, I selected three bars of chocolate and two loaves of bread, bought from women who did not wait until my back was turned to talk about me.

Before reaching Marin's house, I was discovered by Kevin, the boy whom I had met at the Catholic church, who was on his way to the market. Next came Prudence who was simply drifting with the dust. They both fell into step at my side, demanding to know what I was up to. Marin, brushing his teeth in his front yard, saw us coming from a block away. He joined us too, and wanted to carry my pack.

"It's light," he said cheerfully, as we four walked down the middle of the yellow road and ignored curious people who gathered at its edge.

"Probably about thirty-five pounds," I told him.

"It seems much less."

He wanted to know if I planned to walk the entire distance to Etoumbi, how long it would take and where I would sleep along the way. I explained that it was my ambition to travel twenty-one miles each day so that my trek would last only three days. Hopefully, there would be conveniently located villages where my tent could be pitched each night, where potable water would be found, and where food could be bought.

"You must not sleep in the open," Marin warned. "Many of the animals are dangerous at night. Even during the day it is possible to meet some dangerous ones."

"Will I see big cats?" I asked him with utter innocence.

"No," he replied. "But they will see you!" He explained that a large animal was not likely to get close unless it had been wounded by a hunter and it was very hungry. "In that case," he said, "don't worry. Then it will be too late to worry."

When we had gone about two miles, Marin changed his mind about the lightness of my pack. He wished me a safe journey, almost like saying it was nice knowing me and then he turned toward home. Prudence took a turn at the pack then, bending forward as he went. He tried to keep a smile on his face, but my sense was that he was unaccustomed to that particular kind of exercise.

When we reached the road that went behind the abandoned airport, the boys wanted to show me a shortcut. They led me in front of the defunct office, then the storage shed, then between two posts of a broken fence where the road gradually disappeared under vegetation. There it narrowed into a clay trail that cut through the middle of the property. When we reached the tarmac, Kevin took over the pack and grinned at the feel of it.

"It is nothing," he said.

Once across the strip, we followed another trail that snaked through about three hundred yards of head-high grass. Once beyond that, we began a long, gradual descent from which I could see a forested valley in the distance. Ten minutes later we were standing on sandy clay, as we were once again in the middle of the long yellow road to Etoumbi. We had saved about a mile by cutting off that corner, and we had reached a place at which the boys would terminate their part of the trek. Walking alone for another five minutes or so, I glanced back for a final look. Both of them were still standing there watching me go as if my departure was a truly impressive sight. They waved, turned, and disappeared into the grass from which we had come.

Trekking between gorgeous green valleys under the ever intensifying sun, time seemed to gear down and the world around me grew nearly silent. Soon, walking in ruts that my own motorcycle had rolled in before, my boots sank deeply into the sand and squeaked musically with every step. I had expected that my walks around Makoua, sometimes as much as twelve miles a day, would have adequately prepared me for my march. But conditions had been different then. Most of my previous walking had been on hard ground, much of it had been at a relaxed pace, and some of it had been in shaded forests. Furthermore I had not carried a pack on my back, and usually I had been in the company of others who offered diversion. Maybe the psychological impact of what I was doing had begun to sink in, for within two hours my feet were starting to feel hot and my pack seemed to have doubled in weight. Part of the problem was that my boots, straight off the working man's rack at K-Mart, were improperly fitted and thoroughly inappropriate for the task.

I recalled being told by someone during training that my pack was not well suited to hiking because the straps were too narrow and they had no padding. I then realized that the trip could turn out be much longer in reality than it had been in my thoughts. Not having taken any water yet, I stopped at the foot of a hill and lifted my canteen with the realization that consumption would increase rapidly from there on. Knowing the danger of dehydration, I would have to find a source of replacement soon.

Recalling a former motorcycle exploration along the same route, I recognized a long ninety degree turn where smooth clay turned into white waves of sand. If my memory was accurate, that place was about six miles from Makoua. And if so, I was averaging three miles per hour. At that rate, I should reach my first target-village in about five more hours. That was a brisk pace, even better than I had anticipated, but it was early yet. Already the pack was pressing heavily down and cutting into my skin, forcing me to frequently adjust the straps. Furthermore, my feet were already wincing a bit and the sun burned onto my neck with the heat of a branding iron. Already my underarms were saturated, and droplets of sweat were popping from under the brim of my cap. And already the full gravity of what lay ahead was settling in. My adventure just might turn into an ordeal.

Soon I was taking liquid every mile or so, until the canteen was nearly empty. Thirty minutes later I reached a small village that I had once passed on the motorcycle but entirely missed. I must have been going too fast to notice the six mud huts sheltered under a line of trees on one side of the road. Stopping there and calling out the traditional "kokoko," I was very happy to see a middle aged woman approaching. She met me at the wooden gate that guarded the compound.

"May I get some water?" I asked her.

"Yes," she politely responded. "I will show you the spring." She instructed me to leave my pack on a bench and follow her, which I did, but only with her reassurance that it would not be disturbed.

"Nobody else is here to disturb it," she said.

We headed into the thick of the forest behind the village, descending on a damp trail. Momentarily we stopped so that she might grab a basket filled with manioc roots. The load must have been very heavy, much heavier than my pack, but she got her arms through the straps with relative ease and moved on ahead of me, leaning forward as she went.

As we made our way down the valley wall, she suddenly tripped on a root and tumbled violently down a ten foot drop. As her load scattered around her, she wound up flat on her back, moaning softly and holding her knee between her hands. I went quickly to her, fearing that she had broken her leg, but she looked at me with fierce determination and slowly rolled to one side. Pulling on my arm for support, she got back to her feet and gingerly tested the ground with her weight. Soon she was firmly upright, offering no complaint, and without uttering another sound of pain as she waited for me to reload her basket. When we reached the valley floor, she pointed to gurgling water, welcomed me to help myself, then she made her way over the spring and disappeared into the brush.

Fifteen minutes later, on the road again with no idea when the next water might be found, I was acutely aware that my supply must be conserved. Running out too soon could spell serious trouble for a person so far from help, and I had no idea how far the next village might be. Moving steadily on, curve after curve, straightaway after straightaway, hill after valley, miles of yellow clay fell behind me as the hours passed.

All the sights that I had seen up to that point seemed very different from those viewed from a speeding motorcycle, and all of the sounds that I heard were totally new. During rides, it had not been possible to hear the muffled rush of water as it tumbled down a steep drop, or the noises of startled animals hurrying through the brush, or the calls of birds from their hiding places on either side of the road. I did not recall seeing an abandoned hut under a dozen banana trees, or a little burial site with three graves, or even the fresh and wonderful view of forest that faded into the horizon.

Nearly three hours later, I heard human voices among some papaya trees to my right. Indeed, practically at my feet was a trail leading into that direction. Following it a short distance, a tiny village came plainly into view. Three mud-and-thatch houses were on the edge of a grand valley, perfectly concealed from the road. Three men and two very old women were sitting in the courtyard talking, completely oblivious to my approach.

As I drew nearer and finally caught their attention, they all seemed startled as if my intrusion had not only surprised them but unsettled them as well. Surely they could see that I was just a hot and tired traveler, but they did not offer me a drink nor a place to sit. They simply stared. Spying a bunch of fresh bananas in the grass near one of the men, I asked if I might buy a few. The price in Makoua would have been about ten cents each, but those people wanted five times as much. That at least proved that some villagers of the Congo had learned one of foremost rules of capitalism, which was to charge what the market would bear. I was too hot to bicker. I bought one banana, paid for it with exact change, filled my canteen from a plastic container, and walked away as they tried to sell me some palm wine.

Not long after that, my hike took me through a little village that I happened to remember. The huts appeared to have been abandoned when I first rode into it, and it still appeared so. All six of them seemed entirely without life, but for a few chickens pecking in the dirt. Sometimes when young men and women departed those little villages in search of different lifestyles, the old folks who remained were forced to work much harder to survive. And when the last of the villagers died out, their buildings often remained as they stood. Sometimes people would use the old villages as bases, like range camps when hunting or working crops near by, but I felt an eerie sense of discomfort while walking between huts with open doors and windows but with no sign of human life. Passing quickly through, I figured that I must have traveled about fifteen miles by then. Every sight from there would be entirely new.

Thirsty but nearly out of water again, drenched in sweat and craving a good place to rest, one foot still moved ahead of the other as the sun dropped lower and lower in the western sky. A speck of movement appeared far ahead, growing larger as the distance between us narrowed until I could see that it was a man on a bicycle. Dragging his sandals on the clay and wearing a puzzled look on his face, he stopped to greet me. "Where are you going?" he wanted to know. Satisfied with my response, he then told me of a spring about two miles ahead that was good for swimming and safe for drinking. Also, he informed me, there was a nice village for camping another few miles up the road. I thanked him kindly and started moving again.

The rest of the way to the creek came with more than a little pain, and my blistered feet were crying out for rest. But simply seeing the place was rejuvenating. Exactly what I had hoped for, the water was wide and fast, and it looked cold and inviting. The plank bridge was ten of my paces across, relatively new and quite sturdy, such that my boots landed solidly with each step. Stopping in the middle of it to look, I noticed that the water turned sharply a few yards away, and disappeared into the brush leaving only loud gurgles to speak of its fate. Stepping off the end of the planking and onto the shoulder, I made my way down a sandy bank, clinging to the grass for balance, and shed my pack at the bottom. I undressed to the skin, threw my clothes over some bushes, and jumped into the middle of an icy shock. Uncharacteristically, I gave no consideration as to what creatures or objects might be beneath the surface. The water was over my head, and I found it to be cold and sweet to the taste. The experience was wonderfully invigorating.

After only two or three minutes in the water, I returned to the dry sand and took out a loaf of bread and ate it with a tin of potted meat. Appetite satisfied, I then took about fifteen minutes of rest before jumping into the water again. My feet had come back to life, even though I had large blisters on both heels and little ones forming on the tips of each of my toes. Uncertain whether to pop them or leave them alone, I left them alone. Maybe the chill of the water would be therapy enough.

Retrieving my shirt, I discovered that it was absolutely alive with Driver ants. Thousands of them were all over the ground at my feet and crawling all over the bushes on which I had tossed my clothes to dry. They must have been attracted to the sweat. Taking care to avoid the insects on the ground, I grabbed the shirt quickly but carefully and dipped it into the creek, submerging it for several seconds, then I shook it out, submerged it again, and repeated the dunking until every insect had been washed away. Luckily the ants had not found my pants yet, and I had intended to douse the shirt anyway. I gave them a wide berth, clothing in hand, and kept an eye on them as I dressed. Just as I made my way back to the top of the bank, I met another surprise. Two men on bicycles, just then rolling to the foot of the bridge, were clearly shocked to see a white man crawling up the bank. They stopped, they eyed my pack and other possessions, they inquired about my business, where I was going and why, and they listened with great interest to the answers.

They seemed mystified that a seemingly rational person would walk to Etoumbi, for surely nothing was there to attract a person, and even if an attraction existed, surely a rich white man could afford to ride. Taking such a walk "for fun" was a notion that seemed beyond them to fathom. But they did seem to be genuinely impressed. They told me of a village six more miles up the road where it would be safe to sleep, and where plenty of food and water would be available. They wished me luck and rode on, talking vigorously about what they had seen.

Six more miles! Six more long miserable miles! As the two men pedaled into the distance, I actually considered pitching my tent right there by the stream. My feet would have appreciated the gesture. But I recalled Marin's warning about the creatures that could be dangerous at night. Sleeping alone with ants, pythons, big cats, or whatever else might be smacking its lips from inside the forest, was simply not the wisest decision that a person could make. I had no reasonable choice. I would walk the six miles.

My canteen was full of iodine treated water again, my pack was strapped on once more, my cap was tilted a little more forward to defeat the falling sun, and my feet were already burning inside my boots. I would make it, that I knew beyond doubt, but I would probably collapse when I got there. Six more miles!

Before another quarter of a mile was behind me, I was stepping lightly while sweat was boiling from every pore and the straps of the pack were slicing into my skin. I said to myself that if a truck happened along, I just might hitch a ride the rest of the way to Etoumbi. Actually I knew that no truck was likely to come so late in the day, for they did not run at night on roads so rough. Not a single motorized vehicle had come from either direction all day. Short of leaving the road and entering the forest, I was about as isolated as a person could get. Six more miles!

Months ago I had learned to predict the nearness of humanity along most any trail in the Congo, for the signs were always the same. Manioc fields and occasional crops of corn extended outward a few kilometers from each village, well-worn trails leading into them would appear, and a cemetery would be found at one end or both of each community. And as a person drew closer, women and little girls would often be walking along the shoulders of the road moving to or from their crops.

As for a foolish white man with a heavy load, another two hours later I found myself limping past two long slabs of concrete covered with little ceramic squares that looked like floor-tiles. Three mounds of dirt adjacent to those had been adorned with plastic dishes and household glasses, long since broken to bits. A small village was surely near. Just then a woman emerged from the forest about three hundred yards ahead of me. She rushed along the edge of the road without having noticed that I was behind her. Although she was carrying a load of wood on her back, laboring on feet that seemed to move more slowly than mine, the distance between us remained the same until, about ten minutes later, she finally sensed my presence and stopped to see. She turned, looked me squarely in the eyes, and stared for perhaps a half minute. Then she went on and soon disappeared over the hill.

The village of Talengai was one with seven houses and one central paillote, three houses on one side of the road and four on the other, all set deeply back in bare yards. Several children, fascinated and infinitely curious, eased toward me as I went limping into the heart of the village. Their reaction to me was the same everywhere I had been. The boys drew close, but the girls stayed well out of reach always ready to bolt. A tall man who appeared to be in his mid twenties came from the central paillote to meet me, hand extended. His name, he said, was Serge. There was no chief of his village, he told me, but he was in charge even though he lacked the title. He welcomed me to pitch my tent near his own house, have dinner with him, and stay as long as I cared to stay.

Under the close observation of every man, woman and child in Talengai, my tent was erected on a flat piece of ground near the road. The lightweight fabric was designed to open into a broad dome under sturdy but flexible poles that stretched it out. The poles, secured at their tips in canvas pouches, bent upward in the middle lifting the material to its peak and then locked securely in place against the weather. Zippered flaps in the back and front would hold out the rain if any came, while a layer of mosquito netting at both ends allowed air to penetrate without the insects.

Musing over the prolonged "oooooooh" that marked each step of the process, I gave everyone a chance to see inside when it was done. When the front was unzipped to display the mosquito net, a loud exclamation of surprise went up, followed by laughter.

"C'est bon," remarked Serge with his thumb up.

When the excitement died down and we males had all gone inside the grand paillote, I was allowed to rest a few minutes surrounded by silent but hungry children. The men were loudly talking about the strange American who had appeared in their midst, but only Serge spoke to me directly. He explained that he had heard of me already. That was because he often went through Makoua in a truck on which he worked either as mechanic or as a driver. My presence there, he claimed, had more than once been the subject of conversation. Serge was also a "commercant," buying goods along the various routes and reselling them wherever he could find a market. And he was also interested in fish-culture. I chose not tell him that his village was beyond my territorial limit.

Suggesting a bath at the river Serge led several of us on a half-mile walk through the forest over a trail which my burning feet were barely able to negotiate, but I tried to keep my mind on the relief soon to come. Nearing the water, we passed a series of large buildings that Serge said were for storage, although he never mentioned what might have been stored there. Whatever it was, I deduced that it served some purpose related to the transportation of freight on the river. I had not realized before how the "highway" so closely followed the Likouala-Mossaka river. If one had the urge, it would have been possible to float all the way back to Makoua in a pirogue. Establishing villages so close to the river made perfect sense, just as it made sense to have major thoroughfares running through them. The logic was all about need and convenience.

When we reached the water, it came as no surprise that it looked exactly as it did when it passed through Makoua…pitch black, shiny, ominous and bordered by lush green banks. Assuring me there were no crocodiles about, Serge and several of the boys stripped and jumped in. When they had splashed about for a minute or two and made enough noise to frighten away any dangerous creatures, I joined them but took my clothes with me for an equally good cleaning. As always, the river was cold and refreshing, and my body was coming back to life again.

The sun was nearly down when we returned to the village, but Serge was not done yet with his hospitality. He and his friends wanted to show me a special place not more than a hundred feet beyond the edge of the forest. It was a huge fallen palm tree, partially covered at one end with banana leaves where a large hole had been gouged into the trunk. It was a palm wine factory. I was handed a paper cone, filled directly from the container in which the liquid had been captured, and I was treated to a round of the freshest, sweetest and most potent beverage that I had yet sampled in Africa.

Later, shortly after dark and back in the central paillote again, Serge and I were seated before a dinner of saka saka (which some Americans called "grass") and another green leafy delight called "koko," along with cooked fish and a supply of boiled manioc. Not long after that, wined and tranquilized, fed and satisfied, I realized once again just how tired I really was. The time was barely seven o'clock P.M., but I could take no more. I made my excuses and retired to the tent.

As I crawled inside and stretched out on top of the sleeping bag and rubber mat, it came painfully back to me that I had walked nearly twenty-one miles under the blazing equatorial sun without having first conditioned my body to the task. My blisters hurt like cigarette burns, all of my muscles were sore, and every part of my skin that had been exposed to the sun had been cooked by it. Maybe it was the palm wine that gave me relief, possibly aided by several aspirin, but soon my thoughts were focused on creatures of the forest. Mysterious calls provided the perfect backdrop as I stretched out with my hands behind my head and listened to the music of nature. Hardly noticing the hard ground on which my body was resting, I was soon asleep for the night. I didn't even hear the rain.

When I awoke with the chickens and was about to begin day two of my trek, I had been a resident of Makoua nearly four months and I was beginning to feel acclimated to the Congo. When out of the tent in the haze of early dawn, Serge had gone into the forest already and most of the women and girls had gone to their fields. A few small children and two older men were busily moving to and from the grand paillote as if engaged in some important activity that required trips back and forth. As for me, no one seemed interested anymore. A new day had come to Talengai.

I found myself faced with a difficult decision. The tent was thoroughly wet from the night's rainfall, and my clothes, having hung outside all night, were dripping as well. Everything needed time to dry, but on that humid morning, drying could have taken hours which I did not want to spend there. Because the light of day was coming fast and time was ticking, I would either start right then or waste valuable daylight which might become critical as the day wore on. Such waste would also reduce my options in selecting the next overnight stop, and might force me to camp in some abandoned village or in an isolated place on the road.

I would have been content enough to stay another night and enjoy the rest, for Serge had already invited me to do so, but I am one of those persons cursed with a dogged need to follow the plan. There was another more practical consideration. My feet were a mess. There was a chance that a truck would come and I would be able to hitch a ride. However if one happened along while I rested in the village, I would have missed my chance. No truck would wait for me to pack my gear. Furthermore, since one might not come for a day or two, my hike to Etoumbi would probably have been completed by then if only I stayed on the move. The answer was clear to me. I would stick with my goal, even though I would start out in wet clothes that would have to dry on my body.

After packing my gear, and after the customary round of handshaking with those who were still about, an old man with several missing teeth wanted me to give him my cap, my knife, some money, or at least my bandana. I did not believe he would have made a demand like that if Serge had been there. I refused politely and started out, limping on blisters and bruised heels.

Clearly, my progress that day would not be three miles per hour, for my steps were shorter and slower. I tried not to think about that, and tried to stay focused on what the journey would mean to me in the end. I had enjoyed many pleasures so far, but the sounds had been the most striking. I had heard animals calling from the forest as if to warn other creatures that a human was on the move and then I noted utter silence until I had passed. Occasionally a startled creature crashed through the brush, giving me a moment of pause, and once a monkey went sailing among tree branches to get out of sight. Surely there were dangerous animals hidden in there somewhere, but probably because they had learned to fear man, none appeared. The clock continued to tick.

Time was passing at a crawl as the sun climbed slowly and my personal motivation steadily slipped. Several hours into the walk, hills seemed to grow taller as the strip of road went endlessly like an orange streak on a green canvas. Erosion was so bad in places that the road seemed too dangerous for any vehicle to drive over it. That, I thought, might explain the lack of traffic, for if a wheel slipped into one of those ruts it would have to be jacked out. The road was tricky even to walk over, in some of those stretches. That was especially true where the ground was still damp from a night of rain, and water still lay in the trenches.

As time continued to pass and the skies finally cleared, the sun's rays bore down relentlessly on my burned skin while I hobbled down a steep grade where the forest was much thicker, much darker, much damper, much quieter, and somehow more sinister than before. And I froze in my tracks. A sleek, black cat was crossing the road no more than twenty paces in front of me. The beast was about four feet long, probably weighed close to two hundred pounds, and it was deadly quiet as it slipped over the clay. Sensing my presence, it halted in mid-step and turned its head toward me. Its yellow eyes met mine for a long moment, then it simply eased into the brush and disappeared. If it wanted me, I deduced, it would have already taken me. As I crossed over the very tracks of the beast, perhaps only a pounce away, I never felt any sense of danger. That was the Africa that I had come to see.

Three hours into the morning hike, my clothes were finally dry. But my skin was beginning to chafe where the coarse fabric had sandpapered it. Little could I do about that, for my first-aid kit did not include any appropriate medication. All I could do was take breaks now and then, hope for cold swims, and tolerate my self-induced plight.

Having been told in Talengai that I would find a large village about ten miles farther on, it seemed that after so long I should have reached it already. But none of the usual indicators had yet appeared. Maybe I would stop at the next spring for a long rest. Maybe I would set up camp and remain there for the rest of the day. Maybe I would stay for the night. And maybe I would find myself inside the belly of a python. Maybe I would stop whining and just keep moving.

The day before, I had started comparatively late in the day, I had benefited from assistance through the first few miles, and I had walked a considerable distance before having to consume water. But that was then. Having started the second morning just after the first rays of sunlight, walking alone and under a greater state of stress, sweat continually seeped from my skin and I was drinking about two pints of water per hour. I knew, by then, that there was no real danger of dying of thirst in that part of the country. Water was seldom far from the road. However if there was no trail leading to it, the search would have been time consuming and the risks would have been serious indeed. Having no practical choice, when it was time to refill the canteen the first time that morning, it was done from a ditch. I treated it with iodine, of course, which meant I could not drink it for at least a half hour, and it would not last long once my consumption began. Fortunately, just at high-noon, I limped past a very old clearing with fourteen graves. A large village was near.

Bakonga was the large mud and thatch community that Serge told me about. Unfortunately I had averaged only about two miles per hour in getting there. Serge also told me that trucks routinely stopped in Bakonga to buy bush meat, and that a few white people visited there from time to time, usually missionaries and foreign aid workers, so I would not be unique. But the news of the strange man walking to Etoumbi seemed somehow to have preceded me.

When children spotted me coming up the hill, scurrying took place and the assemblage began. Surely the entire village must have been on hand as I walked down the center of the courtyard like a one man parade. Some gathered along bamboo fences or stood under huge palms like characters in an old Western movie, watching the approach of a suspicious stranger. Some stood near open doorways or peeked from behind houses, but none of the adults came to meet me. Some of the older boys met me however, and walked along with me, step for step, five abreast. Young girls were there as well, but as always, safely out of reach.

I stopped at a display of bananas next to the road and asked a man if it might be possible to buy a pineapple, and take a few minutes of rest somewhere in a shady place. Nodding affirmatively, he motioned me to follow him toward a huge paillote where at least thirty young boys followed me inside. They all studied me as I took a seat on a bamboo bench. Gathering closely around me, too closely, crowding me, they stared quietly as I removed my boots to reveal blisters that had increased both in number and in size. The boys might have been more interested in my boots than the white of my feet, but the talking that took place among them was done in whispers and with sideways glances.

When my pineapple arrived already cut into manageable chunks, an ever growing crowd of perhaps fifty people watched me eat every bite. Girls were standing all around the outside of the hut, peeping through spaces in the bamboo walls, while older villagers had assembled to observe from a respectable distance. A young man who appeared to be spokesman for the group encouraged me stay.

"You are welcome to camp wherever you like," he said. "But if you go on, there is no other village for another twelve miles."

That was a tempting notion. Thirty miles lay yet ahead of me before Etoumbi, and a dozen more stood between me and a safe night of rest. Considering my average progress for the day, it would take about six more hours to get there, if I made it at all. But my confidence had taken a beating.

Continuing with my reasoning, if I decided to camp in Bakonga, any possibility of catching a ride the rest of the way would definitely be lost for at least another day. While no truck would wait for me to break camp, the same truck finding me on the road would likely pick me up. Also, in Bakonga I was a one man circus. Rest during the day might not be possible, while sleeping in such a large village would not necessarily be safe from mischief. The ever present reality in Central Africa, was that the people might never before have even seen such possessions as those that I carried on my back. I was a rich white man while they were poor, and the temptation for some of them might have been great. I finished the pineapple while someone refilled my canteen, then I thanked them all for their kindness and moved on. One of the younger boys walked with me for a while but finally said farewell and turned back.

Shoulders on fire under the straps of my pack, movements stiff on aching feet, face sunburned and lips chapped, the next several hours passed like slow motion frames of a war movie as I kept going like a military captive on a forced march. Uphill I went, where sunlit grasses waved in gentle breezes and then downhill I went into patches of musty forest. Next I was trudging over clay and sand, washouts and standing water, and over bridges with stagnant pools beneath them. Late in the day I descended into a valley where a circle of daylight shone far ahead in the brush like a brilliant hole at the end of a tunnel. Inside that tunnel, while enjoying the coolness of the air, I found a little stream of fast water. There I took a seat on a log to bathe my feat, and to eat the last of my food.

Suddenly three young girls stepped onto the road just behind me, probably coming from manioc pools inside the wall of brush. Chattering happily, they failed to notice me for the first few steps, but then they all spotted me at once. They bolted to the opposite side of the road and regrouped there, nervously alert, watching my every move like birds ready to take flight. I tried to dispel their fears with smiles and cheerful words while not moving from my perch. I asked them which village they were from and how far it was yet ahead, but they did not respond. They stood mute at the far edge of the road and stared in near panic. Half expecting them to start running and wondering why they did not, I decided that they simply did not know which way to go or whether I might be able to catch them. Momentarily I gave up, fitted on my boots and watched the girls grow tense as I started out again. I knew that they would remain behind for a time, thus increasing the distance between us, but I did feel better because of them. Finding people was a good sign, even if they refused to speak. The next village had to be relatively close.

Climbing yet another hill and entering a new stretch of plains, I began to notice several different kinds of animal tracks in the road. Dog tracks had appeared throughout that leg of my journey, but I found a few antelope tracks as well, and finally those of a cat. And that cat was big! I moved with renewed spirit. The time was three o'clock in the afternoon, and I had been on the road nine hours already.

Uphill and downhill I went, scattering literally thousands of brilliantly colored butterflies that took flight as my steps fell among them. Some were yellow, some were white, and some were jet black until sunlight shined through their delicate wings to expose rich purple. They must have been feeding on something in the road, for the clay was covered with them as far as I could see. Making colorful waves when they rose before my steps, they flew all about me until I was past their chosen places, and then they settled quickly back in pastel ripples.

Like a scene out of *Tobacco Road*, the highway before me was clay-red mixed with stretches of gravel-white, but there were no people, no fields, no cemeteries yet, and the sun had already fallen to the forest line. My goal had to be close, for even at two miles per hour I had to have gone at least 19 miles since leaving Talengai. Knowing I could not go much longer without rest, and knowing that estimates of the distance to the village might have been incorrect, I decided to climb one more hill and then camp in the next clearing whether it was inhabited or not.

As fate would have it, at the crest of the hill I came upon the telltale cemetery. And soon I saw the first of about thirty thatched houses set back under palm and banana trees. I had made it after all, covering about forty-two miles in two days, and I felt that I had accomplished something significant in my personal quest for adventure. I had also learned valuable lessons. Just then, as I had visions of sleeping inside my tent in a hard rain, I heard a vehicle coming behind me. It was the same old Toyota that I had seen in Makoua several times before.

My decision was instantaneous. If it stopped, I would ride the rest of the way to Etoumbi and never look back. One of the men sitting on top of the vehicle signaled for the driver to stop as if they had expected to find me sooner or later and to take me aboard. I lost no time. Stepping up on the back bumper, I grabbed the crash cage and pulled myself aboard to stand at the very back. There were twenty-two other people in and on the vehicle, counting one man on a fender, one on the cab, and of course the driver and two passengers inside. None of those in the back seemed very happy to have yet another person in their midst. Some of the men greeted me, but the women simply sat on the floor with their children, silently observing the then famous but slightly crazy American from Makoua. All I could do was grin.

The vehicle was a rolling junk heap. Rattling and squawking as it bounced along, it sharply listed to one side over an obviously broken spring. And the driver seemed to be having trouble keeping the wheels in the ruts. Probably the steering mechanism was shot, along with everything else, for maintenance was not a widely practiced concept in the Congo. As we rolled through the village with the brakes applied, I could hear the harsh grinding of metal on metal. Thankfully, we did not have to stop.

The man sitting on the roof was a standard feature on such vehicles. He was the guide whose job it was to blow a whistle when he saw a section of the road that looked too dangerous for the loaded truck. When he signaled, the vehicle would stop and everybody would get out, or off, so that the truck could slowly go through the danger zone. Finally, at the other end, the truck would stop and wait for the passengers to catch up and climb aboard again. A while later, the man standing next to me got my attention. He asked if I had any idea why so many people were dying in the Congo.

"I suppose there might be many causes," I said back, "but I really don't know". The truth was I had not given much thought to the matter, and didn't know what "so many people" meant to him.

"There is only one answer," he said defiantly. "They are dying from sorcery."

"Ah," I responded, as if to say "Of course. I should have known."

"Yes, it is a big problem." As we talked another man nodded in agreement. Finally the fellow with all the information wanted to know why I was walking to Etoumbi, and he quite seriously wondered if I might be out of my mind.

"No," I responded. "I was, perhaps two days ago. But not anymore."

Just as we made it to the bottom of the first hill after the village, the whistle sounded and the routine began. A little girl about eight years old had been sitting on a man's lap where she was cushioned against the violent rocking. When we all unloaded, the wide eyed girl was carried in the man's arms to the next point of reloading. My guess was that she suffered from some condition which made it difficult, or impossible, for her to walk. She looked healthy enough, but I was sure that she was either sick, or weak from some infirmity. As the man climb back on board with her, her lips turned down and her chin wrinkled, but the tears never came.

We passed village after village as we hurried along then, mostly small ones, but each had a large number of graves at its boundaries. Many of those graves appeared to be relatively new, and many of them were covered by very small mounds that indicated children. So many people died in the Congo, I suspected, because medical care was not readily available and because injuries or insect borne diseases were everyday risks. No sorcerer could do a better job than nature.

We did not reach Etoumbi until the sun was almost completely gone, but the town was very much alive as the night marche was just starting up. No sooner did my boots touch the ground than a man approached me to ask if I was looking for Linda, the American woman.

"Yes," I told him. "I am".

"Then you are in luck. She is approaching."

Indeed, Linda was walking across a field from the direction of the Hotel Mea, a complex that looked rather like a small town motel back home, and was perched on a ledge overlooking a magnificent view of the rain forest hundreds of feet below. When she reached me, Linda was amazed to learn of my trek.

"What could possibly motivate you to do such a thing?

"It was for pleasure, mostly," I said back, realizing just how goofy the words must have sounded. As I hobbled along beside her, headed to her house, I marveled at the deep open canyon that we had to cross to get there.

"It must have taken some years to carve that out of the earth," I said as I looked down about fifty feet to the bottom. Evidently some people had decided to make a trash dump out of it, caring naught for the water that went straight into the river less than a quarter of a mile away.

"I guess so. At least one guy died recently when he fell from the cross walk. He was drunk, so they said." The cross walk she mentioned was a pair of heavy planks that had been put over the most narrow place of the canyon.

As we crossed, I was extra careful to keep my eyes on the boards and not on the long fall below. Heights were one of my many weaknesses. Ten minutes later, while I was stretched out on the bamboo bed in Linda's living room and waiting for her to find something in her medical kit to ease my pains, all I cared about was relieving my blisters and getting rest. My mission had been two thirds accomplished, hardly acceptable by my normal standards, but, I mused, when I was completely healed maybe I would make up for it by walking back to Makoua.

The next day we went so see Linda's main work site, which was a flat piece of ground, several acres large, with dozens of old fish ponds. The ponds had been constructed by foreigners years before, but they had not been very productive in a long time. Linda had been working with the owner to turn them into ponds that would meet the rigid specifications of the Peace Corps, but she had not had much success. He had cooperated for a while but then lost interest and abandoned the project. That was a shame, actually, for if he had properly constructed his acreage, he could have become the fish-baron of the northern Congo.

Two days later, mostly healed and ready to travel again, I caught a truck to Kelle, another equatorial village where another volunteer lived and worked. Kelle was located in the high country, and was spread over a radius of perhaps a mile, scattered over hills near the Gabon border. There I moved in with Larry. We walked to a distant village in the forest the next morning, from where it was said that a person could actually see Gabon on a clear day. And then we looked at a nearly completed fish pond on the outskirts of town, where his farmer seemed to have just about lost interest. His was a proper hole in the ground, neatly shaped and sloped, but it had never been completely filled, never stocked, and several children were playing in it that day. Following two nights with nothing better to do than to lie around and read, we talked a little and rested a lot. Finally, during the third day, my American companion was able to find me a ride back to Etoumbi in a government vehicle. So began a two day return to my own post, but I had a whole new attitude and a greatly improved appreciation for the isolated Congolese countryside.

And it would be good to be home.

16

Crash in the Forest

My conviction had long been that any of our leaders visiting from Brazzaville should use the occasion to help volunteers overcome any lingering difficult problems, and also to critique any work that was in progress. Since those leaders had been remiss in that area, it was wonderful to learn that the policy had finally changed.

When Eric arrived in mid-March, only six months after my posting, he was in the company of his own homologue, a Brazzaville resident and government employee named August. The two men slept in my house that night, and arose at dawn the next morning ready to go to work. Makoua had four ponds in progress at the time, with potential for a half dozen more at the same sites. Eric wanted to see them all. Following omelets and sweet coffee at a local cafe, we three started our day at Michel's site which was well under way by then. Michel was a happy farmer to have so much positive attention, and Eric and August seemed truly impressed with what they saw.

Next, we went to Laurrent's place, deep in the jungle. Laurrent and his companion stopped their labors when we arrived, and they stood back to watch while Eric rechecked all of my original measurements. When that was done and the official evaluation confirmed my own, Eric suggested digging the pond as close to the back of the site as we could, farther from the spring head. He believed we could eventually add a second pond on the other side of the source-canal that ran through the middle of the parcel. The farmer was pleased to hear the suggestion, for that was exactly what he already had in mind.

Boreffe's place was next on the list. Everyone agreed that his was a fine location for several ponds, but they were frankly amazed that one man had so quickly cleared and drained the entire property. The pride in Boreffe's eyes said all that needed to be said. He was ecstatic, Eric and August were very pleased and I was brimming over.

Finally we visited Tscendou's cooperative, where six men laboring together planned to build at least three ponds. Standing on the side of the wide hill, looking over the place where one dig was underway and the others were projected, Eric and August were nothing short of elated. The site was perfect, the work being done was truly impressive, and they could not speak enough praise for the men who did it all. Next came a huge surprise. Things were going so well in Makoua that Eric wanted to have an informal meeting with all my farmers that very night. And he was buying.

After the setting of the sun, our gathering took place at a bar where all of the fish-farmers were on hand at the appointed time. A round of beer set the mood, followed by a brief congratulatory speech from Eric, then came another surprise. Eric handed out special fish-culture buttons and stickers to everyone. Rarely receiving any form of tangible recognition for a job well done, those trinkets, made in the U.S.A., were perfect. The Congolese truly loved them. One of the farmers pointed out that he had no glass window to put his four-inch sticker on, but he would find a suitable place to display it. And he would wear his button every day. Surely the next morning, when the buttons were worn for the other villagers to admire, more people would wish they had been included.

Eric and August left the next morning, heading for Etoumbi and Kelle, while I fell deeper into my work. Sometimes Herve was with me and sometimes not, but it had been a busy week. I had visited each of my work-sites at least twice, helping to eliminate any confusion and working to keep the labor on track. I had given several more recruiting presentations, and a number of new inspections had been conducted. Makoua's aqua-culture project seemed to be on a roll.

Michel had been going about town pumped with excitement, telling of his goal to become the community's biggest producer of fish. Indeed, his enthusiasm might have sparked something new, for I began to sense a subtle mood of competition among the project-farmers. I loved it! Competition could do more to move our program forward than any other single influence, and as the competition was generated by the farmers themselves, it would only bring more attention to the work and more quality to the finished products.

Not long ago, our Director, Bob, was replaced by a man named Jaime. Theirs was the product of a normal rotation which, in my judgment, kept people from getting stale at their jobs and helped to prevent such positions from becoming overly politicized. I had already been told to expect Jaime to visit Makoua soon, as he was making a countrywide tour of the various posts. His arrival in Makoua was scheduled for the very next day.

Trying to spruce things up as much as I could at home, and finish any little domestic projects that lingered, I spent some of the day cleaning up inside and some working in the yard. My back yard garden was beautiful, with its long rows of several kinds of vegetables, but it was a battle to keep out the chickens and goats. Herds of goats ran free all over town, no matter how much of a nuisance they were to others, and they did not seem particularly intimidated when I threatened them with rocks.

If someone killed a person's goat in Makoua, the owner of the animal must be compensated according to the owner's stated price. Yet no such compensation was due the owner of a garden that was destroyed. As the farmer was expected to protect his own plot, failure to do so was viewed as his problem. Having that in mind, that morning I erected a crude fence of bamboo and palm branches to deflect the traveling herd of goats. Everything came down when the first animal pushed against it.

Then, caught up with my chores, I had something else in mind for the remaining seven hours of daylight. I had learned of a village that was supposed to be located several miles away along the opposite bank of the river, and that was the only village that I had not yet visited within the boundaries of my territory. Having ridden the national highway many times already, but never having seen a trail leading to the west, it was my plan to find it that day, meet the chief, discuss fish farming, and mark the trail clearly on my map.

The road north was firmer that afternoon, having recently received less rainfall to keep it under water, but a few nasty puddles persisted in the thick of the forest where the ground seldom completely dried. Taking my time, I was riding slowly around the edges of those muddy pools, running carefully through the shallows while trying to keep my boots dry and my pants unsplattered. A close call in one of them almost forced me to drop my feet for support, but my luck held and I made it through without a drop of water on my clothes.

While watching for muddy traps I was also scanning the shoulders for any hint of trails. Six miles fell behind me since leaving my house, but no hint of any path had yet revealed itself. Surely no village would be located on the banks of the river without having a trail close to the currents, unless people were forced to make their way on higher ground. Ah! Stopping in every village to inquire of the "road", I was finally given a clue that seemed real. A woman told me to look carefully to the left just around the next turn. But, she warned, the trail would be difficult to spot the path because of tall grass on either side.

Easing onward another mile and passing through several more "next turns," I finally saw a brown slice in the grass that went sharply to the left. I stopped for a better look. Yes indeed, it was a path that led up a hill of elephant grass. Turning the handlebars sharply, I nosed the front wheel into it and eased to the top. There it opened into a solid strip of sand and clay about twelve inches wide. The terrain toward the river was very low and heavily forested, but directly ahead, conditions were dry as the trail rose and fell over hilly ground. Picking up speed, I was soon zipping through alternating pockets of forests and sandy plains. Fifteen minutes later, slowly motoring down a sharp decline, I suddenly found a large cemetery followed by a field of manioc. A quarter of a mile beyond that stood a peak of thatch, colored like Spanish moss, and then a dozen others came into view. I had found my village.

Tsongo, a community of twenty-five houses standing high above the Likouala-Mossaka River, was a peaceful, picturesque village of about fifty people who made their living fishing and farming. Instantly welcoming me, indeed receiving me as an honored guest, the villagers flocked around me with innocent curiosity. After hearing the story about my mission, they escorted me to meet persons of importance. The chief, however, was not available. He was taking a nap. They next took me to see their school. The building was hardly different from others that I had seen, although it did seem to be newer. However their pride in the school was simply in having one. Its condition was quite beside the point.

When the guided tour was over and a dozen of us were relaxing in a shade that swept gently back and forth over the school yard, some of the men expressed an interest in fish-farming. That interest was vague and unenthusiastic, however, as if they were merely saying what they thought I wanted to hear. But they insisted that I come again one day, earlier in the morning, in order to make a formal presentation with my picture-book. Following that, they assured me, they would decide. After spending nearly two hours with those cheerful, pleasant people, I did promise to return again soon. But for then, it was time to start back.

My ride back toward the highway was exhilarating and very quick, for my speed was limited only by my bravery. I knew that log bridges did not await me along the way, there were no deep puddles to cross, no deep sand traps to slow me down, all aspects of which made it possible to run the entire distance at high speed. However as soon as my front wheel touched the dampness of the national highway, my senses sharpened automatically, the throttle was turned back, and the motorcycle settled into a much slower and safer cruising speed.

The clay was slippery around those washouts where water had been standing, and some of the submerged ground had become more like quicksand. Reaching a place where deep ruts disappeared under two long streaks of water around an elevated hump of mud, I recalled having trouble at that very spot on the way up that morning. I had experienced a close call as my tires sank deeper and deeper, but I made it through without having to wade. Recalling that, wondering if my luck would hold twice in a row, I decided to go straight down the middle between the ruts. That was a huge mistake.

The clay was like axle grease. Half way through it, traction was lost and the motorcycle slipped downward into one of the ruts, then turned sideward, and was about to switch ends. Reacting instinctively, my left foot reached out to maintain balance as momentum was still pushing me forward. When almost through the worst of it, as the machine slid broadside for a second or two, suddenly my boot hit solid ground. The rest was a blur of action, reaction and pain. When the motorcycle snapped around and my foot was hard against the dirt, the full thrust of gravity was bearing down on cartilage and bone. Suddenly my knee felt as if a blow torch was being held to it. A moment passed in slow motion as the bike went down hard, slamming me face first into the rocky clay. Then the machine landed on top of me with the engine screaming and the rear wheel tearing at the road.

Falling was nothing new, but that time I was hurt. My knee was badly twisted, possibly broken, and almost unbearably painful. But I had to get up. Dragging myself out from under the machine with my arms and my good leg, I rolled partially to one side and reached over to twist the key and stop the engine. It died with a cough and a sputter. Leaning over the gas tank then, grimacing in pain, I pulled myself up with one leg while stiffly towing the other. Teeth clenched and lips squeezed shut, it took a long and excruciating moment to stand upright again, and another equally difficult time to balance myself gingerly on both feet. Precariously bending from the waist, I took the handlebar in my grip, and slowly, weakly lifted the machine to its wheels and then propped on it for what must have been a full minute. Suffering a deep chill and an attack of nausea, knowing that I was close to losing consciousness, I was fighting to hold on. But the worst was yet ahead of me. Next I had to somehow get back on the motorcycle, crank it again, and ride it out of the jungle.

One of our second-year volunteers assigned to the other end of the country, had suffered a motorcycle crash several months earlier. At first we were told that he had experienced a simple "wipe out" on a road near his post, and that he was not thought to have any internal injuries. The part about "internal injuries" was true, but the rest of the truth was that bone was poking through the flesh of one arm and he had hardly been able to crawl. Even though he finally made it to a local hospital somehow, the staff there had nothing to give him for his pain and could not set his broken bones. Nearly a day later, he was rescued.

During language training in Bujumbura, we had frequent briefings about some of the risks that we all would face. Realizing just how dangerous a serious injury or illness could be at an isolated post, I used to confound the nurse with questions that always seemed to make her uncomfortable. They were not difficult questions, but they went around the bureaucratic line and drove straight for the point. Similar meetings were held in Brazzaville before we were sworn in, reassuring us that we were always in good hands. Indeed, we were told emphatically that any one of us, anywhere in the Congo, would be no more than three hours away from an airlift if one became necessary. Pressing that point after Chester was hurt, I asked what would have happened if he had been injured even more seriously.

"Someone would have driven down for him immediately," she responded.

Interesting and thought provoking answer, I thought. The drive to Chester's village would probably had taken twelve hours, and another twelve would have passed going back. Furthermore he would have been hauled over roads that were tough on healthy people. Sensing my reasoning, the nurse said that sometimes it might be better to wait for daylight and send a plane. By the time Chester was in Brazzaville and in the care of the embassy doctor, eighteen hours had passed since the moment of his crash. He was treated as best as they could in the local hospital, where they secured his arm and bandaged him up for a flight to the United States. There, he would undergo extensive surgery. Some of us joked after that, that if we got hurt we would need the help of the Africans, the Americans, a good bush pilot, and probably our Maker!

My status after my own crash was desperate. No one was walking along the road to discover me. No one would have heard me if I had called out. Indeed, a day might pass before anyone happened along. Returning home and finding medical help was up to me and me alone, and everything hinged on cranking and riding that motorcycle.

Leaning forward over the handlebar with my injured leg locked beneath me, holding me up, I then swung my good leg over the machine and quickly shifted the weight of the bike to that foot. So far, so good. Pausing then, resting a moment while cold sweat poured down my face, I fought the urge to vomit. Momentarily, trying hard to focus my thoughts, I steadied myself for the next move. I eased my left foot back to the soil again, holding the machine up and keeping it balanced between my legs, I then gingerly shifted the tilt of the machine to the injured side. The motorcycle was not heavy in that position, but my damaged knee was on fire. I positioned the crank-pedal with my right foot and gave it a kick. Luck was with me, for the engine cranked the first try. Sluggish and sputtering at first, after a few seconds it began to smooth out until it sounded completely normal.

Aboard the machine and sitting upright, I needed to shift gears with the toe of that left boot, even thought the slightest movement delivered the sensation that muscle and bone were being shredded. I could press the shift-lever down, but I could not lift it up. That was simply not going to work. Hands shaking from agony, stomach flooded with nausea, mind slipping from faintness, I was nevertheless able to get the motorcycle moving in second gear. Once steadily in motion, I rode slowly to avoid overheating the engine while not changing gears.

Many water traps were still ahead, every one of which was terrifying to contemplate. If I fell again, I knew that my ride would be finished. The faster speeds of a motorcycle enhance control in most road conditions, but my slow velocity at that moment was the product of misery and fear. Facing more hazards, badly hurt, all I could think about was the arrival of help from Brazzaville and whether it would be on time. Or on Africa time.

"Motorcycle, please get me home. Jaime, please don't be late," I said aloud to the wind.

When the next morning came, I had spent the entire night lying on the bed writhing in pain. I had been amazingly lucky to reach home just as Herve and Calixte were walking by. They helped me to get off the motorcycle and to get it inside the house, then they offered me some medical advice. They wanted me to visit a local witch doctor for an application of hot water and a hard massage, which they were certain would cure my knee in a single visit. Culturally sensitive as always, I told them that a bullet in the head would accomplish the same thing. I locked myself in when they were gone, and did the best I could to attend my own wounds.

Almost immobilized with elastic bandages wrapped from calf to mid-thigh, my knee was safe from bending but it was burning with fever. Dragging myself from one place to the next like a monster of the night, and still absorbed with pain, I was forced to either sit, or lie down, and to move as little as possible. Holding the leg stiff like a crutch, I was able to gently swing it around while holding onto things, and slowly make my way from the table to the bed, but nothing more. The slightest wrong move would have dropped me like a rock.

That morning, while trying to step over the elevation between my two rooms, I barely touched the bricks with my left foot before collapsing forward, lunging straight across the floor and crashing one shoulder into my foot locker. Injured again but alert, I made it back to the table and swallowed another handful of aspirin. I was then able to catch a breath, get up again, and open up the house.

As the hours passed and the leg grew stiffer, I desperately needed to move. I got to my feet and inched my way to the front porch where I was able to sit for a while in slightly cooler air. Herve came by just before noon, wanting to know if I had made arrangements to see the witch yet. I told him "No, not yet." Having recalled that I had an appointment with Mr. Boreffe at his work site, I was concerned over the possibility that he might be stood up. Herve promised faithfully that he would go to see Boreffe at the appointed time. I told him it was extremely important that he did so, because Boreffe's motivation seemed to be waning some, and I did not want to lose him.

When three o'clock rolled around, I was beginning to worry a little. Jaime should have arrived hours ago. If he did not make it, I would have no choice but to catch a truck to Owando the next morning, and from there to try to reach Brazzaville. That was a dreadful thought, for the lack of motion was causing my knee to grow stiffer and still more hurtful.

Shortly after having made that decision to get help on my own if help did not come to me, Herve showed up again. When asked about Boreffe's appointment, he admitted that he "didn't get around to it". Thus, driven by a flush of anger coupled with my refusal to let Boreffe down, I slowly and painfully pushed the motorcycle onto my porch and then into the yard, locked up the house, and gingerly climbed on to get it started. Maybe that moment of anger was a good thing, for if I could handle that ride, I might be able to make a longer trip if necessary. I found that being astride the machine was no more uncomfortable than sitting rigidly at my kitchen table, but the movement gave me a psychological boost. Maybe, just maybe, things were not as bad as I had believed the day before.

I found Msr. Boreffe at his site piddling in his garden, patiently waiting for me as he said he would. He listened with grave interest as I explained what had happened, and that he would probably have to make do without me for a few weeks. Trying to avoid discouraging him, I told him that my knee was badly sprained but probably not broken, which implied that I would be back on the job soon and he should keep on with his work.

"I understand," he said rather softly. "I will not quit then." Helping me to turn the motorcycle around and holding it upright while I cranked it, he had some powerful information for me. He said there was a Congolese woman in town who could fix my wound with a hot massage.

Jaime, along with Anne from Owando, Alfred the Congolese driver, and an unfamiliar white woman from Brazzaville, were all standing in my front yard when I returned. Herve and Calixte were there as well, which meant Jaime had already been told of my accident, and everybody was looking at me as if they seriously questioned my sanity. I took about thirty seconds just to climb off the machine, with Herve catching me on one side and Jaime on the other. Someone else had to take it inside.

The unknown woman was from the office of the British Consul in Brazzaville. She had hitched a ride to visit local schools in connection with some foreign aid project. Anne had come along just for the ride. Jaime planned to bunk at my house while the others would take rooms at the Mission. Alfred hauled in an ice chest containing an assortment of ham, eggs, real Coca Cola, huge bars of French chocolate and even a few apples, all kept on ice for a picnic treat, which we all enjoyed while the moment was captured on a camcorder.

Later in the evening when Jaime and I were alone, he said he would take me to Owando the next morning, try to reach Brazzaville by phone for medical instructions, and then decide what to do with me. Because I was able to move about and I did not have tears rolling down my face, he was quite certain that my knee was sprained, not broken, and that keeping it bound with elastic bandages was about all that could be done. He also updated me as to the current political situation in the country, and the money problems that could adversely affect our project. Fearing the worst for political stability, he said that project funds could become hopelessly trapped in turmoil if things did not improve. That gave me a lot to think about beside my knee as I finished the last of the cold drinks and had another bite of candy, but those thoughts did not make the next morning come a single minute faster.

The ride to Owando was absolutely brutal. My leg could not be fully extended and the discomfort was aggravated by every bump in the road. Furthermore the road had eroded even more since my last trip over it, and some places were dangerous even for the Land Rover. Nevertheless, once we made it to Anne's house I was able to move about reasonably well with the leg tightly wrapped.

When morning came, we paid a visit to the local agriculture office, used their phone, and actually reached the nurse in Brazzaville. Although the connection was weak and her voice sounded far away, I was able to describe what happened and to discuss the symptoms that followed. She wanted me to get an X-ray there in Owando if possible and then telephone her with the results. Even a local doctor would be able to recognize a break without a problem, and if the injury did turn out to be only a sprain, then I would not have to make a miserable trip to the city.

Owando's hospital, located on the outskirts of town, was a large complex, two stories high with glass in some of the windows. The place was perfectly hospital-like at first glance, but then, upon taking a harder look, signs of neglect and decay began to show. Because Anne was acquainted with one of the doctors there, who, she insisted, was highly competent, she was delegated to seek him out. Meanwhile, I was compelled to wait in the truck.

When only a few minutes had passed, she and Jaime came back with the news that the X-ray equipment was not available that day. We then returned to the agriculture office, dialed the phone a few times and finally reached Nurse Ruth for the second lucky occasion in a matter of hours.

"You are able to walk?" she asked.

"Well, not actually walk, but I can move around a little."

"And keeping the knee wrapped in elastic bandages helps to control the pain?" she went on.

"I wouldn't say it controls it, but it helps."

"I just don't want you to make the trip here if you aren't forced to make it. Why not lie around Owando for a few days just to see how things progress? Stay off the leg for a while and see if it improves on its own."

"Okay. I'll see what Jaime thinks." Because making a twelve hour road trip was terrible to contemplate, remaining in Owando for a while sounded good to me. Maybe I would get lucky and heal a bit.

"Well, stay in touch. If you have torn a ligament, you'll have to have surgery and that will have to be done in the States. Just use your own judgment and common sense and keep me posted."

When we hung up and I passed along the conversation to Jaime, he gave me another piece of news that cinched the decision for me. He was going to stop on the way back for at least one night in Gamboma whether I went along or not. That meant that my ride would be two days and one night. All I wanted to do was to put my leg up and stay still for a day or two. More riding in that cramped truck and more waiting in Gamboma was not something I cared to deal with.

The next morning, after the others left without me and Anne went somewhere on her motorcycle, I was sitting in a large wicker chair in her living room with my leg resting on a table. Alone in the unusual quiet of the neighborhood and wondering if I had made the right decision, it struck me that it was too late to fret over it. I might as well put it out of my mind.

The two days spent in Owando, trapped in uncomfortable chairs or lying prone on a bamboo bed, was an absolutely awful time for me. Lacking the means to fully immobilize my leg or even to keep it comfortably elevated, and having nothing stronger than aspirin to treat the discomfort. I had been constantly tossing, turning, shifting and rearranging. But my injury did seem to be improving a little. The pain had gone from shooting flames to a steady, localized ache throughout the joint, and I was actually more comfortable when in motion. Keeping it wrapped made it possible for me to use the limb, however stiffly, and to walk short distances. Maybe Nurse Ruth's advice had paid off.

While my most difficult moments came when lying flat, the slightest effort to lift the leg set me ablaze. And turning over during the night would wake me from the deepest sleep until the throbbing passed. Making matters worse, I felt guilty about leaving the shopping to Anne while consuming her privacy. Unable to physically contribute, taking, not giving, I was in the way. And I sensed that she felt the same. Considering all of those factors and definitely not up yet to the rigors of a trip to Brazzaville, I made a decision. I was going back to Makoua. There at least, plenty of food was already stocked in my house, my bed was infinitely more comfortable than her bamboo cot, my own bed was protected by a mosquito net (which I sorely missed), and there I could hire boys to haul water, make trips to the market and even cook my food if it should come to that. Surely my injury would mend in a few more days and everything would return to normal. My fingers were crossed.

My ride back to Makoua was in the cab of the very same truck that I had caught to Etoumbi when on my long trek. An ordinary dead bolt held the passenger door shut, we had no brakes, and the steering system was about to drop from beneath the vehicle. I was glad for the ride, but by the time we had gone four and a half hours, it had badly roughed me up.

During the ride I did learn more disturbing news. Violence in the Capitol had flared up during the night, as ringleaders were trying to stir trouble wherever they could. Because the issues driving the unrest were the same as those that fueled the last period of disruption, conditions could easily worsen and worsen quickly. But our driver was optimistic. The Congolese, he said, were too smart to revolt as the army had recently done in neighboring Zaire. Even so, the fuel supply was growing short again and commercial traffic, at least to Owando, might be in trouble. Anyway, National Highway #2 was so bad that a few more rains might finish it to all but the very bravest drivers.

After they dropped me off at the station in Makoua, my long hobble toward home seemed miles long. I stopped on the way to buy a supply of bread from a street vendor and to pick up a few other necessities from one of the stores, then I inched down the road with short, stiff steps. Coming to the edge of the street along the way, bright eyes shining, grinning cheerfully, children yelled to me in

Lengala and danced African rhythms to greet me. Amused and greatly appreciative of the distraction, I paused to listen and stood there long enough to instruct a large group of them in a proper cheer.

"Fred, Fred. Yea Fred. Yea, yea, Fred!" If they were going to chant for me they might as well say something I could recognize.

Nine days had passed since the accident, and the knee was feeling a little better. Taking aspirin every few hours, keeping the joint tightly wrapped, staying as inactive as possible, and avoiding witch doctors and hot-water massages, I was doing all that I could do to encourage healing. Marin and his brother had both helped me with shopping and chores when I asked them to, but neither Calixte nor Herve had even visited except to discuss whatever business was awaiting my attention.

Finally I tried the motorcycle again. Getting it in and out of the house was the worst part, but once on the road and easing through the gears the ride was actually enjoyable. Visiting work sites for the first time in nearly two weeks, knowing that much of the former momentum had been lost, it was gratifying to find people back on the job and working hard. Their labor had stopped because it was doubted that I would ever come back, but when word of my return spread, progress began anew and things were quickly back on track. Michel had almost finished his pond and would soon be ready for the final inspection. He seemed truly happy, almost excited, to have me back.

One night, while limping along the streets in search of peanuts, a man pulled up beside me on a motor scooter. He had a message. He said that I was to attend a government meeting at eleven o'clock the following morning. He rode off without explaining what it was about, but I didn't care much anyway. Something was definitely not right with my knee. It had started hurting a lot more, in all positions and at all hours, and the fever and swelling were coming back.

I dropped in on Herve on the way home and told him of my encounter with the man on the motor scooter. Herve seemed agitated, almost panicked by the news. He had heard nothing of any such meeting and wondered why no invitation had been extended to him. Evidently the event was somewhat more important than I had guessed. Herve then rushed toward the government building located in the field between my house and the river, to try and find out what was going on. A few minutes later he came back to tell me that he had found a flier on the door. The meeting had been organized by Congolese officials from Brazzaville, whose purpose was to discuss the fish-farming project of Makoua, and the only people invited were those who had a direct interest in the project. Because that had to include Herve, even if he was not formally named, he felt better about things. Still, he wondered.

When Herve and I met the next morning at the appointed hour, we were greeted by Michel, Laurrent, Tscendou, and Boreffe, along with several others including Felix Itoua. All quietly took seats and waited. Soon, the Minister of Agriculture was introduced. He had come to praise our work and also to introduce the Caucasian man at his side, a middle-aged Belgian, who was about to open an office in Owando. His company would offer financial aid to those Congolese whose proposals made sense and who seemed to be worthy of it. The meeting lasted only fifteen minutes and closed with the word that all of us were invited for dinner that night at the home of the Chief of Makoua.

When it was eight o'clock in the evening and time for dinner, Herve and I reached the appointed place together and found that people were already on the front steps waiting to be called inside. Soon we were taken to a large patio in the rear where twenty or more chairs had been placed side by side against one wall. A long table had been prepared with a selection of beer, wine and sodas, along with manioc and bread, beef and fish, saka saka and fish-salad. And, I couldn't believe it, even a small bowl of potato salad that surely must have been prepared for my benefit. Even the order of seating had been preordained, for just as I was about to claim a spot next to Michel, a Congolese man stopped me. I was to sit next to the Belgian fellow, who was next to the Minister of Agriculture, who was closer to the food. Herve was instructed to sit next to Michel. The meal was terrific, the atmosphere was excellent, and the conversation was enlightening. After talking at length with the Belgian and with several of the Congolese, the singular reason for the celebration became clear. Herve and I had begun to make a mark.

The next morning I rode to Tscendou's site and, assisted by one of the men of his cooperative, I went about setting stakes and tying string to create a visual picture of where the dikes had to be, and how the inside walls would have to slope toward the center, and exactly how deep the rest must be dug. Staking it out like that eliminated any need for me to stand over the work, for the completed pond was literally "drawn" in the dirt. I was quite certain that only a matter of perhaps two weeks remained before the time would arrive for stocking. I also learned that Michel had visited the cooperative a time or two, sneaking a peak at the progress of his competitors.

Makoua's phones were down on Monday, so it was impossible to reach Nurse Ruth. I was at a loss as to what to do. I could not be still with the pain, while light work took my mind off it, and the motion did not to affect it much one way or the other. On the other hand, physical stress probably aggravated the condition so that later anguish would be far more intense. During the night I suffered the most, when too tired to stay up and too miserable to sleep. Every night for nearly three weeks, I slept in my bandages so that unconscious movement would not set me ablaze again. I decided to set a limit. One more week without improvement, and I would have to go to Brazzaville. One more week!

The next morning I returned to Tscendou's site, where four members of the cooperative were standing in the middle of it surrounded by my network of stakes and strings, arguing over their meaning. Presumably, the perfectly clear "picture" was not so clear after all. Intending to make my way into their midst, I tried to step over one of my strings, got my sore leg tangled up in it, fell headlong to the bottom, and banged my knee sharply on the hard clay. I almost passed out.

A few minutes later, while shaking off the dizziness and the cold sweat, I was back on my feet again and explaining the meaning of the pickets and strings. Just then Herve strode up with Calixte and a well dressed Congolese man whom I recognized as the regional Minister of Agriculture from Owando. The three of them greeted the rest of us in an offhanded, aloof and incidental manner, then they strolled around the site, inspecting it, discussing it among themselves. Herve, acting as tour guide, went about explaining the meaning of the stakes and how they would help the farmers to dig the perfect pond. No more than ten minutes later, the three of them started back toward the trail.

"We are going for a beer," said Herve with innocent candor as he turned his back on us and left. I stayed behind long enough to straighten out the confusion over the stakes, made sure that everybody understood and then accepted their assistance back aboard my motorcycle for the ride home.

That night, sitting alone in my house and watching movement in the street lights, I noticed that every lamp appeared to show something like snowflakes drifting to the ground. Hobbling out to see it up close, I learned that the "snow" was actually composed of swarms of termites with great wings of white dancing in the light and falling in shimmering pools to the street. They were God's creatures seeking the light of man, only to die by the thousands in the littered clay below.

Not quite four weeks after my accident, I gave in to the need for medical care. My plan was to leave the next day, headed for the Capitol. I caught a bus to Owando, spending five hours on the tough, jolting road, then stayed at Anne's for the night. Finally I caught a bus at eight o'clock in the morning and headed for Brazzaville. What followed were the worst fifteen hours of my lifetime.

When the nurse came into the compound the next morning, she immediately called the embassy Doctor, who happened to be her husband, and arranged for me to have an X-ray. Just a few short hours later, the call from Dr. Cedric came.

My knee was broken! The doctor took one look at the film and said "I can't believe you waited a month to come in for treatment". Thus the nurse was irritated with me, the doctor was something less than happy, and although no mention was made of it, my impression was that neither of them was very pleased with the Director for not bringing me in for treatment when he had me in the truck.

The nature of the break, actually a horizontal tear just above the joint, was a major stroke of luck. The elastic bandages kept it from growing worse and actually helped it to begin healing on its own, but the process was far from over. The ligament was also damaged some, but again, snug bandaging had helped to keep it from deteriorating. Surgery would not be necessary, I was told, and my treatment regimen, starting at that very moment, was a combination of medication, more elastic bandages, plenty of bed rest, and staying off the leg ninety percent of the time for the next several weeks. Herve would have to manage without me for quite a while.

Six weeks passed slowly but with relative comfort since reaching Brazzaville. My wound had healed except for a little ache that still shot through the leg when it was moved wrong, and for the most part I was ready to get back to work. I was taken to the bus station in the Talengai quarter, where I was fortunate enough to catch another Coaster Deluxe. I was heading home to Makoua.

Laying over at Anne's house and hoping for a ride the next morning, I walked toward the night marche for something to eat, and there I ran into none other than Herve. He was on his way to Brazzaville for his own formal indoctrination into fish culture. The course was to be taught by Tom and Eric, following which Herve would finally be issued a motorcycle. I suspected that our entire project had been put on a fast track, in anticipation of a time when we Americans might be forced to leave the country.

Interested in all the news and feeling guilty about being away from my post so long, I offered to buy him a beer. The offer surprised Herve to the point of being silly about it. ("Me? You want to buy ME a beer?") We went to an open air place on the main avenue, where metal chairs surrounded wooden tables facing the street, and there we sat together and talked about how things had gone during my absence.

My four pond-sites were being worked at a rapid pace, he said, and at least two of them were almost done. My house was just the way I left it, sealed shut, but my garden had gone to weeds and the grass was two feet high. He also said that I had been missed.

Changing the subject to political matters, I told him that trouble was brewing in Brazzaville again, and it seemed inevitable that the situation would worsen before it got any better. Herve shook his head negatively, insisting that my conclusions were all wrong. He was certain that his people would never revolt against the government. When the beer was gone, we shook hands and I left him with the mocking warning to be careful on his new motorcycle during the long ride home.

The next morning, riding to Makoua in a little truck with twenty people on board, my thoughts were focused on that moment, that ride, and that road which was then nothing better than a canyon in the jungle. Former ruts had become deep gashes where water stood, holes had become craters, and eroded shoulders had been transformed into dangerous ditches. Just beyond one small village, we slowly approached a tree that had been dragged across the road. A man was standing in front of his barricade with a machete in his grip.

We stopped in front of it and rather patiently waited for the man to approach us for money. Our driver paid him one hundred CFA, roughly forty cents,. The tree was dragged out of the road by one end, and we continued on our way. Barricades of that type were common all over the Congo. Boys or men would throw a few shovelfuls of dirt over a particularly bad spot, tamp it down a little and then block the road with a tree to demand a money from every vehicle that happened along.

I recalled riding with Eric once in Djoumouna when we came to such a barricade. He stopped the truck, put it into low gear and rumbled over the tree like a tank. I thought it was funny at the time, but I understood his reaction perfectly. He was in no mood for roadside extortion. I was never in a mood for it. If the people were going to set up toll stations, they should at least do enough work to make a visible difference in the road.

We reached Makoua in less than five hours that day, which was actually better than I had dared hope. Because we had two large boxes of my food and supplies on board, for which I was compelled to pay an extra fare, the driver delivered me to my door and even helped me to get my things into the yard. That, I thought, was a deal! I stood at the road for a minute or two after they had gone, amazed at how my once trim parcel had given itself back to nature so quickly. Stalks of withered corn were dying in the shade of my banana tree which had grown from a mere sprout to a height of about twenty feet. All the rest of my vegetables had been picked clean and the plants had withered among goat-tracks.

Although my house had not been vandalized, it was a mess. New spider webs hung everywhere, a new layer of dirt covered every surface, rat and bat manure coated my furniture, and a new insect hill in one corner reached almost to the ceiling. Opening the shutters to air the place out, I scrubbed it until nearly nine o'clock in the evening, just in time for familiar calls from the attic.

My house was evidently chock full of bats.

Marin's brother Prudence, helping to weave a blind on my porch.

17

Evacuation

Nearly ten months after I first arrived in Makoua, I took a ride to visit all of my fish farmers and found nothing but good news. Msr. Laurrent had accomplished more than I would have thought possible, having turned his former swamp into a relatively dry field with a canal of swift water running through the middle of it. Having already heard of my return, Laurrent was very pleased to see that the rumor was true. He and all the other farmers had slowed their work during my absence, but they had not given up on me.

"Now we will move quickly," he said.

Michel's site was remarkable. The man had done more hard labor than I could have accomplished in threefold the time. His pond was basically finished, needing only a compost bin, some shaping of the dikes, and the cutting up and discarding of some tree trunks that were felled too close to the back. Soon we would scatter a layer of charcoal over the bottom to kill unwanted life forms, then we would be ready to fill the pond and wait for an algae bloom to activate the oxygen and carbon dioxide cycles. Also soon, I would have to make my first cross-country ride for fingerlings. Explaining to Michel how that would work, I told him that I would travel about one hundred miles on the motorcycle to another post where fingerlings were available. About two hundred of the tiny fish would be put inside a pair of ten-liter plastic bidons filled with fresh water and carried in burlap sacks hung like saddle bags over the back of the motorcycle. Stopping along the way as often as necessary to change the water and to cool down the fish, the trip would be a long and arduous one, but it would also mark the beginning of a new day in Makoua. Michel was excited. So was I.

Boreffe was back at work again, and in a big way. He had completely rechanneled the feeder-canal around his site, drained the formerly spongy ground, and he had sifted most of it to get rid of the humus. Very soon, I would stake out the dimensions of his dig, and he would be on the way to having a very large plot for several ponds.

Tscendou and the men of his cooperative were a treat! The pond they dug was truly a model. The dikes were properly sloped, the bottom was properly shaped, the entire site was clean, and they too had channeled a fast source of water to one side from where they could fill several ponds as needed. Once a compost bin was in place, filled with plant and animal matter, and once the pond was treated with charcoal, the final step would be to open the flow of water.

"Ten more days and you will be done," I told them.

"Will we be the first?" Tscendou asked innocently, making me grin broadly at the spirit of competition.

Only one troublesome matter might have interfered at that point. Tscendou was gravely concerned about what was going on in Brazzaville. He said that the streets were growing tense again, and there was a possibility he might have to go there in the next few days on "business". I never knew just what that business was, but I sensed that his mission would be one of importance. And as expected, Makoua was out of water again. Much rain had fallen during the last few weeks, bringing the river to the highest level since the year before, but the diesel supply was gone and no water could be pumped. Hydro-Congo was out of everything except kerosene, and virtually everyone was speaking negatively as to when fuel might arrive. Even Calixte was openly doubtful.

"The road is treacherous now," he said glumly. My sense was there was more to it than that.

Having been warned by our Director to buy extra gasoline and to keep it on hand in case the local supply ran dry, and in case an emergency arose, I had made it a point to comply with that logical and practical instruction. Although I had hoped to do it discreetly, some villagers had watched me hand-carry the heavy cans to my house. Furthermore, people from the Hydro Congo station had been talking about me, disclosing that I had been storing fuel inside my house. Ordinarily, that would have been trivia from my point of view, but in the face of increased tensions and short supplies, I suspected that some might recall where to find gasoline if times grew tough. I would remain alert. Marin came to visit in the middle of the afternoon, but something was weighing on his mind.

"Kevin and Prudence and I watched your house while you were gone," he announced, "just as you told us to do." Indeed, he and I had agreed before that he and the boys could take anything they wanted from my garden, but anyone else was to keep away from it. "But the policeman's wife stole most of it before we had a chance. I saw her doing it."

No surprise there, I thought. It was a shame that the most corrupt people in the entire village were the people with the most authority, who could do as they pleased with no repercussions whatsoever. But nothing could have changed it, for that was the way things were done in Makoua. Regarding another matter, I asked about the little slave-girl who lived in the police compound and whom I had not seen since returning.

"Yes, yes," Marin said cheerfully. "She still lives there. She works very hard."

"I feel sorry for her," I put in.

"You should not feel sorry," he insisted. "She is well fed and has a place to sleep."

By ten o'clock the next morning, hot and disheartened from trying to defeat the elephant grass that had taken over my yard, I decided to take a break. Just after finishing a splash-bath and changing into dry clothes, two teenaged girls walked onto my porch.

"Kokoko."

One of them had been there before with Kevin, but the other girl I did not recognize. They wanted to know if I would help them, because, they said, they had been injured. They did not look hurt. No dripping blood was to be seen, no cuts were visible, no bone was protruding from torn skin, but I invited them to sit at my table and tell me about it.

The older girl, tall, slim and athletic, was about fourteen. Her friend, much shorter and stockier, was probably a year younger. They said they were both beaten by a school teacher while in class and while standing in front of all the other students. Because they had neglected their assignments, their teacher decided to teach them a lesson. I saw a wound then. The older girl had a knot on her forearm the size of a golf ball, and several lumps on her shoulders and back where she had been struck with a wooden paddle. Her friend, who was hit on the buttocks and legs, had no similar evidence that she cared to display. Nevertheless she claimed to be in pain and wished I could do something for her. Looking at the broad welts and swollen places on the first girl, my reaction was one of anger and disgust at the incredible stupidity that would lead to such an act. Yet I knew that their beatings were justified in a culture where violence was tolerated and in fact never more than a mood away. My meager medications were of little help to the girls, but I gave them each some soothing lotion for the tender skin, two aspirin each to swallow with filtered water, and a few pieces of candy to elevate the saddened spirit. The treatment seemed to help, for they were very appreciative.

Shortly after the girls had gone away, Prudence came to the door sporting an egg-sized lump on the side of his head. His class assignment had not been completed either, and he had also failed a test. His teacher pulled him by his arm to the front of the room and then knocked him flat with a wooden board. Following that, the boy stumbled out of the room and headed straight to my house. Soothing lotion would be of no help to him, but he took the aspirin with gratitude. He also took my advice, promising to talk to his father, or at least to Marin, about the mistreatment.

Marin came two hours later. He had seen his younger brother, he knew the story of the abuse at school, and he had been told of my advice. "Prudence should have done his lessons," he said simply. "He knew he would be punished if he did not do as told. It was his own fault. He deserved what he got."

"Nobody deserves that kind of treatment, Marin," I replied. "Except maybe the teacher." Having said that, there was nothing more I could do. I understood the logic of the situation, but it was still hard for me to take.

Marin had news on another subject. He had learned via the radio that hand grenades had exploded in the Capitol the night before, rapid-fire weapons were heard for several hours, and some people were killed in the streets. Maybe, he mused, it was all over then, because the army had taken control once again. One of the people killed was the wife of the Minister of Commerce, and the Minister himself was missing. People were being warned to stay off the streets and to take precautions, especially in areas where violence had already occurred. Seeing the worry in Marin's eyes, I didn't believe it was over. I believed the violence had just begun.

Living in a land of stark realities where outside interference was discouraged, I passed the time every new day simply by doing my job. I worked with my farmers if they were working, I solicited new business when the opportunity presented itself, or I worked on my own domestic improvements. I also spent a lot of free time listening to my cheap little Chinese-made radio, bought in a Brazzaville market, but the news had only been bad. Throughout Makoua, people seemed more pensive than usual. Men gathered in the streets with a great sense of solemnity, while women moved about in subdued conversation.

Because one of the priests from the Mission asked me if I might be willing to locate a good site for a fish pond there, I went about doing that, knowing full well that the project would not be reportable to my own leadership. That in mind, the water source could have been from their own cistern, draining could have been accomplished with PVC piping, and maintenance could have been the duty of anyone assigned to do it. The priests were quite serious about the project, and, having little else to do, I was going to help them get it done. Thus, walking about the grounds with two of the priests, we located a beautiful, high piece of ground near their cistern where a dozen ponds could have been built. The priests liked the site, they were eager to begin, and they wished me to return as soon as possible to stake out the dig.

While walking back to the Mission compound, they told me that two of their number had been planning to leave the next day for business in Brazzaville, but the trip had to be canceled. Violence had been increasing to such an extent that nobody was safe, and the national mood seemed to suggest more of the same was yet to come. Eighteen deaths had been reported so far and barricades were up again all over the city.

Kevin, almost breathless, came to my house later that day with urgent news. The Catholic church had been radioed a message. All Americans in the north end of the country were to immediately ride their motorcycles to Owando "for a reunion". Reunion, indeed! Code for, "This is it!"

I spent only an hour packing my most treasured possessions in the metal foot locker and then packing my duffel with the few items that I dared not leave behind. However, it took a bit longer to visit the Mission, the church, and the homes of everyone whom I must bid farewell. Those visits were hasty and abrupt as I motored quickly from one place to the next, saying goodbye, shaking hands, wishing people good fortune, cranking up and moving on. The mood probably did not show on me, but a degree of sadness was there. I would miss some of the people of Makoua, a few of whom had become good friends. And I was pretty sure that some of them would miss me. As for the rest, my departure mattered not at all.

The tank of the motorcycle was always kept full during those days, and I had stored twenty more liters of gasoline in my bathroom. My intuitive side was telling me that the extra fuel might yet come in handy, but it could not be taken with me to Owando unless some of my other things were left behind. That was out of the question. My most essential tools for the road were packed into a wicker basket that was tied to the rear fender. The machine was ready, my duffel bag was strapped onto the back of the seat, my rain gear was draped over a chair, all of the money I had was stuffed into my deepest pockets and the rest was up to fate. Mine would be a long, sleepless wait until morning.

I would have left during the night had I not known better than to try it. The roads would have been impossible without sufficient light, but the best of lights would have been useless if the rain came again. A half hour before sunrise, lightning began streaking across the southern skies and thunder was pounding all around. I knew that I was going to be in for a tough go of it.

The threat of a storm would have been enough to keep away those who might have sought to make trouble on the road, but rain would make the ride as slippery as grease and dangerous beyond any of my past experiences in Africa. Deciding to wait no more, hoping to at least get out of town before the storm began, I rolled the motorcycle out of the house, padlocked the door, and started to ride just as the first drops began to fall.

No one was anywhere to be seen as I rode one last time past the tables of the grand marche, past the little stores and the place where the night market started on the edge of the road every night. Suddenly the rain was falling hard, pelting my helmet and dripping inside my rain coat. As I followed the last curve heading out of town, no adults were watching me and no children were out to cheer for me or to wave goodbye.

Water was already streaming down the last hill going out of town, where the clay in my quivering, jiggling headlight glistened like liquid gold. Easing over terrain that was low and nearly always wet, but was then under wide puddles of water and craters of mud, I steered carefully and moved slowly. Even wearing the rubber rain coat, I was wet to the lap already. Forced to ride with my visor up, at least until daylight, rainwater was flowing down my cheeks and neck, but I kept going because there was nowhere to stop.

By the time the sun came up, the rain came at me in waves and the road had turned into runny Jello. But I kept doggedly on until fifteen miles had passed behind me. I stopped in a little village to dry out some and to wait under the thatch of a large paillote, but the rain seemed to come even harder under black skies. Finally giving up on the weather and returning to the road, water pelted my visor like bits of gravel and the mud slurped at my tires like the tongue of a great monster tasting lunch. I went down twice during the morning and fought back a dozen near misses farther on, but after six miserable hours, the bridge of Owando finally came into view. When I reached Anne's house and the rain was still coming down, I was sopping wet to the waist and I was dirty, tired and hungry. And yes, even thirsty.

One other volunteer, Paul, had arrived before me. Anne, having just gotten the message a few hours ago herself, was worried that some of the others might have trouble getting there. Owando had no diesel fuel and no gasoline, which meant that the only vehicles that traveled there had to carry their own fuel. And because the road toward the airport had been blockaded, traffic from the direction of Brazzaville might not be able to get through anyway. Momentarily we got the word that other barricades had completely sealed off the National Highway.

A radio message from Brazzaville reached us via the local Mission. We were to report to the Mission at eight o'clock the next morning for a radio-rendezvous. Until then, we were to group together, stay together, hold tight and wait. The situation was not good. While waiting, we learned that some bridges had been blown up around Brazzaville and that the railroad had been sabotaged by welding the wheels of cars to the tracks. One never really knew how much to believe of stories like those, but they could not be disregarded because all were within the realms of possibility. Also rumored, was that President Lissouba had brought in mercenaries, and that the Congolese army was fracturing, taking sides, making ready for major conflict.

When eight o'clock the next morning came, we three were at the Mission. Owando's Catholic Mission was at the end of a dirt street a few blocks from the grand marche. The building must have been magnificent when its three stories of European design were first built, but like most things in Central Africa, it seemed somehow dismal as we strode across the five acre field in front of it. Several boys were cutting grass with machetes near a group of buildings to the left, and two trucks were parked in front of another complex to the right. Those quiet scenes presented a false image of tranquility, as if order persisted at the Mission no matter what happened elsewhere in the world.

We three volunteers were eager to hear from our distant leaders and to learn what was planned for us. The radio was a base station, used to coordinate important activities with other Missions and churches throughout our part of the country. Located in a plain, shabby room on the ground level facing the field, we walked right in without asking permission from anyone. The radio was being operated by a Congolese man in street clothes, who ignored us when we went in. When our call came, right on time, the radio operator handed the microphone to Anne and we all gathered close to listen to what Tom had to say.

"Things are tense around here," he started, "but relatively quiet at the moment. This will probably all blow over, but we have been ordered to get out of the country just in case. Is everybody there yet?"

"No, only three of us are here. And we are hearing that the highway is blockaded south of town."

"That's not good. We're still trying to get word to everybody, but we're not getting a lot of feedback. A couple of you better ride out to try to find the others if you can." Those words were met with a pause, followed by a simple "Okay."

"We can't assume that they all heard the news. We sure can't wait until the last minute to get it to them," Tom added with trepidation in his voice.

We were to maintain contact by radio at prearranged times each day, but the most important item was to assemble everybody as soon as we could and be ready to move when the order came. Walking back to the house again, we three discussed our options. Anne should stay close in case any new instructions came, while Paul and I would have to figure a way to start a search for the other people. Motorcycles were our only means of contacting the others, but as we talked it over, we learned that Anne had not stored any extra fuel, Paul had not brought any with him, and all we had was in the tanks of our three bikes. Only one motorcycle could go.

Paul could have ridden south and tried to get through the road blocks, but then what? Many roads from other posts connected with the national highway and he would only have been able to travel any one of them until his tank was half used. On the other hand, there was only one practical route from Kelle and Etoumbi, which was the highway that went through Makoua, and I had plenty of gasoline in my house. Thus we decided to rob fuel from two of the motorcycles to fill one. I would ride back to Makoua, and if necessary, go on to Etoumbi and Kelle.

Acting with a strong sense of urgency and traveling light, within fifteen minutes I was ready to ride. At that moment the skies were clear. If a little luck came my way, it should be possible to reach Makoua by noon, Etoumbi by dark, Kelle by mid-morning the following day, and Owando once again by Saturday night. I could only hope that Linda and Larry had stored extra fuel, for if not we might all three be in trouble.

Once my tires touched the dirt of the open road once again, I felt good. Conditions were still wet, but the sandy places were drying out fast and puddles were already shrinking toward their centers. Caution thrown to the wind, I was flying! Feeling more in control than ever before in Africa, I was tearing through deep sand as if it posed no barrier at all. Water was splashing to the road on either side of the machine as puddles and washouts fell behind me, for I was taking them straight on then, ready to ride the bike down in case of a spill. Coasting through the mud, hugging shoulders and banks to get around the most eroded places, I was zigzagging all over the highway but moving rapidly on. Sometimes completely airborne, sometimes submerged to the axles, sometimes throwing plumes of sand behind, it took only two hours and fifteen minutes to reach the outskirts of Makoua.

Having spent my time thinking while riding, I hoped that Larry and Linda might already be en route and I must not run the risk of missing them while in town. My first stop was Marin's house where I asked him to stand guard at the road and to watch for any vehicles on which the Americans could be riding.

"Flag them down," I said to him, "and tell them I have gone to my place. If they are in a truck and are passing straight through on the way to Owando, be sure to find that out and let me know. If they are on motorcycles, tell them that it is very important to find me before they go on."

All the children of the neighborhood waved wildly as I rushed by them on the way to my house, but the people at the police compound only watched me with unrevealing, serious expressions. Hurrying inside the house, I refilled my tank, strapped on a spare bidon of fuel and started out again, next stop Etoumbi. There was a chance there might be fuel there, for its supplies were sometimes hauled across the border from Gabon. Racing toward Marin's house for the second time in twenty minutes, I found him standing at the shoulder waiting for me.

"I don't know how you could have missed each other, but your friends are right now walking to your house. They came by truck."

"Oh, no. All right, thanks Marin."

"Good luck," he called after me.

Speeding toward my house again, I was glad on the one hand to have found them so easily, but on the other hand amazed that they did not have their motorcycles. I certainly could not carry them both on mine. Nearing my house again, I saw them standing in my yard, waiting patiently. Larry explained that they had both been uncomfortable with the notion of riding their bikes so far on roads so bad, so they elected to leave their machines locked up in Linda's house. Luckily they had been able to catch a truck that morning, and they seemed confident they would have similar luck the next day. My feeling was that their plan was fraught with risks, but there was nothing else that I could do. I wished them luck and started back toward Owando.

Four hours later, after having to fix a flat tire on the road, the bridge at Owando appeared like a phosphorescent streak painted across the dark horizon. My luck had held. The hour was late, but I had made it. The streets of town were dark as I eased through, for there was no fuel to operate the generator. However, the metallic clatter of a small private generator came from the largest bar in town where loud music was blaring and people were gathering for the last of the chilled beer. Many people were walking about, almost invisible in the night, and street vendors were working their tables by candlelight as if nothing had changed for them at all.

Anne's house had become a very busy place, for all but three of our number had arrived finally. I told them I had no clue whether Larry and Linda would arrive as planned, but they were healthy and well. We could only wait and see. As it happened, everybody managed to make it to Owando by the next morning. None the worse for wear, we had all staked out claims on bunks or on the floor and we simply waited for the evacuation to begin.

Rumors were flying as usual, with some of the more interesting ones reaching us through the local agriculture office. They said that a bottle of beer in Brazzaville had taken a quantum leap to two dollars, and gasoline was up to eight dollars per gallon. The jump in the fuel price stood to reason, for if the rails were out of service and the highways were blocked, goods could not be transported from the port cities. Beer was another matter, however, for the several brands were all bottled in Brazzaville and should have been plentiful for at least a few days. The price increase was probably because people would pay it. I decided that democracy might come more easily to the Congo than I had expected.

Mile upon mile of the highway toward the Capitol, was said to have been blocked with trees felled from either side of the road. How incredibly strange it was to me, that the people had taken such self-abusive action. I could not understand whose vehicles they were trying to stop, nor what was feared from them, but it was obvious that if trucks could not get through with food and other supplies, people in the most rural villages were going to suffer.

We had been told by staff members that such political hostility was actually a tribal matter, wherein President Lissouba represented one tribe and ousted parliamentarians represented the other. But it was a mystery to me how the people knew which tribe they belonged to, except by geographic assumption. We had always heard that tribal loyalties were more important than nationalism, which was an important key as to why African countries tended to be constantly suffering from strife.

Sunday was the day of our intended air lift. We had been told to be at the airstrip by eight o'clock in the morning and to wait there for a flight to Brazzaville. Arrangements had been made for trucks to pick us up just after sunrise, and locals had already cleared us with the guards at the blockade. All of our motorcycles had been taken to a back street storage-barn used by the local government, and there we locked the machines and left them to an uncertain future. Thus when morning came, no one had much to say as we readied for our last trip out. Personal possessions were quietly stuffed into bags, wallets and money were checked, critical papers were put into handy places, and it was all done underneath a mood of pensive inwardness.

Incredibly, our rides came right on time. The driver of one of them was the Japanese man who was to go with us on the plane. The second vehicle, an open pickup truck driven by an African, was right behind and driving close. Neither driver had anything to say as we threw our things into the pickup and then climbed into the Land Cruiser for the short ride ahead. Luke, Anne's homologue, was riding ahead on his motorcycle as if to handle any resistance that we might encounter. So far so good. The time was seven-thirty A.M.

Owando was quieter than usual that morning. Few vehicles were about and only a few of the usual venders had set up at the grand marche giving it a look of gloom. The women there, sitting or standing about their displays, were watching intently but silently as we passed, all knowing but none reacting with more than a stare.

Cruising down the main street past the playing field, rounding the sharp curves toward National Highway #2, we stopped at the intersection where Hydro Congo was on the right. The station was closed, of course, having nothing to sell. We turned onto the highway and sped toward the airport. One more mile lay before the roadblock that guarded the town's perimeter, and that was the only known obstacle between us and our destination. When it came into view, I counted a dozen people standing guard like soldiers expecting tanks to clatter into view with busy turrets.

The blockade, made of planks resting on the tops of barrels, appeared to be manned by civilians. One or two uniformed men were in the crowd, but a young woman, who interestingly enough seemed to be in charge, was motioning for us to stop. She approached the driver's window, took one look inside, and immediately began protesting. And then the entire congregation closed around us to participate. We soon understood that she was upset over the presence of the Japanese man in our midst, because she did not want him to leave with the rest of us. The reason was never stated and it was never even vaguely clear to me.

Members of our team argued that the man was simply being helpful, driving us to the airport, and was therefore no threat to the security of Owando. Finally, when everyone seemed satisfied that we were not up to intrigue and subterfuge, the planks were withdrawn and we were allowed to pass. Just a few minutes later, we reached the airport. We drove onto the tarmac and followed a crooked path between barrels, pieces of wood and assorted junk that had been scattered from one end to the other as booby traps for incoming aircraft. None of it made any sense to me, for it seemed as if the disruption was being done for the sake of disruption itself, and done by people playing war games with neither rules nor order. Since we Americans had no political power, nor even any interest in causing trouble for anybody, one would have expected the people to have been perfectly indifferent to our activities, if not happy to have us out of the way. But that was not the reality.

Finally, when the debris was all removed, we parked at the edge of another wide stretch of pavement about three hundred yards off the runway. That rectangular extension of the tarmac was a place where a plane could taxi to a stop for the loading or unloading of passengers. Perhaps they had planned to someday build a terminal on that spot, and never got around to it. At that moment, it served only as a place to park trucks, scatter baggage, and wait.

Finally at eleven-thirty, our plane arrived. Resembling a converted sea plane with its upturned underbelly and boxy lines, the aircraft appeared thoroughly incapable of the task that it was to perform. But it had flown the distance before, so we were told, and it would surely do so again. With its two engines throbbing and its propellers screaming, the plane taxied close to the trucks and spun around to face us. When the door swung open and the stairs dropped, several African men stepped down with baggage in their hands. One of them was Herve.

Herve and the other men, all of whom had been in Djoumouna for the training program, were sent home early. Herve called out to me with a cheerful grin and rushed to my side with hand extended. He only wanted to know where my motorcycle had been hidden. I told him and then headed for the plane.

Losing no time, our French pilot energetically motioned the rest of us to get on board. We tossed our bags into a rear compartment that was set aside for that purpose and then stepped up the ladder to find yet another surprise. The four Park-volunteers from the far north were already in their seats, waiting. I had entirely forgotten about them, but that explained why the plane was so late. The plane had first flown to Ouesso to pick them up. Laughing and giggling as we joined them, they certainly seemed pleased about the way things turned out. One of them even had a miniature bottle of whiskey on which to sip once we were in the air. A few minutes later, all aboard, seated and ready to go, sixteen Americans and one mysterious Japanese man were all strapped in and eager to fly. And when our wheels finally left the ground, the moods among us ranged from Anne's almost hysterical tears to excited gibberish and outright elation.

The three hour flight to Brazzaville's International Airport was incident free, and inside the airport we moved along almost without notice. However once in the parking lot, we were reminded why we were called in. Waiting for us were Jaime and Gary with the latest news. Violence was rampant all over the city. Hand grenades had been exploded, automatic weapons had been fired, and many people had been killed or wounded so far. Furthermore, road blocks were up in every quarter of the city, and the military seemed to have taken control of the streets.

As we loaded our things into the vans quickly but calmly, most of us were upbeat, as we were living another adventure that most of us were excited to be a part of. Moving onto the main street, we only went a few blocks before reaching a makeshift check point. As we approached, several soldiers pointed their weapons at us. They were motioning for us to pull over. NOW!

Ordered out of the trucks, we were made to empty our bags onto the grass and stand there like good boys and girls while two soldiers went through our things one item at a time looking for weapons. As each bag passed the search, its owner was permitted to pack it again and return it to the van. We all had a good laugh when someone mistakenly grabbed a bag belonging to one of the guards, and threw it into the truck. The guard, chuckling along with the rest of us, wanted it back.

Once through the search without complication, we did not encounter any other road blocks on the way to the compound, but the emptiness of the streets delivered a clear sense of the sinister and ominous mood of the city. Soon we were behind familiar guarded gates where armed men were on duty to protect the compound. Dragging our bags up the stairs into the bunk rooms, we knew we were relatively safe then. Even so, it was impossible to deny the irony of having moved from the comparative safety of the rural countryside into the very epicenter of tension.

Right away we were told to assemble in the large meeting room for a complete update. And minutes after that we were told that the situation throughout the Congo was dangerous and unpredictable. We were being evacuated to another African country far to the north. The immediate plan was to transport us to Mali, where we would wait a few weeks to see if things returned to normal in the Congo. No one was ready to say that our project was finished, for that decision would be up to Washington, but many of our number were headed home regardless. The second year volunteers were terminating slightly ahead of schedule, and it was unlikely that new people would be brought to take their places unless conditions returned to peace and harmony throughout the country. The rest of us were being given the opportunity to terminate early without prejudice, or to wait in Mali and then decide.

Two nights passed in Brazzaville before we were put on board a special flight of Air Afrique that would take us to Bamako, Mali. There, they told us, we might see such picturesque extremes as the Sahara Desert or sailing craft on the Niger River.

The African nation of Mali is very different from the Congo. It is nearly twice the size of Texas, although the bulk of that is either desert or semi-desert, which reduces productive land to a far lesser value. The country is not an oil exporter, but it does mine gold, and sells a lot of cotton. The national economy is primarily dependent upon agriculture and fishing. Its population is ninety-percent Muslim and the bulk of its people live below the poverty line. Flat, sandy, and with sparse natural vegetation, much of the countryside is colored red, yellow and dirty brown as everything takes on the color of earth.

The capitol city of Bamako was different from anything I had seen elsewhere in Africa. Thatch on mud seemed to be the prevalent style of home, but entire blocks of houses were protected inside high walls as if each compound was an independent village. As we rode along the paved streets where life was bustling, we passed black people in mule drawn carts, black people on horseback seated in leather saddles, black people in motorized vehicles of all descriptions, and black people on bicycles and on foot. Farther on, we saw herds of cows, many horses, and a few goats. We also saw *men* tending crops or turning soil, while women and girls marched beside the roads with loads balanced on their heads.

"Tubani So," the name given to the Peace Corps training center, was located about twelve miles out of town on a smooth, wide highway carved out of dirt and rock. Much of the property around the center was covered with low brush and grasses, two acres of which were dominated by offices, workshops, a school facility, and housing for dozens of teachers and staff when training was in progress. We were informed that volunteers did not live on those grounds when they were in language training. They were instead required to take up housing with local families and then to travel there each day for required activities.

The two dozen thatched huts, shaped rather like igloos, had little windows shuttered with metal, and screened entrances that were secured with steel doors. The huts were arranged in twos such that each pair was connected by a thatched overhang that shaded both entrances and provided a place for the residents to sit in cooler air. Each house was made of mud with a cement glaze that made it nearly permanent. Each was about twelve feet in diameter, each had a cement floor, a pair of bamboo bunks under mosquito nets, two footlockers, and each was wired for electricity. A single light bulb dangled from the ceiling, and each unit had, of all things, a ceiling fan.

Because the place was unoccupied when we arrived, we had more huts than we needed. Mine was about ten steps from a faucet that was positioned to serve four units. Our water came from a cistern that was refilled each day from an underground supply. Water was potable at the pipe, our local leaders told us, and after a few hours of exposure to the sun it was warm enough for a comfortable bath. We also had boiling hot water for washing clothes, heated in iron pots over open fires. Even the outhouses were unique. Each resembled a tiny mud hut and each was connected to another little stall of the same design in which bathing could be done in private. We were warned that the temperature, even at night, could exceed a hundred degrees, and if we had to take splash baths to cool down we should be careful to watch for snakes. The good news was that clothes would dry quickly because of the prevailing winds and the low humidity.

Our cafeteria was an immense brick building like a school auditorium, where a dozen long tables and scores of chairs were arranged under a very high roof. Meals were prepared in a huge kitchen on the other side of the back wall, and the food was served buffet style without restrictions as to quantity or selection. That first night, our menu was fresh bread, beef stew and rice, along with a variety of beer and sodas that were sold on the premises. My first impression was that Tu Baniso was not going to be bad at all.

The training center was even larger than revealed at first glimpse. Several single-story buildings near the cafeteria functioned as offices, storage facilities, a library and a medical clinic. Another pair of structures were across the street from the dining hall, while two large barns were there for working on machinery and storing supplies and equipment. Several large huts around the perimeter functioned as classrooms. And then there was the "hangar".

The hangar was an open barn-sized rectangle with a roof supported on brick columns. Electric light fixtures hung from naked rafters above a floor of loose sand and gravel, over which the steady wind blew without obstruction, keeping the space relatively cool. The only wall in the place spanned the north end, behind which was space for storage. We spent most of our first day in the hangar, listening to speeches and announcements of one kind or another from the Peace Corps staff of Bamako. They gave us a lot of information about muggers and thieves, and of leprosy (which was very common in Mali), and of places to which we should not travel, including Timbuktu. And they made it perfectly clear that we were NOT welcome in the crash house in town, for that was reserved for their own volunteers. My sense was that they were not excited about having us there.

Meanwhile, no good news had come from the Congo. Washington had classified our evacuation as "ordered" (as opposed to voluntary) which meant that we would not likely be going back to our posts. The second year people were to process out immediately, while the rest of us would wait a few weeks just in case the situation changed. I saw everything as an opportunity, for those of us who did return to the Congo would be in positions of better choices, higher regard, and quite possibly improved chances for the future.

Walking about the grounds with an African guide that afternoon, some of us ventured about a mile to the banks of the Niger River, which was very wide, swift and muddy. Fishermen were moving along the copper surface in pirogues fixed with sails on the bows, like spinnakers, while steering the little boats with tillers on the sterns. The scene was truly a picturesque sight, but it was more than that. Mali was one of the poorest countries in the world, yet the people manage to feed themselves from their labors and they appeared to be far more progressive than the rural Congolese. One had to wonder why that was so.

Surely the cultures of both African countries played a major role in moving one of them forward and holding the other in place. Malians had harnessed animal-power for both work and transportation, they used the wind to propel their boats, and the men worked alongside the women as if they were proud to do so. The change of pace was a treat to witness.

My first night in Tubani So, sealed inside my mud igloo, was hot and sticky and still. As I lay there and baked hour after hour without relief, I then understood the importance of the ceiling fan. Even with the fan, the hut was miserably hot, but without it, the dwelling could have been used for a bread oven. Since the metal door had to be kept shut for safety's sake, and since the two little windows fixed high on the walls offered the only sources of fresh air, the environment was simply stifling. Suddenly, just at eleven P.M., my fan stopped and heat swelled throughout the hut.

We had been warned that electrical power would be switched off each night to conserve fuel, but none of us realized the significance of that at the time. Stopping the fan was crazy! It was not just a convenience. It was an absolute necessity. Somehow in Africa there seemed always to be a downside associated with each and every uptick, as if to terrorize those who came, and to escort out those who decided to go. I might have slept two hours before daybreak, and my mattress was drenched in sweat. I soon learned that everybody else had suffered equally.

Following breakfast each morning, we were told to expect a briefing on the situation we left behind. That first morning, the information was that President Lissouba's opposition forces were organizing a parallel government to be based in Point Noire. If true, that action would surely split the country's loyalties down the middle and possibly lead to all out civil war.

Back at my hut later in the afternoon, as heat pursued me in the shadows, the sky grew suddenly dark, and fierce winds begin to whip through the thatch. But, to my shock, it was not rain that slapped across my face. It was sand! Wasting no time to make my retreat, I was amazed at the amount of sand that was blasting through the windows. Even with the ports sealed and the door shut, I still felt sand in the air all about me. After about fifteen minutes of blowing dirt, the wind relented for a time as if the storm might have passed. But no, it was only the sand that had passed. Next there came a mighty rain that assaulted my roof as the world quickly cooled down beneath a raging storm.

During our second day we were delivered into the city to where departing volunteers were taking care of business related to termination, and where the rest of us were free to explore for a while. The Mali Peace Corps offices were in the Nairla quarter of Bamako, inside a secure, guarded compound. Buildings inside that walled area stood like a fortress, facing each other across a small rather cramped courtyard with barely enough room for vehicles to drive through and for a few to park. A long building on one side had steps at both ends leading to offices where executives worked. Situated between those suites was an open verandah with a floor of concrete and a roof of tin, where several couches and chairs formed quadrants, giving people a place to gather in relative comfort or to move about from office to office as need dictated.

Across the courtyard to one side was a library. The bathroom in the back of it, intended for coed use, was ugly but relatively clean. Also inside was a littered desk, a telephone, and a dusty sofa. We were given permission to use the telephone if we wished, but only to receive calls, not to place them. Thus, we had to go elsewhere to make contact with anyone back home and then arrange a time for him or her to call the telephone in the library.

Two local volunteers were about to take some of us to a bustling market near the U.S. Embassy. When a special truck came along, the girls told us to climb in. The little pickup truck served as a taxi and was called a "Bache" (bah-chey). The fare, twenty cents per passenger, was paid to a man in the back who slapped on a rear fender when it was okay to move again. We crowded inside and jammed ourselves among other people seated on narrow benches. No one was able to stand, for we were sitting inside a cage covered with a sheet of plywood. A little girl across from me was half-standing, half-sitting against the very edge of the bench, pressing backward for balance, grabbing people's knees when she was nearly bounced to the floor.

Bamako, smaller and less ritzy than Brazzaville, lacked glitter even where banks and embassies were located. Yet there was something about it that seemed more vibrant and alive, more purposeful, suggesting real human energy. There surely was a plan in the constant motion, and perhaps even commitment and drive that pushed everything along. Our Bache dropped us at the very steps of the American embassy. We would all go there for medical tests before leaving the country, but at that moment we newcomers all wanted to visit the big market that we had heard so much about. The beginning of it was just a few blocks away, and it was definitely worth the walk.

The market was a huge and bustling place on both sides of a major thoroughfare. Perhaps five blocks long and as many wide, it was literally squirming with hundreds of merchants selling everything imaginable. Thousands of people were shopping, browsing, bartering, or trying to work through the crowds. Dozen of wooden kiosks dominated the sidewalks, more or less in rows, with narrow passageways between them and behind them. In those little alleys were displayed all manner of electronic gadgets, tobacco products, jewelry, trinkets, fabrics, leather goods, African art objects, and just about anything else a person might like to buy. Young girls wandered through the crowds selling slices of coconut or fresh mangoes and little plastic bags of frozen beverages like popsicles. Other women and girls, often bare to the waist, indifferent to Western modesty, were selling raw vegetables and meats that were cooked on the site.

A long building across the street was divided into a maze of stores and shops and display zones, featuring imported fabrics, leather goods, and jewelry made on the spot from silver and gold. Beautiful pieces of carved ivory and bone were there, next to displays of tribal artifacts and millions of little beads and incidentals used in the practice of sorcery. Fabrics were woven before one's eyes and wood carvings were done while-you-wait. One could buy a python skin there, as well as the skins of antelope or even leopard. Hand made knives and Tuareg swords could be bought on the street, where hustlers were also pushing chess-pieces made of ivory or bone or wood, as well as jewelry boxes made of engraved leather.

An extension of the shopping zone farther down the street had freshly picked vegetables and freshly butchered meats that were sold in the same manner seen in Central Africa. But entirely surrounding that open market were literally dozens of conventional stores with excellent inventories of diverse and useful products on their shelves. My early impression was that men tended to be the storekeepers and street merchants of hardware and dry goods, while the women and girls were in charge of foods and beverages. Both were actively engaged in commerce in a most aggressive fashion, but it was interesting chaos. The products being promoted were certainly varied, their prices were right, or at least negotiable, and the overall atmosphere was perfectly suited to my taste.

When it was time to leave for the day, we had to go to a place called the VOX Cinema in order to catch transportation back to Tubani So. The dirt field in front, serving as a kind of central station for buses and trucks, had about a dozen of them parked side by side and going to all points. As prospective passengers, we went from vehicle to vehicle asking for a ride to Katiabougou, which is the next village past Tubani So, then upon finding the right truck, we climbed aboard and waited. Each Bache could seat perhaps fifteen people without excessive discomfort. But, as in the Congo, people were brought on board until it simply was not possible to squeeze another body inside.

Baches did not run after about six o'clock in the evening, which was a fact of crucial importance. If one missed the last truck out, one was in for a very long walk through villages where unguarded strolling would have been dangerous; or, one would have been forced to stay overnight in a hotel. We were warned that local hotels were not inviting places, and only the brave should stay in one. Two friends and I, made it a point to reached the station in plenty of time to catch a ride home.

By the time we had been in Mali two weeks, many of our number had left the country and several others were about ready to abandon any notions of ever going back to Brazzaville. I planned to stay to the end, and let fate take its course. When another week was behind us and no official decision had yet been made, some among us were growing edgy, frustrated, letting tempers fly in all directions. Most were still complaining about the lack of electricity at night to drive the fans, not only because of the heat, but also because the sudden change in noise and breeze would awaken a person from a sound sleep. When we received the news that a man and a child were killed in a crossfire in Brazzaville, it was finally announced that we were definitely not going back to the Congo. All of us were going home.

Nearly a month into our sojourn, I was told to see the company doctor for my termination physical. The regular doctor was out of the country, so a replacement had been flown in from elsewhere for the task. He was a thin, bearded, middle-aged man with a case of the tremors. As if to apologize for that, he said he arrived at three o'clock that morning, he was out of his element there, and he was tired and he couldn't find anything. He definitely seemed confused and disoriented as he set up for my examination, but we got on with it soon enough. He handed me a questionnaire, on which I was to report every medical condition that I ever suffered before traveling to Africa, and every one since…like amoebic dysentery, salmonella, Carpal Tunnel syndrome, pink eye, broken knee…that sort of thing. I pointed out that my vision had changed significantly and that my glasses didn't work anymore. He looked at the file. "Yes," he muttered. "There is a notation from several months ago about such a complaint." He looked at me, put his hand to his cheek, and literally whispered, "Do you want to see an ophthalmologist when you get home?" Staring back at him for a moment, I whispered back in the affirmative. He made a note.

When the examination was done and all the conditions that needed followup had been documented, I was sent to the embassy for blood tests. That was the end of it. Only money and a plane ticket remained to be settled, and those would be done very soon. Because we would be flying to different destination in the

U.S. and also because some people planned to travel a bit more before going home, most of our departure-schedules were different. I didn't mind.

Leaving Tubani So was done quietly and without fanfare. A few volunteers saw me to the bus and wished me a good journey, and then the compound faded quickly behind me. As the African driver rushed me to the airport with nothing to say, I thought about Makoua again, and the people, and the work I left behind. Whether or not my tenure there had served any beneficial purpose, would depend entirely on Herve and his sense of commitment to finish what we had started. I was sorry to abandon the farmers with whom I had worked, but I could only hope for the best. I then had a vision of Herve, sporting about the forest on a fire-engine red Yamaha, DT 125, riding wherever he pleased for whatever purpose that suited him, with nobody to complain.

Our ride to the airport took only twenty minutes. My driver helped me to get my bag out of the truck and to the ticket counter, and then he left me to my fate. Soon, with ticket and boarding pass in hand, I was alone again, a stranger among dozens of strangers, and perfectly content to have it so.

I spent the last of my local currency for two beers in the restaurant and then took a seat in the passenger's lounge where hardly anyone else was present. Several Malian boys, wandering about with shoeshine boxes, approached me one after the other, each at least once. But I did not bother to explain that I only had American currency and a U.S. dollar was too much to pay for a shine. I simply told them no thanks. When the last of them gave up and rejoined his friends across the room, it struck me that they were probably the last of the African hustlers I would ever encounter. When my flight was announced and I headed toward the stairs, I waved goodbye to the boys. They nodded back, but they could not possibly have understood.

My flight was not crowded at all. Indeed, I even suspected that the seat next to me was going to be vacant during the trip. Carryon stored above, seat-belt fastened, seat upright, shoe strings loosened for the long hours ahead, I was ready. Our wheels left the ground promptly at nine-thirty P.M., exactly on time. Soon the seat-belt warning would be off and I would be able to order a mixed drink, which would be something familiar and tasty with an instant kick to it. Soon an English-speaking hostesses would bring me a microwaved dinner, perhaps seafood or maybe beef prepared a special way with interesting sauces, and it would taste good. It would be a treat and it would be wonderful.

By the time we would next land, a new morning would have arrived. The sun should be breaking over the horizon, and Africa would be a continent behind me. I would be in Belgium, and only a change of planes away from the United States.

Soon, shiny cars and chrome-covered vehicles would race before me instead of donkey-carts or broken down dump-trucks loaded with gravel, sand and people. Soon the sounds I would hear would be the screeching of rubber on asphalt instead of the dragging crunch of rubber sandals on the dirt. Soon I would be listening to background music played in shopping malls, instead of repetitious percussion played painfully loud over blown speakers.

Soon my world would be one of fast-foods in air-conditioned places where seats were colorful and reasonably comfortable. Soon I would see movies and eat popcorn, and buy double scoop ice-cream cones, chocolate-chip cookies, and soft drinks over ice. Soon mine would be a world of business suits and shined shoes, of spiked heels and short skirts, of elevators, escalators, ringing telephones, hustle, competition and achievement.

I leaned back and closed my eyes then, wearing a little smile on my face that would not go away. It was a terrific, warm feeling to contemplate the hours ahead, for my adventure on the Dark Continent was over.

Things are different in Africa. God bless home sweet home!

978-0-595-33204-5
0-595-33204-8